10/11

AND NOTHING BUT THE TRUTHINESS

ALSO BY LISA ROGAK

Michelle Obama in Her Own Words
Barack Obama in His Own Words
Haunted Heart: The Life and Times of Stephen King
A Boy Named Shel
The Man Behind the Da Vinci Code

AND NOTHING BUT THE TRUTHINESS

The Rise (and Further Rise) of Stephen Colbert

LISA ROGAK

THOMAS DUNNE BOOKS
St. Martin's Press
New York

THOMAS DUNNE BOOKS.
An imprint of St. Martin's Press.

 Printed in the United States of America. For information, address St. Martin's Press, 175 Fifth Avenue, New York, N.Y. 10010.

www.thomasdunnebooks.com
www.stmartins.com

ISBN 978-0-312-61610-6

First Edition: October 2011

10 9 8 7 6 5 4 2 1

For Michael Murray

AND NOTHING BUT THE TRUTHINESS

INTRODUCTION

I used to make up stuff in my bio all the time, that I used to be a professional ice-skater and stuff like that. I found it so inspirational. Why not make myself cooler than I am? I once told an interviewer that I'd been arrested for assaulting someone with a flashlight. And I said that I drove a Shelby Cobra. They totally swallowed it, and I felt bad. Then I thought, it doesn't matter. It'll make a better story.

—Vanity Fair, *October 2007*

I'm a super straight guy. I grew up in Charleston, South Carolina, and I am perfectly comfortable in blue blazers, khaki pants, Brooks Brothers suits, and regimental striped ties. It's just genetic. I love a cocktail party with completely vacuous conversation, because I grew up in it.—Campus Progress, *October 2005*

WILL THE REAL Stephen Colbert please stand up?

Colbert has been messing with the truth for years now, both in and out of character. This hugely popular comedian with a biting wit and rapid-fire skill for calling up obscure figures and events in everything from Greek history to light opera has largely built his career on messing with people's minds. And most of the time, they don't even know when he's doing it.

No other comedian has so blurred the line between his real character and his on-screen character.

"My name is Stephen Colbert, but I actually play someone on television named Stephen Colbert, who looks like me and talks like me, but who says things with a straight face he doesn't mean," he said in his commencement address at Knox College in 2006. "I'm not sure which one of us you invited to speak here today. So with your indulgence, I'm just going to talk and let you figure it out."

Good luck with *that*. Even his own mother knows that's an impossible task: "I can never nail him down as to exactly what he is," said Lorna Tuck Colbert when her son was well into his forties.

Stephen Colbert grew up in a large tight-knit Catholic family, essentially as part of a tribe where he was the youngest of eleven children. "His humor is an accumulation of the eccentricities, mannerisms, and jokes of his ten older brothers and sisters, a medley that trickled down," said one Colbert staffer.

The constant bantering endemic to his family often assumed a slapstick quality, as evidenced in a 2009 interview with Stephen, his mother, and several of his siblings when asked about their name's pronunciation:

Elizabeth Colbert-Busch: What did I say my last name was?
Margo Colbert Keegan: Coal-*bear*.
Elizabeth: I did? No, that's not my name.
Margo: Yes, you did. You said Coal-*bear* Busch.
Elizabeth: That's not my name.
Margo: You said Coal-*bear* Busch.
Elizabeth: Roll that back. That's not my name. My name's Elizabeth *Coal*-bert Busch, and I'm not telling y'all how old I am.
Lorna: Oh, I have no idea what my name is.
Margo: What?
John A. Colbert: You're Mom.
Lorna: Well, I don't know.
Elizabeth: You have a vague inkling, okay?
Margo: You're *Coal*-bert or Coal-*bear*?
John: You're *Coal*-bert.
Stephen: You're Coal-*bear*, you're Coal-*bear*. Come on.

Elizabeth: Well, I was Coal-*bear* until I was twenty-three. It followed me all the way through college. I finally gave up. I was intimidated.

Margo: Tom claims he was the first to go Coal-*bear*, is that true?

Lorna: Who was?

Margo: Tom. He was the first to go Coal-*bear*, he claims.

Lorna: Oh, I don't know.

John: He might have been.

Elizabeth: I think it would be Dad.

Margo: Yeah, but it didn't stick.

Stephen: [To interviewer] Have you any questions?

Margo: Oh, yes, Brooke.

John: [To interviewer] See, this is what happens . . .

Obviously, the rapier-sharp wit that Colbert demonstrates regularly on *The Colbert Report* had its roots early on.

Like virtually all comedians, his humor developed in the face of tragedy, and Colbert's great tragedy is that his father and two older brothers were killed in a plane crash when Colbert was just ten years old. His tribe was smashed apart, and he's spent his life trying to re-create it. At first, he found it in high school, then at Second City with his friends Paul Dinello and Amy Sedaris, and again with Jon Stewart on *The Daily Show*. But try as he might, he has never been able to exactly replicate it. He has admitted that he has never completely dealt with their deaths, and he's said that he sometimes expects the three to walk right back through the door.

Unlike many other comedians and celebrities, Stephen Colbert is a genuinely—perhaps shockingly—good person. Time and again during my research, friends, colleagues, as well as complete strangers have told of his generosity when it comes to his time, spirit, and money. Above all, he's never been shy about proclaiming his love for his mother, both on camera and off. "She's bright, not just intelligent but bright," said Colbert. "She shines. She's hopeful, indefatigable, and has great faith. And

On September 24, 2010, Colbert testified before a House Judiciary subcommittee on the subject of immigration reform, citing his experience working the fields as a migrant farm worker. Some in Congress were not amused. *(Courtesy Reuters/Corbis)*

she's tough: she raised eleven kids, and she raised me after my father and two of my brothers died. And she's Irish, *so* Irish."

Despite his quickness to announce his love of family, Colbert guards his personal views closely, and if you watch the show carefully you'll see subtle digs at everyone across the political map. "I'm not entirely a commie," he says. "I don't mind putting things in that might be perceived as conservative that I actually believe, but I don't know if the audience needs to know *which* of them I believe."

At the same time, he cheerfully admits that he's biased. "I don't have to pretend to be impartial. I'm partial. I'll make fun of anybody. We're all about falling down and going boom on camera," he said. "I'm not someone with a particular political ax to grind. I'm a comedian. I love hypocrisy."

In the fall of 2010, he testified before a congressional subcommittee to offer his views on migrant farm workers, where, by staying in character, he was able to show his thoughts on the subject: "Generally speaking, if you slap me across the face at 3 A.M. and say 'What are you?' I'd say I'm a liberal." Some of the congressmen in attendance got the joke, while others frowned and viewed Colbert's appearance as little more than a publicity stunt.

But after reading his prepared statement, Colbert turned serious, breaking character in response to a question about why he chose to testify on this particular issue. "I like talking about people who don't have any power, and it seems like one of the least powerful people in the United States are migrant workers who come and do our work but don't have any rights themselves," he said. "Migrant workers suffer and have no rights."

"Stephen is one of the smartest people I've ever met," says Allison Silverman, the former executive producer and head writer at *The Colbert Report*. "He's brilliant." In fact, he's eager to share his knowledge with anyone who wanders into range.

Indeed, members of the studio audience have been treated to Colbert's warming them up by reciting poetry, singing a Gilbert and Sullivan tune, and spouting Latin epithets. His breadth of knowledge is prodigious. In a conversation with his family and in-laws, his mother mentioned that their father spent time in Beirut with the army while another sibling corrected her to say, No it was *Bayreuth*, a town in Germany, not Beirut. Stephen asked, "Isn't that where the big Wagner festival is, Bayreuth?"

Unlike his more acerbic comedic counterparts, Colbert is a happy family man who completely embraces the mundane routine of suburban life. He's not hurtling down the path of swift self-destruction like other Second City alums Chris Farley or John Belushi. On the contrary, he's Everyman in a Brooks Brothers suit.

"His basic decency can't be hidden," said Jon Stewart.

"I have a boring baritone. I have boring hair. Every decision that I've made in my life is the middle decision," Colbert told Morley Safer in a *60 Minutes* interview.

"I have a wife who loves me, and I am oddly normative," he said. "I live in a bubble. I go to work and then go home, and I don't get together with people in groups that often."

Plus, he's probably the first hugely popular comedian who makes no secret of his deep commitment to Catholicism. "I love my Church," he said. "I'm a Catholic who was raised by intellectuals, who were very devout. I was raised to believe that you could question the Church and still be a Catholic. What is worthy of satire is the misuse of religion for destructive or political gains. That's totally different from the Word, the blood, the body, and the Christ. His kingdom is not of this earth."

He even teaches Sunday school, and it's clear that he draws some inspiration from his charges. "They immediately ask questions that you thought were so deep in college, like 'What's beyond time?' 'What came before God?' "

"Stephen is a happy man," said Ben Karlin, who served as executive producer on *The Colbert Report*. "He goes home to a lovely wife in New Jersey, a dog, and three beautiful children, and he knows his way around the kitchen."

"His own family is very, very important to him," said childhood friend Chip Hill. "The typical story is a guy gets famous and loses perspective on his life. He works very hard to stay grounded."

Fans are not the only ones who adore him. By and large, the media not only follow him but thoroughly respect him as well, even given his status as a fake newsman. "Colbert is more than an entertainer, he's a force of nature," said Julio Diaz, entertainment editor for the *Pensacola News Journal*. "He's influenced the way we look at the news and even the way we speak. Whenever a major news story breaks, one of my first thoughts is what's Colbert's spin on the story."

As a biographer, Colbert's constantly shifting chameleon persona—both in character and in real life—created a challenge, because he even does many of his media interviews in character. "I like preserving the mask," he said. "Stepping out from behind it doesn't do me any good."

"There couldn't be a huger difference between the character Stephen and the real Stephen," said Richard Dahm, a head writer at *The Colbert Report*. "The real Stephen is an amazing guy. The character Stephen—well, I wouldn't want to be working for him."

"He always said he was going to major in mass communications and start his own cult," said Chip Hill.

"I drive myself home at night," adds Colbert, who lives on a cul-de-sac in suburban Montclair, New Jersey. "The network would happily send me home in a car—after all, they don't want me running off the road. But I'd work the entire way home, and I need more than the 30 seconds from the car to the front door to become a dad and a husband again. So I drive home and I crank my tunes. And by the time I get there, I'm normal again."

CHAPTER 1

When Stephen Tyrone Colbert was born, he was the youngest of eleven children—as well as the last—and the first new baby to arrive in the household in five years, which was an eternity considering that his parents brought seven of those older children into the world in just under a decade.

From the day he was brought home from the hospital, his siblings regarded Stephen in the same way they would a new puppy. "My three sisters had a live baby doll: me," he said.

"He had lots of attention paid to him and was carried around," said his mother, Lorna. "They used to do little tricks with him."

"I was very loved," he said. "My sisters like to say that they are surprised that I learned to walk and that my legs didn't become vestigial because I was carried around by them so much."

His sisters weren't the only ones who spoiled him; in the Colbert household, Lorna served dinner from the youngest to the oldest, so Stephen was the first to eat. "That way, I'd also be ready for seconds first," he said.

"Being the youngest, I always got a lot of attention," he said. "It became an addiction. I need attention."

But the youngest Colbert soon discovered that being cute and cuddly didn't automatically win him points where it *really* counted in the family: being funny.

"It became an addiction. I need attention."

"I grew up in a humorocracy where the funniest person in the room is king," he said. "There was a constant competition to have the better story and be the funniest person in the room, and I wasn't a particularly funny kid."

One time, Stephen eavesdropped on his mother while she was telling his siblings that they had to listen to his stories, even though they complained that he was boring. "And to this day I sort of feel like if I'm doing well with an audience, then Mom's gotten to them and said, 'You *listen* to him.'"

Even today, when the family of Colbert adults gets together, Stephen still takes a backseat. "I'm definitely not the funniest person in my family," he said. "I think my brothers and sisters are so much funnier than me. When we're together as a family, I just listen to them, but I have stolen from them over the years."

He still doesn't think he's as funny as his brother Jay. One example: "He used to do an impersonation of a squirrel taking a shit while it walked, leaving a trail behind him," said Stephen. "He swore there was a squirrel that did this in the parking lot when he was in college, and my sister Lulu would get so incredibly embarrassed when he did the impersonation in a public place, but it's my gold standard when it comes to humor."

Lorna Elizabeth Colbert was born on November 6, 1920, to Andrew and Marie Fee Tuck. Andrew was a lawyer and had previously served as a major in the army, while Marie was a housewife who had been educated by nuns. "The Ladies of Loreto, who are very hoity-toity French Canadian nuns," her grandson Stephen would say years later. "You had to be of means to be educated by them."

Lorna joined a three-year-old sister by the name of Mary, and Andrew

III would arrive two years later. The Tuck family lived in a spacious apartment at 130 Claremont Avenue in the Morningside Heights neighborhood of Manhattan, a relatively prosperous area near Columbia University that overlooked Riverside Drive. They were wealthy enough to have an African-American woman named Eliza Hart serve as their live-in maid.

The neighborhood was filled with white-collar professionals and artists: musicians, writers, and lawyers filled the apartments. The Juilliard School—founded in 1905—was right next door, at 134 Claremont Avenue. Although in Manhattan, the neighborhood was still considered rural for the time; anything north of Central Park was considered to be the country, yet it was easy enough to commute to a downtown office.

The 1920s were booming economic times, and there was much work for an ambitious lawyer with a new family to support. Attorney Tuck did so well in his practice that he moved his family to Westchester County, purchasing a house at 54 Chatsworth Avenue in Larchmont, a growing suburb seventeen miles north of the city; in 1930, the house was valued at $30,000. Their neighbors were engineers, business owners, and bookkeepers, with a few secretaries and apartment superintendents thrown into the mix. The Roaring Twenties brought great wealth to the growing families of the new Victorian and craftsman-style homes that lined the leafy streets of the bucolic village.

The Tucks attended Saint Augustine's Church, a few blocks away from their house, and shortly after her confirmation, Lorna was sent away to a convent school in Providence, Rhode Island.

Boston Post Road passes through Larchmont, which had once served as a summer resort town where upper-class New Yorkers could escape the oppressive heat of Manhattan. Once the roads connecting Larchmont to New York City were developed and improved in response to the growing popularity of automobiles—by 1925 over two million of the ubiquitous Model T Fords were sold each year—an increasing number of summer residents decided to make Larchmont their home year-round. Located on Long Island Sound, the village's several pleasant beaches made it an even more attractive place for upper-class families to settle.

Larchmont also beckoned as an attractive address for celebrities of the day: the playwright Edward Albee and the silent movie stars Douglas Fairbanks and Mary Pickford all chose Larchmont as their home.

Fifteen miles away, in the New York City borough of the Bronx, James William Colbert, Jr., was born to James William Colbert and Mary Tormey on December 15, 1920, along with a twin sister, Margaret. The twins were the Colberts' first children.

The family lived on Jerome Avenue, surrounded mostly by families whose mothers and fathers were born in Russia, Hungary, and Ireland, and whose first language was not English. By contrast, James Sr. was born in Illinois, and Mary was born in New York.

As a sales manager who sold glass bottles for Owens Illinois Glassworks, James hustled to provide for his family, and he did very well. "He evidently had a misspent youth, because he was very good at cards and very good at pool," said his grandson Stephen years later. "He knew some dicey characters."

"[My grandfather] evidently had a misspent youth, because he was very good at cards and very good at pool."

As was the case in the rest of New York City—and the country, overall—the 1920s brought bustling times to the Bronx in the aftermath of World War I. The New York subway system was extended into the borough, which helped ease some of the overcrowding in the traditional enclaves where immigrants first settled, like the Lower East Side and Brooklyn. Many new large tenement houses were built, especially along the Grand Concourse, and some immigrants headed north, where they could live in New York City but easily commute to their jobs.

The Grand Concourse was the name of a street largely regarded as the "Park Avenue of middle-class Bronx residents," according to the *WPA Guide to New York City*. "A lease to an apartment on the Grand Concourse is considered evidence of at least moderate business success." Indeed, in planning its design, the French engineer Louis Risse used the Champs-Élysées in Paris as his model for the thoroughfare that ran four miles in length when it first opened in 1909.

Once the first subway line was brought to the neighborhood, it set off a construction boom given over to stately six-story apartment buildings built in a suitably grand art deco style in the 1920s and 1930s, including uniformed doormen and elegant lead-glass elevator doors (those touches weren't seen on the Jerome Avenue that the Colberts knew).

Nevertheless, James was doing well, so in the mid-1920s, the Colbert family moved from Jerome Avenue to a larger apartment at 2877 Grand Concourse, where they paid about a hundred dollars each month for rent.

At the same time, the Concourse was also a magnet for upwardly mobile Jewish families. In fact, by the mid-1930s, Jews would make up about 45 percent of the total population of the Bronx. Since the Colberts were devout Catholics, they belonged to a distinct minority in the neighborhood. "When [James Jr.] turned thirteen and didn't get Bar Mitzvahed, he knew he wasn't Jewish," his son Edward Tuck Colbert would relate years later.

The Catholic population in the Bronx was small and tightly connected. In the 1920s, prejudice against Catholics was commonplace, from Protestants, who viewed Catholicism as a pagan brand of Christianity, to the Ku Klux Klan, who believed that since Catholics answered to Rome, they would never put America first. The 1928 presidential campaign featured the first Catholic candidate of a major party, Al Smith, a Democrat from New York. His religion was cited as a major factor for Republican Herbert Hoover's landslide victory; Hoover carried forty states, Smith only eight.

Sometime in the early 1930s, New Yorkers began to get restless and uncertain as the roots of the Depression began to take hold. Irish Catholics began to leave the Bronx, despite the fashionable Grand Concourse address, and headed for the relative calm of the developing suburbs in Westchester.

In the early 1930s, the Colberts joined the first wave of Irish-Americans to leave the Bronx, and James and Mary moved their family to Monroe Avenue in Larchmont, just a few blocks away from Lorna Tuck's house. James Jr. enrolled in junior high at Saint Augustine's School in Larchmont, where he also served as an altar boy. He later attended Iona Preparatory School in nearby New Rochelle. But Saint Augustine's was where he would meet Lorna Tuck.

Lorna spent most of the year at convent school in Providence, Rhode Island, but whenever she came home for vacations or weekends, she kept her eye on the altar boy at Mass. Though they'd occasionally see each other around the neighborhood, their exchanges were mostly limited to greetings in passing and mutual glances during church services.

They finally met for more than a brief moment at a dance class in 1932, when both were just twelve years old. Lorna was invited to the cotillion ball, a gala coming-out event for young women. Despite the economic strife of the Great Depression, they were still in fashion and held regularly throughout the New York metropolitan area among the upper classes. Debs and their potential escorts took classes in the finer arts of polite society, from table etiquette to dancing lessons.

Lorna and a girlfriend invited young men to classes so they could practice their dance steps. Her girlfriend just happened to bring the altar boy from Saint Augustine's. "I brought a very nice, handsome guy who was a monitor in my school," Lorna remembered. "He was very tall and good-looking, but Jim Colbert was a much better dancer, so that's what stuck with me."

Afterward, the young couples headed for a neighbor's house for cupcakes, and Jim made sure to sit next to Lorna instead of her girlfriend. They talked for several hours. Lorna had to return to the convent in Rhode Island for school, but she kept her eye on Jim. She liked the fact that Jim was an optimist and that he always had something good to say compared with other boys, who always had something negative to say about the continuing economic misery afoot in the world—despite the fact that in the rarified world of upper-class Larchmont, many families had managed to hold on to their wealth; both the Tucks and Colberts were relatively unscathed by the Depression.

Her crush intensified during high school. When Lorna came home from school, she and a friend would ride down to the beach on their bicycles, and she'd make a point of passing by Jim's house on Monroe Avenue. But she'd get so nervous that she wouldn't look for him when they pedaled by. "I'd ask, 'Was he there, was he there, did he look at me?' "

Lorna also liked that Jim put his studies first. As a straight-A student, it was obvious he had a brilliant mind and was destined to go far in life, though he rarely flaunted it over others. "He was always bookish but he didn't mention it that much to me because I wasn't so bookish," said Lorna.

She dreamed of becoming a singer and actress, and Jim also proved to have an artistic streak. His son Jay later remembered seeing a drawing that Jim did of a nautical scene, which he'd entered in a high school art contest with an honorable-mention ribbon on the back.

Despite their mutual attraction, they weren't officially a couple and would only see each other at church or on the street. "There wasn't a big to-do with the parents," she said, "but they weren't really alike. They're both very nice, very lovely, but they just weren't the same type of people."

One day when Lorna was around fifteen years old, she decided to take charge. She was scheduled to return to Larchmont for a few days, so she asked her mother to call Jim and ask for a date when she came home. The Tucks belonged to the Westchester Country Club, and Lorna invited him to have a drink at the bar, where she ordered a scotch and water and he ordered a sarsaparilla, a popular health tonic of the day.

In 1938, Jim graduated from Iona Prep and proceeded to the College of the Holy Cross, in Worcester, Massachusetts. While he was in college, he weighed different career tracks, and even though he loved philosophy and would have preferred to pursue that path, he decided to enroll in medical school at Columbia University.

"He really didn't want to be a doctor," said Lorna. Though his parents wanted him to pursue a profession, he didn't want to become a lawyer, so he turned to medicine as a default move, and because, as his daughter Margo would later say, "It just seemed to be the thing to do at the time."

His relationship with Lorna quickly intensified during college, and he graduated in 1942 with a bachelor's degree in philosophy. That fall, Jim enrolled in the College of Physicians and Surgeons at Columbia University with a focus on immunology and infectious disease. A year into the rigorous program, he asked Lorna to marry him. She told him yes, and they began to plan their wedding.

Lorna's younger brother Andrew was serving as a first lieutenant paratrooper in the 101st Airborne Division in World War II and couldn't make it home for the wedding. He wrote a letter to Jim where he sent his regrets. "I wish terribly that I could be there to 'hold the ring' for you," he said. "I'll be proud to call you brother. It's just as well that I'm over here, I'd probably trip in the aisle, lose the ring, and get disgracefully pickled at the reception."

They married on August 26, 1944, and Jim and Lorna moved into a third-floor walk-up apartment at 630 West 168th Street, right around the block from Columbia's medical school. It was only two miles away from Lorna's first apartment on Riverside Park, but it might as well have been a world away since it was a definite step down from what she was used to. "It was just a terrible apartment, with a fire escape outside the window that blocked the view," she remembered.

Within a few months of the wedding, Lorna was pregnant. She had little to do all day since Jim was off at medical school, sometimes for days at a time—he'd sleep in one of the dorm rooms upstairs from the medical school where students and residents slept when they were on call or between rotations—and besides, she missed her friends back in Westchester. The couple soon moved back to Larchmont, and after a brief stint living with Lorna's parents, they moved to an apartment a few blocks away, at 12 Chatsworth Avenue.

In the spring of 1945, Lorna was only a few months away from giving birth to their first child when Jim graduated with an MD from Columbia. During World War II, medical schools crammed four years of education into three because they expected that all new physicians would be shipped overseas as soon as they graduated. When the war was declared to be over in June 1945, the couple was thrilled that Jim could stay close to home for the birth of their first child. However, their euphoria was shattered when news arrived that Lorna's brother Andrew had died. He had made it through the Normandy invasion and the Battle of the Bulge, only to be killed in a car accident in Austria at the age of twenty-two, just a month after the war had officially been declared over.

For Lorna, it was almost too much to bear. She was near-term and had been cautioned to stay off her feet for most of her pregnancy, so she decided to spend the summer at the family vacation home in Seventh Lake Inlet, in the Adirondacks Mountains of New York. There, she could rest and grieve the loss of her brother. Jim stayed with her but commuted to the city, where he would start his internship at Bellevue Hospital in Manhattan. James Colbert III, their first child, was born on September 1, 1945, at Columbia Presbyterian Hospital.

After Jim completed his internship in 1946, he signed up to serve for a year with the U.S. Army Medical Corps. Lorna decided to stay at the vacation home in his absence, but before he left, Lorna became pregnant again. Their second child, Edward, was born on January 20, 1947, while Jim was overseas.

When he returned from Germany in the spring of 1947, the Colberts packed up and headed for New Haven, where Jim would do his residency at the Yale University School of Medicine. There he began to develop a specialty in infectious diseases and immunology. Thus began a fast track for Jim and his career.

Mary Colbert, their first daughter and third child, was born on January 1, 1949, in New Haven. That same year, Jim re-upped with the army and headed back to Germany, but this time his family would come with him for the two years he'd be stationed overseas. He specialized in hepatitis research and headed up the lab at the German epidemiology hospital. While he was still in Germany, he was named an instructor of medicine at Yale and then an assistant professor of medicine. And he and Lorna would have another child while in Germany; Billy was born on May 12, 1950, in Munich.

No matter where they were living, Jim liked to take some time off each summer so that he could give his growing family his undivided attention. However, he couldn't seem to stay away from the hospital. Instead of his usual research and study, he liked to use the time to see patients since he didn't have time for clinical practice the rest of the year. Even here, he made an impression.

One summer, he was treating a patient with a rare fungal infection that was fatal for patients with compromised immune systems. However, the patient was rude and uncooperative, and though Jim prided himself on getting along with almost anyone, this patient sorely tested him. Lorna remembered that Jim would come home after dealing with the patient and say, "I'm just so inclined to just let him have this disease."

Remembering the Hippocratic oath, Colbert kept his mouth shut and treated the man, who fully recovered. As it turned out, the patient was the first man to actually survive and be cured of the disease.

Jim later found out that the man had been so hostile to him because he was an anti-Semite and for some reason thought that Dr. Colbert was Jewish. A few months later, when he found out that he had made medical history, the patient had a change of heart and joined the Israeli army because Colbert had cured him. "He said he was so grateful to him that he wanted to do something for his people, so he went to Israel and joined the army," said his son Edward Tuck. When Jim found out, another doctor recommended that he tell the patient he wasn't Jewish after all, but Jim disagreed. "There's no point," he said. "Don't ever tell him."

Shortly after the family returned to New Haven in 1951, Jim was appointed assistant dean of the Yale School of Medicine. As usual, Lorna was pregnant, and they needed to move to a bigger apartment. But there was one big change: Now with four kids—and pregnant again—she no longer was picky about how fancy an apartment was or if there was a fire escape blocking the view of a window. All she cared about was making a good home for her family and protecting her kids. Besides, she had already moved several times since the birth of her first child, so she had the routine of packing and unpacking cribs, furniture, and clothes down to a science.

After they returned to New Haven, the Colberts moved into an apartment at 205 Livingston Street, near the medical school. The previous tenants had left behind a feral cat that had just given birth to a litter of dead kittens in a box in a bedroom in the new apartment, and the mother cat would hiss and snarl and try to attack anyone who tried to come in the room.

Lorna called the city animal control department to remove the cat from the premises, but the guy who showed up thought the cat was too wild to handle. Lorna would have none of it. She was hugely pregnant and tried to play on his sympathies, but the animal-control official refused to deal with the cat.

Lorna grabbed a bag from him and marched into the bedroom. A few moments later, she came out of the room with the cat in the bag and handed it over.

The family continued to grow. Numbers five and six followed in short order: Margaret—aka Margo—was born on May 25, 1951, and Tom arrived a little over a year later, on July 21, 1952.

In his relatively short career, Dr. Colbert had already built a national reputation in the field of epidemiology and was a sought-after speaker at association meetings and at other medical schools. Jim regularly received job offers.

He turned them all down until the Saint Louis University School of Medicine—today, part of Washington University—called to offer him the position of dean of the medical school. If he accepted the job, at thirty-two years of age, he'd be the youngest person to be dean of a medicine school at the time.

Dr. Colbert credited his military service with his desire to take the position, which he later explained to his son Edward.

"They made me a captain in Germany so I could order everybody around," said Jim. "I've got people working for me, I'm in charge of an entire wing of a hospital, and then I come back to be an intern or resident and go to the end of the line with a nurse telling me what to do?"

"There was an entire generation of men his age who went over to

Germany who were put in charge of things very quickly," said Edward. "That's what made him want to keep moving up. He said that his whole generation was very impatient because of the war."

So in October of 1953, he left New Haven while Lorna—eight months pregnant—packed up a house and six kids and moved halfway across the country, into a house at 6211 McPherson Avenue, St. Louis. Days after they arrived, John—aka Jay—was born on October sixth.

When he arrived in St. Louis, Dr. Colbert hit the ground running. His first assignment was to hire the best physicians and researchers he could find. Indeed, it was not unusual for the younger Colberts to sit at the dinner table while a Nobel Prize winner regaled the family with stories as they passed the peas. Colbert not only recruited several physicians and researchers from Yale but also helped design and build one of the first chronic-care facilities to be based at a major American university. The concept was radical for the time; Colbert believed that the patient rooms in a chronic-care wing had to be dark, a world away from the bright, airy rooms that were standard for all patients at the time. He also did away with nurses' stations, because he thought it reduced the time nurses spent caring for patients; without them, nurses were more inclined to spend time in a patient's room instead of gabbing with one another.

After Jay was born, the first Colbert born in St. Louis, three more children—Elizabeth (who was also known as Lulu), Paul, and Peter—followed in quick succession. Despite Dr. Colbert's tough schedule and long hours, he always made a point to spend time with his constantly growing family, especially on Sundays. They attended Mass every week, no matter where they were, although by the time Peter—the tenth Colbert—was born in 1959, they had long ceased to fit into one car.

"We had to go to church in two cars, there were so many of us," said Margo Colbert Keegan. One time, she remembered, they were heading out of the driveway of the church and Lorna saw a parishioner hold up a little boy who was crying. "I remember Mom say, 'Oh, that poor little boy's . . . oh my gosh, that's Paul!' "

After that, Dr. Colbert counted noses whenever the family traveled together, but that only worked for a short time. "When we had eight kids he started to count to eight," remembered Edward. They may have gotten to *eight,* but they weren't necessarily all Colberts. One time, somebody was left behind because one of the kids who had responded was a friend, and not a Colbert.

"After that, we had to answer by name," said Margo.

"It was just like being in the army, with roll call," added Edward.

Later on, Stephen would get big laughs by breathlessly reciting the chronological list of his siblings, from oldest to youngest:

JimmyEddieMaryBillyMargoTommyJayLuluPaulPeterStephen

In 1960, in addition to his other duties, Dr. Colbert signed on to be chair of the St. Louis chapter of Doctors for Kennedy, to support John F. Kennedy, Jr., the first Catholic to have a good chance at becoming president of the United States. The photograph of the two of them shaking hands—with Jim absolutely beaming—was displayed prominently in his office at the medical school, and visitors often commented on it. Though they were lifelong Republicans, he and Lorna voted for Kennedy. Later on, the photograph was hung in the Colbert home; Stephen later commented, "In our house, the Kennedy picture was like a religious icon."

Despite negative feedback from some old-school physicians and nurses on the changes that Dr. Colbert had implemented at Saint Louis University, overall the new building was enthusiastically received by staffers. So after several years on the job, he felt ready to take the next step. The medical school was not accredited, and in order for that to happen, the physicians who were affiliated with the hospital had to start seeing their patients at the hospital instead of at their private offices, which had long been the practice at the university. That way, the students could start working with patients, which was the only way the school could receive accreditation. Colbert asked the physicians to start seeing patients at the hospital, but few altered their ways. He asked a few more times, only to be met with the same response.

With the approval of the board and the president of the university, Dr. Colbert sent every physician a letter to inform them that if they were not going to see patients at the hospital, then the university would have no choice but to end their relationship.

As expected, there was a huge uproar. Not only did Dr. Colbert become persona non grata at the hospital, but his kids went through the same thing at school. "A lot of us had friends whose parents were doctors, and they were affected," said Edward, who was in his freshman year at Saint Louis University High School in the fall of 1961. "My freshman year of high school was a living hell, because we were now the enemy, the sins of the father and that sort of thing."

When Eddie and Jimmy came home from school at the end of another long day of taunts and teasing, Dr. Colbert took the boys aside to explain what was going on. But he also presented them with a few scenarios and options, asked for their opinion, and used them as a sounding board. "The thing that I loved about him is that we were kids, but he would talk about what was going on," Eddie remembered. "We were all very family oriented. It was the only thing that mattered. We weren't really school oriented, and neither Jim nor I were particularly athletic so we weren't on teams and we didn't have this rah, rah school thing."

Margo, who was only ten at the time, was also on the receiving end of the taunts of her classmates. When her father explained what was going on, he repeatedly said that integrity and dignity were important. "I'm just a little kid, I thought, what are you talking about?" she said. "But as I got older, I realized this is where it all came from. You keep your integrity and dignity at all times."

Lulu remembered another piece of advice her father gave her: Take every legitimate adventure and don't be afraid. "As a young girl it was very important to be pretty and popular," she said. "I remember sitting down and having a conversation with my father—which were rare because there were so many of us—and he said to me, 'Lulu, there's nothing sexier than an educated woman.' "

Despite having the support of the president and the board, the uproar from the physicians and their own staff was so complete that the school caved into the pressure and fired Dr. Colbert from his position. He had been with the hospital for eight years.

"The university hand-delivered a letter of termination to the house on Christmas Eve, 1961."

What made matters worse is that they delivered the news when he was out of town on a business trip. Instead of waiting until he returned, the university hand-delivered a letter of termination to the house on Christmas Eve, 1961.

"The medical profession today offers one of the few real chances for dedication of life," Dr. Colbert said in 1960. "It is the exact opposite of the materialistic drive that dominates most Americans."

Regardless of this, with ten children and a wife to support, Jim had to look for a new job. Fortunately, once word got out that he was looking for a new position, requests for interviews came pouring in. "He was really so academically oriented and research oriented that he could have any one of these jobs and make a ton of money," said Eddie. One came from Bristol-Myers, a major pharmaceutical and consumer-brands company even then. "They wanted to hire him because they wanted to use his reputation for integrity to bolster the company."

So Jim went to talk to them. "He came home with his coat pockets full of these little plastic white balls," said Margo. Those balls were for the Ban roll-on deodorant that Bristol-Myers manufactured, and he gave them to his kids to play with.

"They wanted to hire him," said Eddie.

They *all* wanted to hire him. And even though the money was better than anything he had made up to that point, he just couldn't bring himself to do it. "I specifically remember him saying they wanted him to be a front man for the company and he didn't want to be that," said Eddie.

"And that was the end of the plastic ball supply," said Margo.

Dr. Colbert also received a job offer to work with a friend at a plastic-surgery practice out in Beverly Hills, but he turned it down because he didn't want to live in Hollywood and be a plastic surgeon. Other job offers came in, but they would all require him to sacrifice some degree of his personal integrity. It was incredibly stressful to be out of work, and he lost a lot of weight. So when the National Institutes of Health called with an offer to become associate director for extramural programs at the National Institute for Allergy and Infectious Diseases, he jumped at the chance. Once again, Lorna packed up the house and ten kids and headed to 9011 Honeybee Lane in Bethesda, Maryland.

In his new position, Jim's budget for research was fifty million dollars a year, and Jim would spend much of his time traveling around the world. He loved the job.

Old Fashioned

2 oz. whiskey

1 sugar cube

1 dash Angostura bitters

1 lemon twist

1 slice orange

1 cherry

In an old-fashioned or rocks glass, combine the sugar cube and bitters. Dissolve sugar with 1 teaspoon of water. Add whiskey and stir. Fill glass with ice cubes and garnish with fruit.

When Jim did land back at home for a few days, the kids fought for the chance to make him an Old Fashioned. "Oh, that was a thing of honor, if you got to make him an Old Fashioned," said Margo.

As before, no matter how busy he was, Dr. Colbert always made time for two things: church and his family. "Mass for this family is like breathing in and breathing out," said Monsignor Harry J. Byrne, who would become familiar with the Colbert family a few years later.

More often than not, church was followed by a relaxing drive in the country. The custom of Sunday drives soon became legend in the growing family.

They all piled into a 1957 Ford Country Squire station wagon (a car that could finally fit them all) and headed out. The kids loved ice cream, while Dr. Colbert loved battlefields, particularly those from the Civil War. And although he didn't always stop for ice cream, much to his children's dismay, he always stopped for a battlefield. But the potential for an ice-cream cone was always there, if you could just make it through the interminable drives past fields and hills.

Once they were settled in Bethesda, the Sunday drives intensified; after all, there were countless Civil War battlefields a short drive away, including Gettysburg and Harpers Ferry. Once they arrived at said battlefield, all twelve would pile out to look at what was not much more than a hill. Jim would explain what had happened there, and then they'd all pile back in, the kids quiet and obedient because of the promise of ice cream.

Eddie remembers another time when they were driving through a park at a fairly slow speed when his father abruptly told them, "Look at this, look at this!" when suddenly he heard two clicks, followed by the sound of rushing air. To see what everyone was looking at, Jay had pulled himself up by grabbing the door handle. The door swung open, Jay fell out, and before anyone could react, the door closed behind him, and the car kept going. "Everyone is screaming at Dad to stop the car, but he kept driving because he was deaf in one ear," said Eddie. "We finally went back and got Jay and put him in the car and the next day, Dad took it to the shop to get childproof locks installed. After that, you could only open the door from the outside."

Into this spirited mêlée, the eleventh—and last—child of James and Lorna Colbert came into the world.

CHAPTER 2

STEPHEN TYRONE COLBERT WAS born on May 13, 1964, at Georgetown University Hospital in Washington, D.C. Both Lorna and Jim were forty-three years old.

As the first new baby in five years he was welcomed into a family that already had its routine down in terms of its sheer chaos, activity, and the propensity of children and adults alike to finish one another's sentences and participate in a kind of one-upmanship when it came to being funny.

"It's hard for me to imagine a family any other way than chaotic," he later said. "It allowed me to not imagine that things would be perfect at holiday time, because there was no way for Christmas morning to go off without a hitch with that many kids."

From a very early age, as the baby of the family, he also got away with murder. December 15, 1966, was Jim's forty-sixth birthday, and the family was getting ready to celebrate. Stephen was two and a half. "I heard this excited voice coming from the dining room, and went to look in, and there were two perfect little footprints right in the middle of the cake and a trail of frosting leading out the door," said brother Jay. "But my father let it go."

Jim let a lot of things go, primarily because the older kids were becoming more independent and spending more time away from home—Jim Jr., the eldest, had just turned eighteen—which reduced some of the stress, but also because he finally had a job he loved and that didn't require him to make excuses for his principles. As a result, Dr. Colbert mellowed a bit, and he spent a little more time with his youngest son than he had with the others. "He adored Stephen," said Jay. "They were especially tight."

However, Jim was no less demanding of his children's intelligence, especially at the dinner table. He demanded that all of his children possess an insatiable curiosity that was as natural as breathing. "We weren't allowed to read, whistle, or sing at the table," said Stephen. Jim would also spring pop quizzes on his children at dinner, and he'd ask his youngest son the same question every night without fail: "What are the three layers of a glacier?" Inevitably, because the Colberts were devout Catholics, religion would be discussed. "My father's idea of fun was to read aloud from a book of French Christian philosophy," he added. Given Lorna's early interest in singing and acting, "Singing around the house was highly encouraged," said Stephen.

When Stephen was around eight years old, he watched *Man in the Wilderness*, a 1971 movie about fur trappers set in the early nineteenth century. When the main character is mauled by a bear, his buddies figured he was dead so they buried him. But it turned out that he was alive after all, so he dug himself up and tracked them down to kill them. The movie shook young Stephen, so he went to his father because he was afraid of going in the woods and thought he'd find a bear there. Instead of telling him that he had nothing to worry about, Jim said that if he was ever attacked by a bear, modern medicine would sew him right up, and he'd be just fine.

"My father's words kinda stoked my fear about bears."

But the stone was cast. "My father's words kinda stoked my fear about bears," he would say later.

. . .

During his tenure at the NIH, other companies and hospitals continued to try to recruit Dr. Colbert. He enjoyed his job, but as the decade came to a close, he decided it was time to look for another position. He needed to increase his income now that several of his oldest children were away at college; after all, despite the perks and the travel, the federal government didn't pay enough. So instead of automatically saying he wasn't interested, Jim started to listen to his suitors and even put feelers out. He soon received three offers.

One was from the pharmaceutical company Eli Lilly. While the money was definitely good, as with some of the offers that came in the last time he was job hunting, he felt he would have to play front man and sacrifice his principles. So he turned it down. Then in 1968, another offer came in from the American University in Beirut, Lebanon. At the time, Beirut was known as the Paris of the Mediterranean, a cultured, literate city. As Jim described it to his kids, he said they would fly all over Europe and go to Swiss schools and live a cosmopolitan life.

Not surprisingly, the kids loved the idea. "We all wanted to go to Beirut for the adventure," said Eddie. It looked so promising that Dr. Colbert even bought each kid a caftan to help them get in the mood.

In the fall of 1968, he traveled to Lebanon for the interview, but when he came back his mood was decidedly different. He sat the family down at the kitchen table and told them they wouldn't be moving to Beirut after all.

"He told us it was an armed camp ready to explode," remembered Eddie, "that the tensions there were just phenomenal, and at some point in the very near future, it was going to blow up." In fact, someone threw a Molotov cocktail over the wall at the university while he was there. A couple of months later, on December 28, Israel raided Beirut International Airport, a move that touched off battles and skirmishes that continued until the mid-1970s.

The third job offer arrived from the Medical College of South Carolina in Charleston. President William M. McCord, MD, invited Dr. Colbert to Charleston to interview for the vice president for academic affairs, a new position.

"The Medical College is an old medical school," Dr. McCord explained in a letter to Dr. Colbert. "We had a reorganizational program two or three years ago [which] calls for an academic vice president. We have had much to do and have been keeping our eyes open for an adequate person. Your name has been suggested to us."

At the time, the entire campus of the medical college had only six buildings, and many of the clinical and residency offices were run from the offices of local physicians. The administration was ready for an overhaul, and they were specifically looking for someone who would deliberately shake things up, as Dr. Colbert had attempted in St. Louis. Jim went for the interview, and after he got back he gathered the family around the dinner table again, but this time he announced they were moving to Charleston. Essentially, he asked for the sky and they gave it to him. Their initial salary offer was $35,000, he countered with $40,000, and they agreed. "They gave me everything, so how can I turn it down?" Eddie remembered him telling his family.

"Having come from Yale and St. Louis, Dr. Colbert understood academic medicine in ways that we didn't," said Layton McCurdy, MD, dean emeritus of the MUSC College of Medicine. "The hospital had only been open for about fifteen years before he came here, and we hadn't yet learned how to integrate academics with research and patient care. He understood how to do that, in both a strategic and pragmatic, nuts-and-bolts sense."

In fact, they wanted him so badly that they also courted Lorna. "They sent me a tray of Spanish moss with camellias set on top of it," she said. "It was so Southern."

Dr. Colbert accepted the job, and once more they packed up house and kids and headed for a new part of the country. Lorna's job was a bit easier because she only had to deal with moving six kids. It was 1969, and Jim, the oldest, was twenty-four and had not lived at home for several years. Mary was engaged to be married the following summer in Washington, and Ed was a senior in college. Margo stayed in Washington to finish out her senior year in high school and moved in with a cousin.

Dr. Colbert and Lorna packed up Tommy, Jay, Lulu, Paul, Peter, and Stephen and left Washington on January 29 in the middle of an ice storm. Eddie came along to help with the move. When they arrived in Charleston two days later, it was seventy-eight degrees.

The Colberts saw the first sign that life was going to be different in Charleston when they crossed the border from Virginia into North Carolina.

There, on the side of the road, was an enormous billboard with the figure of a Ku Klux Klan member dressed in sheets and a hood riding a horse. It was designed so that the head of the Klansman rose high above the billboard. The sign read, "Welcome to North Carolina, home of the Ku Klux Klan. Help stamp out integration, communism, and Catholicism."

"My mother said to my father, 'Where are you taking us?'" Stephen remembered. "But we kept going."

The family settled into the Holiday Inn on Calhoun and Meeting Streets in downtown Charleston for a few days until they could move into their house on James Island a few miles away. For the staff at the hotel, however, that day couldn't come soon enough. More than once, the front desk called up to Jim and Lorna's room because Peter and Paul were outside climbing on the rail of the hotel.

When they headed out to their new home, they received a few more hints that life would be different from what they had left behind in Washington, D.C. They drove by a pharmacy and everyone gaped at the signs hanging over the doors. One said Whites, and the other one said Colored.

"Welcome to the South," Lulu remembers thinking.

Dr. Colbert's first day as vice president for academic affairs at the Medical College was on February 1, 1969. He was immediately accepted among his medical colleagues; no doubt the natural way he communicated with colleagues and his family—with reason and respect—translated well when introducing himself into a new community.

The first thing he did was start to recruit nationally recognized faculty members to the school. "He believed the faculty was the University and it would rise or fall on the strengths of its faculty," said Marion Woodbury, former vice president for administration and finance.

Dr. Jim Colbert was a rising star from the first day he was hired at MUSC. *(Courtesy of the Waring Historical Library, MUSC, Charleston, South Carolina)*

Lorna and her kids did their best to acclimate to life in the South, despite their initial impressions of the racial divide in their new home.

Shortly after they moved into a house at 728 Willow Lake Road on James Island, Lorna took the kids to do some shopping. They'd only been in Charleston a few days and didn't have a chance to register the car yet; it still had Maryland license plates. A woman came over to her in the parking lot and barked out, "It was perfectly fine before all you Yankees got down here." This, despite the fact that Maryland is below the Mason-Dixon Line.

Some of the other changes were cultural. Compared with Washington, D.C., Charleston was still a small city. In 1970, the population of the metropolitan area was just 336,000; Washington was ten times as large. "I remember walking around with my jaw hanging down because it was so different from living in a big city," said Eddie. "The food was different, the people were different, the accents were different, and all that Spanish moss and the old buildings."

"James Island was like moving to the moon," Stephen remembered.

"It was very sleepy, with dogs sleeping in the street. When I read *To Kill a Mockingbird*, I pictured the town where I grew up. It had dirt roads and some really ramshackle neighborhoods where the black people still lived, essentially in the houses where their ancestors had been slaves. And there were cotton fields and peanut fields and tomato sheds."

In 1969, there were still blue laws on the books in South Carolina, legislation that prohibited retail stores from being open and that also banned the sale of alcohol on a Sunday. Though blue laws had been in effect when the Colberts lived in St. Louis and Washington, they'd been repealed while they were living there. "It was like a time warp," said Eddie. To make matters worse, everything shut down after ten o'clock.

Despite the differences, the family did their best to settle into everyday life. The kids enrolled at school, and Lorna set about turning the house on James Island into a comfortable home for her family.

Stephen enrolled in the first grade at Stiles Point Elementary School. "We started every day with a prayer long after it was illegal," he remembered. "But they didn't care. I crossed myself after the prayer and once a boy next to me asked me if I was a Catholic. When I said I was, he said, 'My mom says you're going to Hell.'" Another time, a classmate asked him when the ghosts came out of the statues.

"My mom says you're going to Hell."

Margo encountered the same thing. "I remember one girl said to me, 'You're Catholic? You're the second Catholic I've met. But you're nice, too.' Back then, people thought that Catholics were strange people," she said.

Shortly after moving to Charleston, Stephen started to have trouble with his right ear. It was discovered that he had a tumor in his ear, and it was removed along with his eardrum. He'd be deaf in that ear. After his surgery, he was cautioned not to get his head wet or allow water to get into his right ear for any length of time.

It was just one more thing to set him apart from the kids in Charleston, many of whom had been sailing and swimming since they were toddlers.

The racial and religious strife the Colbert family encountered when they first moved to Charleston had a long, tragic history, of course. The ongoing tension on both sides was palpable. However, what the Colberts didn't know was that it was about to get a lot worse. The year before they moved, five African-American students at South Carolina State were killed in rioting in Orangeburg, a small upstate town about eighty miles from Charleston. The killings would become known as the Orangeburg Massacre.

The police were absolved of all blame in the shootings, but that didn't satisfy the black community in South Carolina, or the country. The tension continued to simmer. The massacre, the growing civil rights movement, the visibility of the Black Panthers, and the general revolutionary mood of the country at the time all combined to create a tinderbox that would blow up soon after Dr. Colbert arrived at his new job. In fact, dealing with the offshoot of the violence would be the first real test of his tenure; his new job would be to ease a long-simmering racial divide.

Unskilled hospital workers who happened to be African-American made $1.30 an hour, compared with their white counterparts, who received $1.60 an hour—which was the federal minimum wage at the time—for performing the exact same jobs. The previous fall, Naomi White, one of the African-American employees, asked the AFL-CIO union for help and started signing up co-workers to demand that they receive the same wage as white workers. A couple of weeks after Dr. Colbert started working at the college, the union set up a meeting with Dr. McCord, a South African native. He agreed to meet, but when they showed up, he was nowhere to be found.

The black union members held a protest at the hospital, for which they were promptly fired. This, in turn, created a domino effect where hundreds of black employees walked off their jobs in protest, for which they were subsequently fired. A week later, over a hundred other African-American employees at Charleston County Hospital also walked off their jobs. Picket lines were set up at both hospitals, and the national media headed to Charleston to cover the strike. National civil rights leaders like Reverend Ralph Abernathy and Coretta Scott King—whose husband Martin Luther King, Jr., had been assassinated less than a year earlier—came to Charleston to show support for the workers.

When the strike was first called, Dr. McCord locked himself in his office so Dr. Colbert couldn't reach him. But Dr. Colbert couldn't get to his own office, since he normally entered through McCord's. So he had to go in another way, through the boardroom. "And that was filled with strikers, and little children were dancing on the table," said Lorna. "He told me he told the people, 'It's getting kind of hot in here,' because there were so many people there. And some woman yelled out, 'Well, it's going to get a lot hotter.' "

Once the strike started, his family rarely saw him, even though Lorna spent days at the hospital helping with the babies in the nursery.

The strike dragged on, with neither side willing to negotiate. At one point, Reverend Abernathy arranged a meeting with Dr. McCord, who didn't want to talk to him without having Dr. Colbert by his side. Abernathy walked into the office with his assistant Andrew Young, and McCord said, "Oh, so I see you brought your boy." He then pointed at Dr. Colbert and said, "Well, this is my boy," to introduce him.

Dr. Colbert didn't say anything during the meeting, but afterward, he went over to Reverend Young and apologized for McCord's calling him "boy." Young accepted his apology.

"He always tried to be the calm voice of reason and a model of stability when others around him appeared to be losing their heads," said Marion Woodbury, who worked at MUSC at the time.

"He had this vision, and he could persuade others," said Layton McCurdy another MUSC colleague. "He was marvelous in that way. He was a wonderful man and he did it with humor, with gentleness, and persistence."

"Dad was not impressed with Mr. Abernathy, but he told us to watch Andrew Young," Margo remembered. " 'Watch him,' he said. 'He's going places.' "

After the others left, Dr. Colbert and Andrew Young stayed behind to talk. "We talked about it for a long time, and we both agreed that we'd continue to talk if no one else was," said Young. "If we could work together [to end the strike], then neither one of us could get credit for settling it. And that was the only way it could get settled." And that's exactly what happened. "Nobody knew that he had been involved in bringing it to an end," said Stephen years later. "They only knew that he was involved in supporting the strikers."

Dr. Colbert also worked behind the scenes. None of the other hospital administrators were reaching out to Charleston's African-American community, and it's hard to say what they would have said if they knew Colbert was going into the local African Methodist Episcopal churches to speak to the people. "He told me what a wonderful experience it was to speak in these churches because they talked back to you," said Jay Colbert. "The feedback from the audience was just wonderful. He said if you ever get a chance to give a speech in an AME church, take it, because he just thought it was terrific. He loved it."

"By contrast, you get up and give a presentation in a Catholic church and when you're done, you could hear a pin drop," said Eddie.

The strike ended one hundred days after it had begun. The hospital rehired all the employees it had fired and started to pay them the same wages as their white co-workers.

"We worked out the strike so everyone thought they had won but nobody got any credit," said Young. "Dr. Colbert was a Southern gentleman from New York. That's very unusual."

And the following month, the Medical College received its accreditation to become the Medical University of South Carolina in July 1969.

Not long after moving to Charleston, Stephen worked hard to eradicate any signs that he'd grown up south of the Mason-Dixon Line.

"At a very young age, I decided I was not going to have a southern accent," he said. "Because when I was a kid watching TV, if you wanted to use a shorthand that someone was stupid, you gave the character a southern accent. And that's not true. Southern people are not stupid. But I

"At a very young age, I decided I was not going to have a southern accent. Because when I was a kid watching TV, if you wanted to use a shorthand that someone was stupid, you gave the character a southern accent."

didn't want to seem stupid; I wanted to seem smart." He decided to pattern his new accent after news anchors and reporters not only because he could detect no southern accent in any of them, but also because they all sounded smart. After all, they were delivering the news.

Another aspect of pronunciation he started to become aware of revolved around his last name. Stephen said that his father always wanted to pronounce his last name Col-*bear* but that his own father didn't like the French pronunciation because they were Irish. So Dr. Colbert told his own kids, "Do what you want. You're not going to offend anybody." But Stephen decided to hold off on making any radical moves on that front. Since he was working hard to eradicate his southern accent, he filed the Col-bert/Col-bear option away for the future.

He also became aware of the culture around him: the protests against the Vietnam War, changing racial and sexual politics, which of course at the time were impossible to ignore. When he was only eight years old, he hung a 1972 Nixon campaign poster on the wall.

"He was the first president that I was aware of," said Colbert. "I have great warm feelings for Richard Nixon, even though I was a little upset with him because when I'd come home in the afternoons from school, instead of seeing *The Munsters* or *The Three Stooges* on TV, it was Senator Sam Ervin. And while his eyebrows were hilarious, they weren't quite as good as Herman Munster's."

"I have great warm feelings for Richard Nixon."

Sam Ervin chaired the Senate Watergate Committee that investigated Nixon for his role in the break-in at the now-infamous Washington hotel. The hearings were televised live every afternoon, and favorite daytime shows from black-and-white sitcoms to soap operas were preempted for weeks since all three networks broadcast the hearings.

Later on, Colbert said that the poster also served as a symbol of when he first became aware of not only how politics can be twisted by those in power but also how humor can help both temper the outrage and make other people pay attention to you. "He was such an important cultural figure and object of comedy," said Stephen. "Everybody made Nixon jokes when I was a kid. When Watergate happened, I first became aware of the world and started to understand the concept of irony and satire or sarcasm. After all, he was the ultimate punch line."

Jim and Lorna Colbert regularly made the rounds at MUSC social events. *(Courtesy of the Waring Historical Library, MUSC, Charleston, South Carolina)*

Years later, he would defend Nixon. "He was so liberal!" he exclaimed. "Look at what he was running on: He started the EPA, he opened China, he gave eighteen-year-olds the vote. His issues were education, drugs, women, minorities, youth involvement, ending the draft, and improving the environment. John Kerry couldn't have run on this! What I wouldn't give for a Nixon!"

For the first time in a long time, things were relatively peaceful for the Colberts. Jim loved his job, the family was settling into Charleston, and the older siblings were establishing new lives of their own.

It also looked like a few years down the road, Dr. Colbert was likely to become president of the university when McCord retired. It wasn't part of his original job description, but after the strike was settled, Dr. Colbert started to assume some of Dr. McCord's responsibilities. He wasn't doing them to suck up or to make himself look good, but the truth was that many administrators and legislators up in the capitol of Columbia—after all, it was a state school—didn't get along with Dr. McCord and thought he was overly abrasive. Just as was the case during the strike, people asked to deal with Dr. Colbert instead of McCord because Colbert succeeded in making everybody walk away feeling like they had won.

In fact, over the next few years, the family was drawn into the culture of MUSC. In 1971, when she was sixteen, Lulu landed a job working in the audiovisual department, and Stephen would occasionally accompany his father to the office.

While his two older brothers Peter and Paul were involved in high school activities and out of the house most of the time, Stephen was the only little kid left at the house. With both his parents' attention freed up, they, especially his father, doted on Stephen.

With his future firmly in place as the president of the medical university, Jim started to relax. He loved Charleston. In fact, despite being in a completely different culture, he grew to love it within six months. He said it was the best move he ever made and that he'd never move away.

"Dad really did love it here," said Jay. "And one of the things he loved to tease us about was that he was going to get himself a dog and name it Calhoun after the street where we stayed when we first moved to Charleston." That's the advice he always gave his children: Throw yourself into it, don't do it halfway. Embrace the culture.

Paul liked to go for a walk at low tide off Fort Johnson Point near the house, and sometimes he'd actually walk to Fort Sumter, the site of a Civil War–era fort in Charleston Harbor where the first shots of the war were fired back in 1861. The fort became a national monument and part of the National Park Service in 1948, and today it is a popular tourist attraction. Once Paul walked out and got stranded when the tide was coming in, and the harbor patrol had to rescue him.

Dr. Colbert bought a boat to start exploring the waters around Charleston: the Ashley and Cooper rivers converged only a stone's throw away from their house on James Island. He named the boat the *Galaxy*.

Even though he'd grown up in the city, Jim loved going out in the boat and fishing. His family was surprised. "We'd put the boat in the water and go down to the Wappoo Cut, and Mom said she was convinced that he was just going to point the boat toward Spain and we'd never see him again," said Eddie.

And he loved to take his youngest son out to spend the day on the river, catching little hammerheads and other fish. Once Lorna accompanied them. "Jim and Stephen and I were in the boat, and I did not think of Jim as being a big sportsman so I was a little worried about where he was going," she said. "Uphill and downhill, it was a very rough day."

"Once we were crossing the harbor right by Fort Sumter where the rivers converge, and Dad said, 'Don't worry, Lorna, we won't let you out here, these are shark-infested waters,'" said Stephen.

"He was also a natural-born swimmer," said Jay. "He loved to body surf in the waves."

As they'd done with all of their kids, Jim and Lorna encouraged Stephen to find something he loved to do, and he never felt pressured. "They were very supportive of anything I eventually decided to try to do as long as it could pay the rent."

"Even though my dad was a doctor, he was always saying, 'Go be a whaler. Be an ice climber. You don't want to be a lawyer, go raft the Amazon.' We were not people of means, but the rule in our house was: Never refuse a legitimate adventure."

His was an idyllic childhood, one that was rapidly disappearing. Stephen Colbert grew up along a dirt road on James Island, a small town just across the harbor from Charleston, but one that might have well been worlds away given the differences in its people and culture. When he wasn't in school, he spent most of his waking hours riding bikes, fishing, and playing with his friends, normal kid stuff. That is, until everything tragically changed one day in 1974.

CHAPTER 3

JUST BEFORE SIX IN the morning on Wednesday, September 11, 1974, Dr. Colbert and two of his sons left the family's house on James Island and headed to the Charleston International Airport. Paul, eighteen, and Peter, fifteen, were the second- and third-youngest of the eleven Colbert children, and Dr. Colbert was taking them to New Milford, Connecticut, where they would enroll at the Canterbury School, a prestigious Catholic high school founded in 1915.

Dr. Colbert made a deal with his sons: He'd travel with them the first time so they knew how to get to the school, and on subsequent trips, they'd go by themselves.

With his brothers gone, only the Colberts' youngest son, ten-year-old Stephen, would remain at home with his parents, both of whom were in their early fifties. He would be the only child after ten years of sharing his parents with his siblings.

Once they departed for the airport, a twenty-mile drive from their home on James Island, Lorna got Stephen ready for school. He'd just started in the fourth grade with Mrs. Angela Katsos Kiehling, and he'd already made his mark with her and his classmates.

"He stood out because he was so bright and creative," she said. "He had a phenomenal vocabulary, even in fourth grade. Once I gave him a test with some pretty difficult words, and he could tell me what they all meant. Plus the other children liked him. It wasn't like he was in his own little world that he couldn't interact with the other kids."

While preparing him for school, Lorna suddenly felt sad. Stephen, always concerned about his mother, picked up on her melancholy. Though he was excited about the new school year, he couldn't ignore his mother when she was feeling down, since it was so rare. So he gave her an extra hug before he left for Stiles Point Elementary School, about a mile and a half away. Lorna, for her part, shook it off as a natural reaction to Peter and Paul leaving the house. After all, she'd had children underfoot for almost three decades. Stephen would be home for eight more years, but she already knew how they flew by.

The three Colberts stepped onto the silver-blue twin-jet DC-9 around 6:30 A.M. Dr. Colbert was a regular on Eastern Airlines number 212, a businessmen's commuter flight that was typically filled with Charleston executives and Marines from the nearby naval base on their way to points further north, after first connecting at Charlotte Douglas International Airport in Charlotte, North Carolina. The flight would continue on to Chicago. Twenty-six-year-old senior flight attendant Collette Watson greeted the seventy-eight passengers on the flight that morning along with the other flight attendant, Eugenia Kerth, who was twenty-five years old. Captain James E. Reeves was forty-nine years old and had worked for Eastern since 1956; Reeves had more than twelve thousand hours of flying time.

First Officer James M. Daniels, Jr., thirty-six, served as copilot and had been with Eastern for eight years.

The flight took off on time, and everything about the thirty-five-minute trip was ordinary. The plane began its descent into Charlotte around 7:30, and they were set to land on runway 36. A dense fog floated above the ground, but it was nothing the veteran pilots hadn't dealt with before.

The first officer flew the aircraft manually while the captain handled radio transmissions and ticked tasks off the checklist. They announced the imminent landing over the PA, and after first checking that passengers' seat belts were fastened, the flight attendants took their seats. The fasten-seat-belt light was on, but the no-smoking light hadn't yet been illuminated, giving smokers a few more minutes to enjoy their cigarettes. Since Watson was the senior attendant on the flight, she took the jumpseat next to the cockpit while Kerth sat in the back of the plane.

. . .

The first people to realize something was wrong were on the ground. Whether they lived near the airport or were driving to work, when they heard a low-flying plane—or saw it roar by overhead, they knew something was clearly amiss.

Jim Stanley lived a few miles away from the airport and was heading to work at the time. "I heard the jet and saw what looked like the tail section going into the fog, and then I heard an explosion," he said.

Survivors would later tell of glancing out of the plane expecting to see a runway, but instead they looked below onto a county road and saw cars driving into ditches to avoid the low-flying jet.

"All of a sudden, I felt a real hard jolt," said Collette Watson. "I thought that the landing gear had come down and that we were on the runway. But then I looked up and saw flames." The jolt she felt was the plane hitting a white pine about eight inches in diameter.

"I saw a tree go by the window, and a fraction of a second later we hit," said one passenger, Francis Mihalek of Charleston.

The plane skidded through a cornfield for about a hundred yards before it plowed into a dense clump of forest. Watson was tossed from side to side as the plane mowed through the trees, and passengers heard the first explosion before the plane came to a stop at the edge of a ravine overlooking a barn.

"I felt a wing tip down, then it hit some trees and I felt heat," said passenger Robert Burnham of Charleston. "I must have been thrown out of the plane. I got up, looked around, and started running through the woods."

"Everything was on fire," said Charles Weaver, who was hanging upside down from his seat when the plane finally came to a stop. He scrambled out of his seat and crawled toward the front of the plane.

"As I unbuckled my seat belt, I realized fire was all around me because my hands were burning," said Mihalek. "The right side of the plane was all ripped open, and I saw nothing in back." He crawled up the aisle and out the hole in the side of the plane, which was "just big enough to squeeze through." There, he found Watson trying to pull Daniels out of the left sliding window of the cockpit. "We could tell the copilot was alive, and he kept repeating, 'Get the people out, get the people out.' "

After a neighbor frantically knocked on his door around quarter to eight to tell him that a plane had crashed nearby, Robert "Tink" Lawing, Jr., ran out of his house. He knew exactly where to go: He just followed the clouds of black smoke billowing up from a nearby farm. He met up with Jim Stanley as he was rushing to the crash site, and they headed over together.

"As we were going through the woods, we saw bodies and parts of bodies, just scattered all over," said Stanley. Then we heard a lady scream. She was hollering for help, and she was helping people that were hurt."

He helped drag people away from the plane but couldn't get to those inside the plane.

After Watson and Mihalek pulled Daniels from the plane, Watson went back to help others, but she was stopped by a second, much larger explosion that resulted in a fireball that roared through the entire plane.

"There were tremendous numbers of people making cries from inside," said Johnny McDowell, who owned the farm where the plane had crashed. "Then there was a tremendous explosion and a flash fire. The massive hysteria was silenced."

Reeves and Daniels thought they were 1,650 feet off the ground when their altitude was actually 650 feet. The pilots had no clue they were in trouble, which explains Reeves's last words before the crash: "Now all we've got to do is find the airport."

The airport was two and a half miles away from the crash site. Reeves survived. Daniels didn't.

Rescue forces mobilized immediately. At 7:35, a controller in the tower at the airport saw the smoke and called the airport fire department. Three fire trucks left immediately and arrived at the scene five minutes later, after some difficulty making their way through the forested terrain. The

Steele Creek Volunteer Fire Department and the Charlotte ambulance service also rushed to the crash site.

Emergency physicians and nurses at Charlotte Memorial Hospital went on high alert shortly before 8:00, invoking the facility's disaster plan, with a total of thirty doctors ready to go. The first eight survivors of the crash arrived at the hospital around 8:10.

The story hit the local news shortly after 8:00 A.M., and as soon as word spread, residents of Charlotte and the surrounding towns flocked to the hospital to donate blood. Some waited in line for hours.

However, just after 9 A.M., the emergency staff at the hospital were told they were no longer needed. It was clear that there would be no more survivors. "Rescue activities were confined to those persons outside the aircraft because there were no signs of life from within the aircraft wreckage when the fire and rescue equipment arrived," read one report.

By 4:00 P.M., five hundred pints of blood had been donated, all for naught.

After Stephen left for school, Lorna luxuriated in finishing a second cup of coffee, which she never seemed to be able to get to in the typical morning rush when there were several kids to see off to school, and turned on the TV to watch the morning news.

Shortly after 8:00 A.M., a newscaster came on to announce that a plane had crashed near Charlotte and that the loss of life had been substantial. Initially, they didn't name where the plane had originated.

"My first reaction was, 'How terrible,'" said Lorna. Then it hit. Remembering her earlier premonition, she picked up the phone and dialed the main number for Eastern Airlines.

She received the news that, yes, it was flight 212 that had crashed, though the airline didn't go into detail about the severity of the accident at that point.

After Lorna hung up the phone, she called Lulu, who was nineteen and a sophomore at the University of South Carolina in Columbia. Because Lorna hoped for the best—after all, they hadn't yet confirmed the names of the dead—she gave her daughter clear instructions: "You need to come home and pick up your father and brothers in Charlotte. There's been an accident."

First, Lulu picked up Jay and Tom, who also went to USC, but instead of heading to Charlotte, they headed for Charleston.

Stephen remembered the day quite clearly. "My brother Billy picked me up from school, but he didn't say anything so I knew something was wrong," he said. "We went home, and everybody was there, so I knew something was up. I went upstairs, and my mom told me there'd been an accident. I knew that my father and my brothers were going off to boarding school, and I immediately made the connection. After that, I remember the house filled with people and food."

The Eastern Airlines office in Miami was in charge of notifying the families of the survivors as well as the next of kin. However, they tempered their words by describing the list of casualties as those who had "purchased tickets and were not among the survivors."

As Lulu, Tom, and Jay drove, they listened to radio reports on the crash. "We hit the Summerville line—about twenty-five miles from Charleston—and the radio announced the list of survivors. There were thirteen. And that was it. The three of us kept screaming, 'Come on! Come on!'"

None of the Colberts were on the list.

Sixty-nine people died at the scene, and three others died within a few days. Of the seventy-two, thirty-eight were from Charleston. Only ten people survived.

Mayor J. Palmer Gailliard ordered all flags to fly at half-mast throughout the city. The crash of Eastern Airlines flight number 212 was North Carolina's second-worst air disaster since 1967 when eighty-two people were killed in a midair collision over Hendersonville.

The casualty list read like a who's who of the Charleston community. "It affected everyone in the city because everybody knew so many of the people who were on the plane," said Frank Ford III, who lost his father, Frank Ford, Jr., the president of Ford's Ready-Mix Concrete Company, in the crash. Also among the dead were John Merriman, the news editor for *CBS Evening News with Walter Cronkite*, three executives from the *Evening-Post* newspaper, and Wayne Seal, the news director at WCIV-TV.

The navy was hit disproportionately, since the navy base had a significant presence in Charleston at the time. Rear Admiral Charles W. Cummings, commandant of the Sixth Naval District, was killed along with two submarine commanders and three enlisted men.

In addition to Dr. Colbert, MUSC had lost the nursing instructor Martha Jean Sloan, and several MUSC employees had relatives who were killed. Linda McCarter, who worked in the department of obstetrics and gynecology, lost her husband, Martin, and mailroom employee Jack Ratliff's daughter Stephanie Ratliff Bolin and her husband Sergeant Curtis J. W. Bolin were both killed. They were flying back to their Illinois home after they buried their infant daughter in Charleston just one week earlier.

Ben Hutto served as organist and choirmaster at Saint Luke and Saint Paul's Cathedral on Coming Street in downtown Charleston, where a community memorial service was held to remember the thirty-eight Charlestonians who had died in the crash. It was his responsibility to select the music and lead the choir for the service.

"It was really wrenching for the entire community. But everyone was aware that the Colbert family had suffered the greatest loss of anyone in Charleston."

"It was really wrenching for the entire community," said Hutto. "But everyone was aware that the Colbert family had suffered the greatest loss of anyone in Charleston." Hutto lost his best friend from high school, Harold Newton, the brother of the Piggy Wiggly founder Buzzy Newton.

"That was one of the hardest things that I ever had to do as a church musician, because so many people had suffered in Charleston. I knew that service would be the toughest in my life, and I knew I needed to be strong for it."

The eulogies for Dr. Colbert poured in. "We concentrate on his medical achievements while realizing the great difficulty of separating the man from the physician," said H. Biemann Othersen, MD, a MUSC colleague. "He possessed compassion and understanding and never lost his sense of humor. The visitor in his office never felt as if he were being ushered out. His duties and obligations left little time for hobbies although he was an ardent if relatively unsuccessful fisherman and he avoided activities which might diminish the time that he had with his family."

Funeral services filled the following days. Some Charlestonians did nothing else but go to funerals and memorial services for an entire week. The city was drained.

The Colberts' three caskets were displayed at the McAllister Funeral Home at 150 Wentworth Street, on Saturday and Sunday, with funeral services held on Monday, September 16, at the Cathedral of Saint John the Baptist on Broad Street, where the Colberts were parishioners.

Angela Katsos Kiehling, Stephen's fourth-grade teacher, attended the service. "It was heartbreaking seeing the three caskets up there," she said.

"Unlike so many people of our time, Jim Colbert was not torn, not divided, not driven," said the priest. "He had a great sense of the comic and a sense of the majestic. He was fond of saying, 'Remember, there is no substitute for intelligence.' Yet, in the face of human foibles and weaknesses and yes, stupidities, he could see the comic. His laughter, so characteristic, was never malicious, nor hostile, nor mocking. It put things in perspective. He was not a negative person but ever positive and creative."

Of Peter and Paul, Father Byrne said, "They were true sons of their father and shared his ideals and his outlook. Their very names say so much: Paul and Peter, and they were on their way to Canterbury. Canterbury is a school in Connecticut, and it's also a medieval shrine in England, the goal of pilgrims in an age of faith. They have arrived."

The next day at the burial at the Annapolis National Cemetery in

Maryland, the monsignor continued his tribute: "There is nobility from their intelligence, from their solidarity and love, from their faith. It is somehow refreshing, too, that in this military cemetery surrounded by men who fell in war, these three died on a mission of peace and education and growth."

At ten years old, Stephen felt anything but refreshed. With this, losing a role model so young, his father's godlike image was "trapped in amber."

Very early on, the focus of the investigation was on pilot error. "Experience has shown that mechanical failure—particularly, failure of the crucial altimeter system—is exceedingly rare," said one investigator.

During the plane's descent, the two pilots were participating in what was known in flight terms as "nonessential chatter," where they were gabbing about desegregation in the schools, rising gas prices, and President Nixon's impeachment hearings instead of focusing on landing the plane.

"I must have misread the altimeter," Daniels said later, though he added that it was Captain Reeves's task to keep tabs on the readings. "I thought I was above a thousand feet. Or perhaps I missed a cycle. I don't know, I'm no expert on altimeters."

In his testimony, Reeves also said that he didn't see the runway lights because they were obscured by fog, but during the subsequent hearing, the FAA interviewed two other pilots who landed minutes before flight 212, and they testified that the runway lights were indeed visible.

"It is noteworthy that the terrain warning alert sounded in the cockpit, which should have been particularly significant to the crew," read the report. "If heeded, it would have made them aware that the aircraft had prematurely descended. Based on pilot testimony taken at the hearing, it appears that the crew's disregard of the terrain warning signal in this instance may be indicative of the attitudes of many other pilots who regard the signal as more of a nuisance than a warning." The report cited five similar recent crashes on descent "as examples of a casual acceptance of the flight environment, reflecting serious lapses in expected professional conduct."

The National Transportation Safety Board concluded that the "probable cause of the accident was the flight crew's lack of altitude awareness at critical points during the approach due to poor cockpit discipline in that the crew did not follow prescribed procedures."

Partly as a result of the crash, soon after the FAA instituted mandatory rules against nonessential chatter in the cockpit.

CHAPTER 4

THE FUNERAL AND BURIAL had been surreal. But in the immediate aftermath the reality of how life had so fully, irreparably changed hit home for Stephen.

After the burial, the family gathered at Stephen brother's Ed's house in Washington D.C., where Stephen came down with a nasty headache that he just couldn't shake.

"I went into a spare bedroom to try to get rid of my headache, and there was a science fiction book up on the shelf," he recalled. "I picked it up and was instantly hooked. I proceeded to read about a book a day."

It was a great escape, and one that school couldn't provide. He became detached immediately after the funeral and stayed that way for years. And though he earned average grades in his classes, according to his own estimates, he said, "I don't think I did homework a dozen times between the time I was ten and eighteen."

Science fiction saved him, and that's where his learning came from. "I learned things at school accidentally, not because I did any work," he admitted. "Nothing seemed important, and any threat that a teacher could present to me seemed pretty ridiculous after they died. At one level, it made me lazy because you need threats to have discipline, and nothing seemed threatening to me," he said. "I escaped my teen years and all that grief in books.

"I was detached from what was normal behavior of children around

"I learned things at school accidentally, not because I did any work."

me," he added. He would later observe that his experience at school helped him to develop a sense that accepting the word of an authority figure without question—as many fellow students had—had no place in his world.

His detachment extended to how he regarded his own trauma. "Everything that happens to you as a child seems normal because you have no reference point," he said. "This is what happens and it all seems normal. It obviously was sad and shocking, but I didn't feel like something strange had happened to me, because what else did I know?"

Overnight, the home on James Island had gone from a raucous, chaotic, busy mix of two parents, three smart, rambunctious boys, and frequent visits from nearby siblings to an unearthly quiet house that contained just one grieving mother and a traumatized, hurting child. With Peter's and Paul's deaths, Stephen Colbert's closest sibling was now nine years his senior. Until he left for college eight years later, Stephen, who'd spent the first years of his life in a household overflowing with brothers and sisters, lived alone with his mother.

"The shades were down, and she wore a lot of black," Stephen remembered. "It was very quiet."

But he wasn't so withdrawn that he pulled away from his mother. On the contrary, he worked overtime to help her and turned to the age-old Colbert talent for making each other laugh, and says that he did his best to cheer his mom up. While she appreciated her youngest son's efforts, Lorna found great solace in continuing to go to Mass, usually on a daily basis. Stephen often accompanied her.

"My mother found great strength—I don't know about peace—by going to Mass. Because it was just the two of us at home, I was often there with her. And that made a powerful impression on me. It was a constant

Little "Stevie" Colbert on the playground in fourth grade, taken a few months after his father and two brothers were killed in a plane crash. (*Courtesy Angela Katsos Kiehling*)

search for healing. My mother gave that gift to all of us. I am so blessed to have been the child at home with her."

"I don't see how I could have made it without my faith," said Lorna. After her husband and sons died, she could have returned to Washington, D.C., where she had friends and a couple of her children lived. But after five years in Charleston, like her husband, she felt rooted there. "I felt very solidly ensconced down here," she said. "Besides, I had a child to finish raising." Jay and Tom were close by in Columbia, and Lulu dropped out of USC that fall to move in with her mother and Stephen.

Despite her great losses, Lorna pulled herself together to help her surviving children. She approached MUSC's Dr. McCord to help pull a few strings to secure Lulu a summer internship in Washington with Senator Ernest F. Hollings of South Carolina for the summer of 1975. And she asked Dr. William H. Patterson, president of the University of South Carolina, to keep a special eye on Jay and Tom, both juniors at USC, after they returned to school from the funerals. They wanted to live together in the same dorm room, which required a bit of shuffling in mid-semester.

"As you can imagine, we all have bouts of extreme depression and such deep sorrow that it is physically and mentally draining," she wrote to Patterson. "The triple tragedy is almost more than any of us can bear, but when we have each other there is a kind of comfort."

The Colberts weren't the only ones affected by the loss of Dr. Colbert. Since he was being groomed for the top spot at the hospital once McCord retired, his death threw the entire administration into disarray. "MUSC entered an eight-year period of chaos and confusion that would not have occurred had he survived," said Marion Woodbury, who worked with Colbert during his entire tenure. "The progress that began under his leadership was delayed for at least ten years."

Probate papers were filed on November 27, 1974, in which Lorna was listed as administratrix. Dr. James Colbert's estate was valued at $112,400 in 1974, which wasn't much for a renowned and highly respected physician who had been practicing medicine for three decades.

About a year after the plane crash, Lorna decided that the best thing to do for herself and her son was to move from rural, bucolic James Island to downtown Charleston, into a Federal-style home at 39 East Battery, known as the George Chisolm House. Built in 1810, the five-bedroom house had more than six thousand square feet and came with a carriage house out back. Designed by the esteemed Scottish architect Robert Adam, the Chisolm House was known as a showcase for the nineteenth-century decorative art form called composition ornament, which an artist named Robert Wellford made famous. Wellford traveled throughout the South to create raised murals and sculptures to decorate mantelpieces and complement woodwork. Above one of the home's six fireplaces appears a scene of Cupid bound by the Graces, while the dining room mantel displays a boar hunt. Upstairs in a second-story room—possibly Stephen's childhood bedroom—another mantel shows a scene of a boy herding sheep.

Stephen wanted to stay on James Island. The move to the Peninsula—as downtown Charleston is often called—only compounded the loss of his father and brothers because he was also leaving his boyhood friends and neighbors behind. And even though they were only moving a few miles away, downtown Charleston was a world away from James Island. "I wasn't from downtown and I didn't know the kids there," he said. "I love Charleston, and I love the Lowcountry, but it's very insular. I just wasn't accepted by the kids."

Instead of attending classes at the local public elementary school, Stephen followed in the footsteps of his older siblings and went to private school. Lorna enrolled him in Porter-Gaud, a private college prep school across the river in West Ashley. He entered in the fall of 1976, when he was in sixth grade. Coincidentally, it was also the first year that the school went completely coed.

Porter-Gaud is regarded as one of the best private schools in Charleston. Covering grades one through twelve, it's a small school with Episcopal roots, considered to be the school where WASPish moneyed Charlestonians send their kids. Many of the families whose children attended Porter-Gaud had been in Charleston for generations, and there was an established social structure at the school.

Interestingly enough, several of Stephen's older siblings had attended Bishop England, Charleston's primary Catholic school and the largest Catholic high school in the state, but Stephen was the first to attend Porter-Gaud. Perhaps Lorna thought it would help Stephen better fit into downtown if he went to school with the kids who were among the cream of the crop.

"The faculty was aware of Stephen because of the plane crash, that was a big deal in Charleston," said Dr. Maxwell Mowry, a language teacher at the school. "He had no spunk when he first came here, but he was definitely smart and had a classical training, courtesy of his family, which was obvious whenever he opened his mouth."

Most of the other students regarded him coolly at first, aware of his family tragedy. He was shy, withdrawn, and smaller than his classmates.

After enough time had elapsed, his older, larger classmates called off the hiatus on this new, smallish, bookish kid, and soon Stephen turned into their punching bag.

"I was beaten up on a regular basis," he recalls. "When I was in high school, I was a huge loser, beyond the fringe of high school society. I was stuffed in a lot of lockers, and if there were no lockers handy, they'd just stuff me in the wall."

Mowry said he was unaware of the abuse. "Any student who bullies is going to be really careful that it doesn't cross a teacher's radar," he said.

In 1977, Stephen discovered something besides science fiction novels to help him escape from his misery. *Dungeons & Dragons* is a fantasy role-playing war game where each player takes on a persona and stays in character while developing backstories, solving problems, and pursuing all kinds of adventures with other characters.

"One day at lunch, I overheard my friend Keith saying, 'I listened at the door, and I didn't hear anything, so I went inside and got attacked by a giant rat!' I asked what he was talking about," he said.

Stephen took to *Dungeons & Dragons* in the same way he had taken to science fiction, and soon he was living and breathing the game. "It was a whole new kind of game," he explained. "No board, just dice, just probabilities. It allowed me to enter the world of the books I was reading. I put more effort into that game than I ever did into my schoolwork."

"I put more effort into [*Dungeons & Dragons*] than I ever did into my schoolwork."

He liked the fact that he was able to play the hero; through the game, he had a sense of power that was totally absent during the hours he spent at school. "It's an opportunity to assume a persona," he said. "Besides, who really wants to be themselves when they're teenagers?"

He found a ready group of fans at Porter-Gaud. "We were all complete outcasts in school, beyond the fringe, beyond nerds," he said. "We were our own sub-dimensional bubble of the school, that's how outcast we were."

His favorite part of the game involved delving into his character's personality and history, and then figuring out how that character related to others. "We'd do huge campaigns where each of us would have multiple characters," he said. "I even created characters based on the personalities of my brothers and sisters and my mother and father."

Eventually the characters were all killed off, except for his sister Lulu, who was a witch, who had seductive powers and love potions. "She was my character for years," he said. "All my friends bugged me that my favorite character was female, but I thought it was kind of cool that it didn't matter what sex your character was."

In the South, as elsewhere, the religious community was up in arms about *Dungeons & Dragons.* Preachers called it a cult, saying it was little more than devil worship and that some kids actually thought the game was real. Stephen scoffed at this, thinking, "Who'd be stupid enough to believe this was real?" But at the same time, he also admitted, "I certainly wished it was real at times."

In time, his fanaticism for the game faded. "We started to judge each other based on how our characters behaved, and one Dungeon Master thought we were too greedy and that we wanted too much," he said. "But, within the culture of high school we were the weak puppies and were looking for power. We *wanted* our characters to be too strong. I think by the end we were using the game to express how we felt about each other."

Around the same time, he also discovered J. R. R. Tolkien's *Lord of the Rings* books, which served the same purpose as *Dungeons & Dragons* during his troubled adolescence. He discovered a wealth of great role models in that book, including one in particular who must have reminded him of his father. "Aragorn is an Apollonian ideal of a man," he said. "He's a warrior and a hunter and a poet and a scholar and a woodsman and a healer. Everything in moderation, everything done beautifully. And a peacemaker."

He was so fond of the books that he would read them over and over again; as an adult, he estimated that he's read *Lord of the Rings* more than forty times. "I used to read it, finish the last book, and start the first one all over again," he said.

"His *Dungeons & Dragons* phase was partially a function of his loss," said Chip Hill, a close friend from Porter-Gaud. When he was growing up, Colbert, according to Hill, used to joke about how he "wanted to major in mass psychology and start a cult."

"The thing about Colbert is he's fucking brilliant," said Scott Wherry, another high school friend. "He was always the smartest guy in the room, but he was always smart enough not to let you know he was the smartest guy in the room."

"The thing about Colbert is he's fucking brilliant."

Around the same time, Stephen also started listening to comedy records every night to fall asleep. "I was one of those kids who had every comedy album," he said. He particularly liked Bill Cosby's two biggest albums, *Bill Cosby Is a Very Funny Fellow . . . Right!* which came out in 1963, and *Wonderfulness*, from 1966. He also became hooked on *Saturday Night Live*, which debuted in the fall of 1975, and particularly liked Steve Martin and Don Novello's character, Father Guido Sarducci.

"I read the covers off Don Novello's book *The Lazlo Letters*," he said. *The Lazlo Letters* was a series of letters Novello wrote under the pseudonym Lazlo Toth, who was actually a real person who was mentally unstable and defaced a Michelangelo sculpture in the 1970s. Novello addressed the letters to celebrities, politicians, and big American corporations, which deliberately contained mistakes, jokes, and outright lies, but often what was more funny were the letters he received back, which tended to be very serious and full of hyperbole and misguided advice.

"I loved it so much I wanted to ape it, and actually started writing letters like that myself when I was in college," said Colbert. As the phenomenon of Young Republicans started, he and a friend launched an organization called "Us Young Republicans." "We would write to people the way Novello did. There's some of Lazlo Toth's DNA in what I do," he would later admit. "In fact, I frequently think of him when I think about my character's emotional ignorance."

He also became obsessed with George Carlin's brand of humor—which was shocking for the time—and just about wore out his album *The Class Clown* with his notorious routine "The Seven Words You Can Never Say on Television" from 1972.

Stephen also liked to listen to the comedian and political satirist Mark Russell, because his particular brand of humor—telling jokes about Ted Kennedy drinking, being fat, or womanizing—made it look like it was easy to get people to laugh, again something that had been in very short supply around the house since the airplane crash. "Most of it seemed flippant, like somebody saying, 'Ted Kennedy—enough said,' " Stephen later explained. "There's not really a joke there, just the attitude of a joke, but a lot of that passed for political humor at the time."

During his junior year in high school, after being ostracized for all five of the years that he'd spent at Porter-Gaud, Stephen underwent a radical transformation. It was as if someone flipped a switch. "The beginning of my junior year, nobody knew me at school," he said. "A year later, I was voted wittiest, and people were happy when I showed up at parties."

"He was very quiet and withdrawn when he was younger, and he didn't blossom until later in high school," said Ben Hutto, director of choral activities at the school, who had seen the caterpillar-into-butterfly transformation happen with students before. "A lot of kids are withdrawn up until the 11th or 12th grade. It's as if they're watching and waiting, and once they realize they're different from the other kids, that they have a real talent that sets them apart, then their confidence flourishes essentially overnight and their whole personality changes. Stephen was that

Colbert, with book, holds court with other members of the debate club at Porter-Gaud. *(Courtesy Porter-Gaud)*

kind of kid. All of a sudden, he came out of this cocoon, this private place where he stayed for a number of years in the wake of the trauma, and then he just blossomed."

Athletics were big at the school, but since Stephen was never particularly athletic, he decided to sign up for the debate club. Sue Chanson, an English teacher at Porter-Gaud, coached the team.

"The debate club was made up of a group of boys much like him," she said. "They were some of the brightest kids we had, but they were also off-the-wall in some way." When Stephen joined, the club had only been around for a couple of years, and Chanson found it hard to recruit members, so she scouted out students who had a little bit of an edge and who were willing to try something a little different. "In order to be a good debater, you need to be intelligent and witty and have a strong enough ego

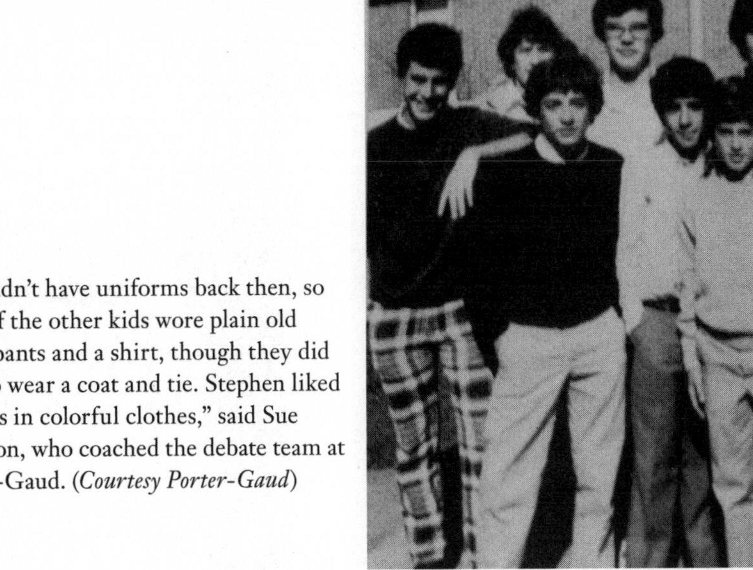

"We didn't have uniforms back then, so most of the other kids wore plain old khaki pants and a shirt, though they did have to wear a coat and tie. Stephen liked to dress in colorful clothes," said Sue Chanson, who coached the debate team at Porter-Gaud. (*Courtesy Porter-Gaud*)

to get up in front of people to debate, and Stephen had all of those traits," she said.

Chanson remembered that he liked to dress in a way to call attention to himself. "We didn't have uniforms back then, so most of the other kids wore plain old khaki pants and a shirt, though they did have to wear a coat and tie. Stephen liked to dress in colorful clothes," she said. Indeed, in one yearbook photo, he's wearing a pair of loud plaid pants.

He also joined the boys' glee club in his junior year and took to it instantly.

"I was surprised that he joined in the first place," said Hutto, who first thought that the only reason Stephen signed up was because some of his buddies were in the club. "I thought he was going to be the guy who's always cutting up, so I was surprised he sang as well as he did and he liked it as much as he did. A lot of the guys in glee club had been together since the fourth grade, so by the time he came along, he was very much behind the pace." While Stephen didn't audition for any of the big parts or

"Every time Stephen walked into the room, there'd be people laughing," said the Porter-Gaud choral teacher Ben Hutto. "You never knew who he'd zero in on—and half the time it was at my expense—but he was always good-natured about it. He was brilliant, a little naughty, and supercharged with energy." *(Courtesy Porter-Gaud)*

solos—he preferred to sing in the background—he was quick to learn the repertoire, which was fairly challenging.

He was a second bass, "a natural musician," said Hutto, who taught the boys songs from musicals like "Nothing Like a Dame" from *South Pacific*, spirituals, folk songs, and classical works by composers ranging from Mozart to Fauré. Since Porter-Gaud is affiliated with the Episcopal Church, they studied a few religious songs as well, including the challenging Missa Brevis in D major by Mozart.

"He was constantly on," said Hutto. "Every time Stephen walked into the room, there'd be people laughing. You never knew who he'd zero in on—and half the time it was at my expense—but he was always good-natured about it. He was brilliant, a little naughty, and supercharged with energy."

After his transformation from the picked-on kid to most popular funnyman in the school, Stephen didn't just focus on developing the more outgoing parts of his personality. He also started to write—for himself, for the school newspaper, for friends, and for potential girlfriends.

He had a crush on a girl at Porter-Gaud, and she made no secret of the fact that she disliked a certain teacher. Stephen decided to entertain her with a series of stories straight out of the science fiction novels he had devoured only a few years earlier. "Almost every day, I'd write her a short story where she would kill him in a different way in sort of a James Bondian kind of explosives in the gas tank of his car kind of way," he said.

Just as Stephen had injected himself into different fictional scenarios with *Dungeons & Dragons*, he began to do so with other media. In 1979, he watched the movie *All That Jazz* and found that it stirred something in him from his dark side. "I thought I'd like to live that dark life," he later said. "I liked how damaged they were and how they used that to create something beautiful. There was something viscerally attractive to me about living the sort of life that might kill you young. I liked these unhappy people. There was [also] lots of drinking and fucking. And that was appealing."

In fact, a dark side was not-so-quietly creeping into the periphery of Porter-Gaud's esteemed reputation. During his senior year, Eddie Fischer, a long-time coach and trainer at the school, resigned after being accused of molesting a male student.

Stephen had a private encounter with Fischer in his sophomore year one day when he didn't feel well and was sent to Fischer's office, which he remembered had a door and no windows.

"He checked me for a hernia and said, 'Turn your head and cough.' And he was pretty thorough. I'm 16, and I'm thinking to myself, 'I just don't see how it could be a hernia.' But he's the trainer. He said, 'No, I don't think it's a hernia, just go to the nurse's office and get an aspirin.' "

Later in his senior year, a student did an impression of Fischer at a school assembly and asked a boy to drop his pants, and the audience burst out laughing. "There was no embarrassed hush," said Colbert. In the early 1980s, pedophiles were rarely mentioned in the media and were not the topic of public conversation. "They didn't make that connection. There was the sense that 'There's crazy Mr. Fischer,' not 'Hey, that guy's a pedophile.' "

The story ended tragically. Even though he was fully aware of the accusations against Fischer, Porter-Gaud's principal, James Alexander, ignored them and gave Fischer a positive reference for another school job on James Island. The teacher would go on to molest more boys for almost two more decades. In the spring of 1999, Fischer was sentenced to twenty years in prison. A year later, after news of Alexander's referral was made public, the principal committed suicide.

On his summers off, Stephen started working part-time at MUSC. One summer, his only job was to clean and switch out all the lightbulbs in the Basic Science Building.

The next summer, he worked in the computer department when the hospital was in the process of converting every employee from using typewriters to computers. His job was to remove the typewriters and wheel in the computers and hook them up. Some of the secretaries had worked at the hospital for twenty-five years and didn't take kindly to having their typewriters whisked away. "I'd put the computer on their desk and turn it on, and they'd burst into tears and quit," he said. "It happened more than once."

Emboldened by his newfound popularity and confidence in school, he decided to audition for parts in local theater productions. In 1981, he tried out for *Babes in Toyland*, put on by Charleston Stage at the Sottile Theatre, and he won a part in the chorus.

At Porter-Gaud, he also started to audition for some of the plays and musicals produced by the drama club each year. He won a part in *The Music Man* in his junior year, and then played the lead, Frank Butler, in *Annie Get Your Gun* during his senior year. He discovered that he loved to hear people applaud for him just about as much as he loved to make them laugh.

He also started to sign up for an impressive list of clubs and activities at school; it was as if he was making up for lost time with a vengeance, and then some. His senior yearbook entry showed that he belonged to the astronomy club, debate team, film society, glee club, French club, Latin club, Rowdy Club, the senior steering committee, the vestry, Delta Delta

Colbert played the lead of Frank Butler in *Annie Get Your Gun* in his senior year at Porter-Gaud. *(Courtesy Porter-Gaud)*

Sigma, and the National Forensic League. In addition, he was a National Merit Scholar and had won an award for his Latin skills.

If this sounds like a lot, it's important to keep in mind that Porter-Gaud was a high-pressure college prep school. Senior yearbook listings for other students showed that some participated in twice as many extracurricular activities as Stephen.

But even back then, signs of the character who would later make him famous would pop up here and there, since sometimes it was difficult to discern whether he was kidding or not; in many cases, one sensed that the truth was somewhere in between, which was the case with his senior year book listing.

"I barely graduated from high school," he said, "but I read so much of what I wanted that I was incidentally able to pass the tests without doing homework."

He had applied to several colleges, including Hampden-Sydney, a

Colbert's senior yearbook entry foreshadows the tongue-in-cheek personality of his famous future character. *(Courtesy Porter-Gaud)*

small private liberal arts college for men in Hampden-Sydney, Virginia, about seventy miles southwest of Richmond. He decided to enroll at the school, partly because his good friend Scott Wherry accepted, but also because with its focus on Latin, great-books study, and the mandatory blue blazers, he thought it would feel familiar to him, just like the genteel Charleston flair of Porter-Gaud and the focus on a classic education.

He was accepted into the class of 1986.

As her son flourished and prepared to go off to college, Lorna also started to pull herself out of her shell. She took a few classes at the College of Charleston and threw herself into volunteer activities, including raising money for local nonprofits like the Gibbes Museum and attending social events for a variety of causes and charities throughout Charleston.

But she never remarried. She and Jim had been married for almost three decades, and she'd known him for almost forty years. They'd raised eleven children together and made a good team.

"It was obviously very tough on her," said Stephen.

She also got involved with the annual Spoleto Festival held each spring in Charleston by helping with fund-raising events and escorting visiting artists around town and putting them up in the carriage house behind 39 East Battery.

Spoleto Festival USA is a major arts festival that features world-class performances in opera, music, theater, and dance for two and a half weeks each spring in Charleston. The festival was founded in 1977 by Gian Carlo Menotti, a Pulitzer Prize–winning composer who modeled it after the Festival of Two Worlds that he'd founded two decades earlier in Spoleto, Italy.

Though primarily a composer, Menotti also wrote several plays, and at Spoleto Festival USA in 1982, he decided to feature *The Leper*, a two-act play, as the main dramatic theatrical work. The play, which he had written in 1970, was his most autobiographical work to date, essentially serving as a plea for the world to accept homosexuals run through the story line of a leper who loves a prince who is also afflicted with the disease.

Stephen decided to try out for the play at the last minute, after the teenage actor originally cast for the part of the king's mute gay lover dropped out. Menotti had written *The Leper* for his adopted son Francis "Chip" Phelan, who played the lead at Spoleto. Even though he was onstage most of the time, Stephen didn't have a line in the entire play.

He was thrilled to get the gig. Only a couple of months after starring as Frank Butler, he'd be performing with professional actors from New York. His high school Latin teacher, Dr. Mowry, remembers the play very clearly.

"He acted rings around Chip without ever saying a word, and he did it all through body language," Mowry recalled almost thirty years later. "I still have vivid memories of the moves he made onstage, they were so arresting. In his very last scene he wanted to tell the audience something, he turned towards the audience, tried to speak but couldn't. There was such pain and anguish on his face. To this day, the only thing I remember about that play is Stephen Colbert."

The reviewers were less than kind, but of course the fact that the play was performed sixteen times during a seventeen-day festival struck many as overkill since many of the other performances received only a handful of airings. Colbert, however, received special notice in one review.

"As Manuel the workman whose leprosy has gained him the love of a king, Stephen Colbert gives a sensitive performance. This strange variation on *The Prince and The Pauper* then is dropped after Manuel commits suicide offstage during the intermission," said a review in the *Charleston Evening Post.*

Stephen was thrilled, especially by the feedback he received from his fellow actors. "They were very encouraging and told me they thought I could do this for a living," he said. "No one had ever said 'You could do this' to me about anything."

CHAPTER 5

In the fall of 1982, Stephen started his freshman year at Hampden-Sydney College. Although one aspect of the school fit like a comfortable old shoe, overall he had a tough go of it from the beginning.

"It was like going to college one hundred and twenty years ago," he said. "We studied languages and all of the Great Books, with a nineteenth-century emphasis on rhetoric and grammar."

Even by Charleston standards, Hampden-Sydney was very conservative. As Colbert would later describe it, the college was "an inorganic rock of ultraconservatism," he said. "The school was so conservative, it made Charleston seem like a love-in."

Even though he had grown up in a relatively conservative home and city, his experience working with professional actors on *The Leper* had given him a glimpse into a way of life that was the polar opposite.

The regimented curriculum meant that a significant number of the freshman class flunked out, but Stephen wasn't among them. "[The professors] hammered you," he said. "It was really hard work." Though he said he was in no danger of dropping out of the school, it made him realize how little he had applied himself in high school. "I knew this was my last chance, so I worked very hard. But I didn't have the disciplinary skills, so it took a lot more time to do the work I needed to do than it took the better students."

Football and fraternities ruled the social life on campus, neither of which Stephen cared for, which made it easier for him to devote himself to his studies. Although most of his classes were in philosophy, he didn't declare a major. Why?

"My dad liked philosophy," he admitted. "I was supposed to be trying to find a father, so I studied philosophy, but I found it very depressing. I studied Western Man in my freshman year, and *The Iliad*, and there was one question on the exam at the end of the year: Is it better to know or not to know? Defend your answer."

Despite the heavy course load, he still found time to gravitate toward the drama department, where he became friendly with Professor Steve Coy. "He was very different from the rest of the teachers at Hampden-Sydney," said Stephen. "He said he went to Yale because the acting students there threw the best parties."

Stephen acted in a few plays at the school, including *Oh Dad, Poor Dad, Mama's Hung You in the Closet and I'm Feelin' So Sad*, by the playwright Arthur Kopit, which appeared on Broadway in 1963 and was made into a movie in 1967. It's the surreal story of a wildly dysfunctional family that travels around the world with the corpse of the dead father tucked into a casket. When they performed the play at Hampden-Sydney, it was a revelation for Stephen. "I thought, this is for me," he said. "These people are saying things in a very silly way and getting away with it."

He also gravitated toward another professor at the college. Stephen was a student in Amos Lee's class on the history of western civilization in his freshman year and found he could confide in Lee. "Since the other students were primarily interested in playing football and sports, being in the drama department put him in a different league," said Lee. "I don't recall him really getting along with the other students at the college. He'd come by my office to catch me up on what he was doing, things he wanted to do, and how the campus was treating him. He knew I liked opera, and he'd tell me stories about Spoleto. Menotti was in and out of his house a lot at parties, and we talked about acting."

In the meantime, Lee became friendly with the rest of the Colbert family. Lorna had converted the carriage house in back of her home at East Battery into a modified bed-and-breakfast, where paying guests could stay for a night or two when passing through town. Whenever Lee visited

Charleston, he'd stay in the carriage house. "Lorna would bring fresh rolls and pastries when I checked in, and we'd chat for awhile," he remembered. "She was a very gracious hostess."

Stephen once told him that he received a commission for the number of people who came to Charleston to stay, and Lee was never sure if he was joking or not. They also talked about whether he should transfer to a larger school with a major drama department and other students he could relate to or stay at Hampden-Sydney until he graduated.

"I weighed 135 pounds, and I was incredibly depressed," Stephen said. It was time to move on.

"He finally realized he needed to be at a bigger university so he could pursue his acting," said Lee. "And one day he dropped by my office to tell me he was going to transfer to Northwestern."

There had been another issue that he didn't bring up before: there were no girls at Hampden-Sydney.

While Lorna continued to attend Mass on a regular basis, Stephen stopped once he left Charleston.

"The minute I went to college, I stopped believing in God," he said. "The minute I had an opportunity to be out from under the constant exposure to my faith, I accepted the opportunity to not believe." He said that the prime factor why he became an atheist during those years was that he still desperately missed his father and brothers. "I wanted to know that I would see my father and my brothers again, and it was heartbreaking to think that that wouldn't happen. I was very convinced of my atheism for a long time, but I was also very depressed about it because I wanted very much to believe."

He continued to pursue his acting in between semesters and during the summers off from college. In 1983, he flew to Spoleto at the request of the director Ken Russell to appear in the stage production of Puccini's *Madama Butterfly*, albeit an updated, risqué version of the opera. Russell, an English movie director, was known for courting controversy in his work; he directed *Altered States* and *Tommy*, by the Who. At the time, Menotti was still in charge of the Spoleto festivals in the United States and in Italy, and he often duplicated parts of the programs at both venues. In 1983, in addition to staging *Madama Butterfly*, Menotti directed *Antony and Cleopatra*, written by his erstwhile lover Samuel Barber. Stephen had a small part in the Italian production of the opera.

The role was a walk-on during a dream sequence that showed a ship landing, followed by people disembarking. Russell had a definite vision for what he wanted, and he thought Stephen would be perfect for the role. Though it wasn't a speaking part, they told Stephen he'd be onstage by himself, and they kept stressing that it was a very important role.

When Stephen went to the costume department to be fitted for the show, he was handed a pair of boxer shorts. Okay, he thought, he could wear them onstage. He got the true picture of how important his role was at the first rehearsal.

"Dear Mom, am having a wonderful time, have met a lot of nice people, and oh yeah, I'm doing a nude scene. Love, Stephen."

"I went out wearing the shorts and immediately heard Ken Russell yelling 'Stop stop stop!' [Menotti] then asked, 'Now Stephen, who said you could wear boxer shorts?' Apparently, Russell wanted me to appear totally nude. *That's* why it was such an important part!" he said. Later on, he wrote his mother a letter about it: "Dear Mom, am having a wonderful time, have met a lot of nice people, and oh yeah, I'm doing a nude scene. Love, Stephen."

In the fall of 1984, Stephen transferred to Northwestern University, which he picked because he'd heard that the school had the best undergraduate program in theater. He was thrilled when he was accepted, and he finally felt like he was on the right path.

"I had discovered that the one thing I liked to work hard at was performing, and when I was working on my craft, nothing else seemed important."

He was on the way to a brand-new life. He'd never been to Chicago before, and no one knew him at Northwestern. He had already made a few changes to his life—losing his accent, for one, and deciding to pursue a risk-laden artistic path—so he figured, what was one more? Even though his father had long ago told his children that it was their choice to decide how to pronounce the family's last name, Stephen hadn't gotten around to deciding for himself until now. His brother Eddie went by "Col-bear" in college, before reverting to the traditional "Col-bert." Then Tom made the switch, and supposedly stuck with it.

On the flight to Chicago, Stephen finally made his fateful decision. "I'd toyed with the idea of changing the pronunciation, but if there was ever a time to do it, it was now," he said. He was upgraded from coach to first class, and sitting next to him was Farrell Corley, an astronaut. They struck up a conversation, and Stephen asked Corley what he thought of the idea.

"I think you already know," he responded.

"When I walked off the plane, I was Col-bear," he said.

Once he arrived at Northwestern and settled in, Colbert realized just what a culture shock he was in for.

"I came from a place where everyone was a doctor or professor," he said, referring both to Charleston and to the families from which the men at Hampden-Sydney came. At Northwestern, in contrast, guys and girls lived on the same floor in the dorms, a quarter of the theater class was gay, and the theater program was an entire school, not just a major, and had separate buildings, dorms, and cafeterias. "Just to have girls living on the same floor and showering near me was remarkable," he said. "And I was calling my teacher not Professor but Anne, and she was coming over and partying at my apartment and crashing on the couch."

The winter of 1984–85 also happened to be the coldest winter in Chicago's history to date. One night, Stephen remembered standing in a phone booth and looking out to see a bank's temperature sign report it was 39 below.

The movie and TV show *Fame*, about a group of students and teachers at New York's High School of Performing Arts, had come out in 1980 and 1982, but Colbert described the atmosphere at Northwestern's theater school as pretty close to that of the movie. "It was like living in an episode of *Fame*, or maybe the pilot," he said. "It was all 'I'm going to live forever' and torn sweatshirts and legwarmers, on both the guys and the girls. I didn't fit that at all."

Despite having a totally different focus, the workload at Northwestern was just as intense for Colbert as the program at Hampden-Sydney because the theater major was a three-year program. Since he entered as a junior, he had only two years to complete it. On top of everything else, even though he had already completed the core curriculum at Hampden-Sydney, he still had to sign up for several nontheater classes at Northwestern.

This was his typical schedule:

Dance class starting at 9:00 A.M.
Acting class
Another acting class
Dramatic criticism class
A class on the history of costume and décor
Scene design class

His classes were back-to-back without much of a break in between, and he had to squeeze in homework. He also had to work backstage on various crews for the shows, which ran practically every night. And to earn money for food and rent, Stephen also worked several part-time jobs waiting tables at local restaurants, including a restaurant in Evanston called J. B. Winberie's. His schedule was hellacious. But he didn't mind because he was finally able to dive into his craft—and not only that, but he was surrounded by people who felt the same way that he did about it.

At the same time, there were some students who buckled under the pressure, but not necessarily because of the workload; instead, it was because of the strain of being required to express themselves in ways that they hadn't previously. Colbert admitted that he came close to cracking under the load several times.

"The point of all of the acting classes was for students to *show* how they feel," he said. "A lot of people came there with some experience and a lot of tricks to entertain their teachers and classmates. But the teachers wanted to strip all those away, and they demanded that students be emotionally honest onstage." In reaction, most students become angry, because it's a defense mechanism against being emotionally honest. "We all build these walls to keep ourselves from showing our true emotions, because they can be seen as weaknesses. And everyone [in the theater program] went through that."

If anyone was familiar with building emotional walls, given the loss of his father and brothers and the relentless bullying he endured for several years, it would be Colbert. Unlike his classmates, who usually proceeded to the crying stage, he tended to get stuck on anger. In fact, Anne Woodward, one of his acting teachers, worried that he would get so angry that he would punch her.

"She insisted that I get counseling or else she wouldn't teach me," he said because he once tried to break a man's hand during rehearsal. "We were improvising, he pissed me off, and I grabbed his hand so hard that I almost broke it. I had a short fuse back then."

"I was constantly asking myself the question, Who am I?, which actors are supposed to do to act as a character in performance," he said. "So while that isn't a bad thing, it can make you insufferable."

And it did, for a while, at least. "I was a real poet-slash-jerk," he admitted. "I had a beard, and I wore black, and I was really willing to share my grief with you."

He also made an attempt to get as far away from his roots as he could: He wore very un-Charlestonian black turtlenecks, a long scraggly beard, and shoulder-length hair. "He was masculine and intelligent and radiated his intelligence," said the author Ayun Halliday, who dated Stephen in college. His newly acquired Hamlet look helped him with his performances. "He had a certain gravitas that he could get across onstage," she said.

"It's like he was born in the blue blazer with the khaki pants."

Regardless of his new look, he couldn't entirely hide his pedigree. "It's like he was born in the blue blazer with the khaki pants," said Anne Libera, who studied at Northwestern with Colbert and now teaches at Second City. "Ayun is such a hippie girl and she would try to make him over. I have this vivid memory of him going into an hour-long rant about how much he hated hummus."

"I can't imagine that we ever went to the homecoming parade or a single football game," said Halliday. "He was not a fraternity boy."

As he settled into the program and grew accustomed to the long hours of work, Stephen began to explore a wide variety of characters to play onstage. While the faculty mostly let students choose the parts they wanted to play, students were naturally attracted to one kind of archetype over another. And Colbert was no exception.

"I like weak characters who feel like they should have a better place in the world, but are too weak to assert themselves in any way," he said. However, there was one character that he'd always been attracted to but didn't get the chance to play: Richard Rich in *A Man for All Seasons*, by the agnostic playwright Robert Bolt. The play is about Sir Thomas More, the chancellor of England in the sixteenth century who chose to be beheaded rather than grant Henry VIII a divorce from Catherine of Aragon so he could marry

Anne Boleyn. "Richard Rich in *A Man for All Seasons* feels like he should have an appointment in court, and his friend Thomas More won't get it for him," said Colbert. "So, he eventually betrays him." In time, it's discovered that the character Rich—who has been angling for a job in the king's court, is spying on More to get in good with Henry. After More is executed, Rich takes over the position of chancellor, which he holds until his death.

However, he did perform in *Pelléas and Mélisande*, an avant-garde story of forbidden love written in 1892 by the symbolist playwright Maurice Maeterlinck. It wasn't until after he'd left Northwestern that Stephen grasped that it was impossible for a twenty-one-year-old theater student to competently perform in such a surreal play. "I had no conception of what to do," he said. "All I knew was that my character had really broad shoulders, so they made me a pour-foam chest. God, I wish I still had it! I'd wear it to bed at night."

Although he tackled meaty roles, since he was in Chicago, it wasn't long until Second City began to work its way into Colbert's life. In fact, part of the undergraduate curriculum included the study of comedy, so that graduates of the program would receive a well-rounded experience in all aspects of the theater.

But since he was determined to be a serious actor, not a comedian, despite the early comedic training he got from his family, he treated it lightly. It wasn't until a fellow student dragged him along to a downtown theater focusing on improv that he began to doubt his original path of pursuing serious drama study.

"I went and saw it once and was stunned by how much I wanted to go do it," he remembered. In fact, he was so smitten by it that, soon after, he formed an improvisation team at Northwestern and called it the No Fun Mud Piranhas, recruiting students not only from the theater school but from other departments at the university, including economics and engineering. Though the group met primarily for fun, Stephen soon heard of a college improv competition and decided to check it out.

The contest was held at ImprovOlympic, a Chicago theater cofounded in 1981 by the renowned improvisation teacher Charna Halpern. Stephen approached her to see about signing up.

The Northwestern team competed against several other colleges, including the University of Chicago and Yale. Though the team from Yale won, Stephen was hooked. He signed up for classes with Halpern and started to seriously pursue improv at Northwestern, too.

"He was relatively inexperienced in improv when I first met him, but he always had amazing ideas, and he could make something out of nothing," said Halpern. "The smarter you are, the better you're going to be at this work. Stephen was so aware of the world around him that he could talk about anything. Once, someone started to narrate a game about Greek mythology, and he was right there. Other students would think, I gotta study my Greek mythology, but he didn't. You've got to know everything to get up on that stage. And he did."

He wanted to soak up improv as if he was a sponge. "He was a great student, and eager to take direction from others," she said. "He'd look up at me after a sketch with his notebook and ask, 'What did we do right and what did we do wrong?' "

Halpern said that she remembers Stephen because he was the most vibrant one in the group. "He would weave three different pieces together to make the whole thing work and make the audience scream because look how all those things came together to mean something," she said. "He was smarmy when he needed to be, and he had something to say politically all the time."

His fellow classmate Anne Libera agreed, to a point. "What Stephen was always interested in was not so much politics as . . . hypocrisy and extreme points of view and the way in which people behave in extreme situations," she said.

And from growing up in a large family, he already knew how to play well with others. "He was a good team player," said Halpern. "Everyone loved working with him because he wasn't out there trying to be the star, he was out there playing the piece. He wasn't standing there thinking, what can I do so people see how funny Steve Colbert is, he would jump onstage to help or heighten what somebody else was doing."

Around the same time, Stephen met Del Close, the artistic director of the ImprovOlympic, who was widely considered the godfather of comedy in Chicago.

Though Close was a brilliant teacher, he had an extremely volatile personality, and no one quite knew how he'd react at any given moment. In fact, in later years, his students began to refer to him as the Ted Kaczynski of modern comedy. Nevertheless, he made a huge impression on Colbert, who was drinking up everything he could about improvisation. "Del used to say, 'If you come across a rabbit hole, don't step around it, jump down the hole to see where it leads,'" said Colbert. "One of the great things about Del was that he was a pagan. When he was teaching, he would take out this pentagram necklace that he wore and flash it at the class. As a result, I've been to my share of new-moon celebrations."

"One of the great things about Del [Close] was that he was a pagan."

Two years flew by, and graduation day arrived. His mother and siblings flew to Chicago to attend the ceremony. When his name was called, Stephen walked onto the stage, and as the dean handed him a leather case, she shook his hand, then leaned over and whispered, "I'm sorry."

He had no clue what she was referring to until he returned to his seat and opened up the portfolio. "Instead of a diploma, there's a torn scrap of paper inside with 'See me' scrawled on it," he said.

He soon discovered that he had never finished an independent study from his last semester, which earned him an incomplete and meant that he lacked enough credits to graduate.

"Let me tell you, when your whole family shows up and you get to have your picture taken with them, and instead of holding up your diploma, you hold the torn corner of a yellow legal pad, that is a humbling experience," he recalled.

He completed the study over the next six months and attended the mid-year graduation ceremony around Christmas. When he went up on the podium for the second time in six months, the same thing happened.

Apparently, this time, the torn yellow scrap of paper was because of an unpaid library fine. Once that was cleared up, they sent him his diploma in the mail. "To this day, I'm pretty sure I graduated from college," he joked.

After graduation, even though some of his classmates moved on to try their luck in New York or Los Angeles, Stephen stayed in Chicago. He began to go out on auditions for serious theatrical roles and plotted out what his next move would be. But money was extremely tight; he could no longer rely on the cafeteria plan at Northwestern. Though he preferred his coffee black, he started to take cream and sugar in his coffee because, as he told his mother back then, "It's food."

He continued working in restaurants as a waiter and bartender, and he also started building furniture, or as he put it years later, "horrible, horrible futon frames. They fell apart on people in the middle of the night and left jagged bits of wood and 4-inch, razor-sharp zip screws sticking into their mattresses."

He also spent a few months traveling through Europe and returned to Chicago flat broke. After he got back, he had no money to rent an apartment, so he had to sleep on a friend's floor. Another friend who worked as the box-office manager at Second City offered him a job answering phones, and he was so broke that he had no choice but to take it. Besides, the endless cycle of going on auditions and not getting called back was starting to wear him down. "I wanted to do something other than try to get an acting job, because I was so afraid of not being hired," he said. "At the same time, I suddenly realized I had chosen something that's damn near impossible to make a living at."

"I suddenly realized I had chosen something that's damn near impossible to make a living at."

Though he loved doing improv at Northwestern and with Charna Halpern, he had long fought the idea of having anything to do with Second City. "ImprovOlympic people looked down on Second City people because we thought it wasn't pure improv," said Colbert. "And we were all very proud of ourselves."

While ImprovOlympic improvisers would build a one-act play around one word, in contrast, Second City actors would tweak and polish their routines by performing the same skits and scenes in front of a new audience every night. They were doing something right; some of the biggest names in American comedy started out at Second City, including the *Saturday Night Live* alums Dan Akroyd and John Belushi.

Second City got its start in 1959 when Paul Sills, Bernard Sahlins, and a couple of other undergraduates at the University of Chicago decided to start a coffee shop where they'd serve coffee during the day and put on comedy shows at night. From the first night, when three thousand people showed up, the die was cast.

The format was simple: "A typical Second City show consists of a series of relatively unconnected scenes, some music, a funny song, a blackout, then another scene," said Sahlins. "But it has to be aimed at young people. And to this day, audiences and the actors remain young."

Another key to Second City was the idea of cooperation; after all, Second City is an ensemble theater company. "The notion of ensemble, of you depending on your fellow actor and he depending on you, was drilled into every actor by Paul," Sahlins added.

After Stephen started working at the box office, he learned that he could take classes for free, so he dove right in. "I liked the atmosphere, and I liked the fact that a lot of people who worked there were sort of damaged," he said. He also let go of his ImprovOlympic snobbery when he discovered that Second City actors were indeed improvising, contrary to what he thought in college. They were just doing a variation on the theme. It was still improv. "I saw what they did, I didn't care whether they were really improvising. I wanted to do it."

Stephen and his ImprovOlympic classmates had learned long-form improv, while Second City actors relied more on short-form. "In long-form, a group of performers receive one suggestion from the audience and then create a whole piece around that subject," explained Allison Silverman, who took classes at Second City in the 1990s and would later write for Colbert on his show. "There are three acts, each with three scenes. This method teaches that you shouldn't go for the immediate and easy punch lines." Short-form, in contrast, goes for the quick and easy gag, and that's what Second City stressed.

Colbert started to spend every waking moment at the theater. But even though he loved working and taking classes at Second City, he still viewed it as a stopping-off place, convinced he belonged in serious drama. "In my mind, I had a loft with only a steaming samovar as my furniture and was an incredibly self-important, pretentious person," he said.

Stephen spent almost two years working in the box office and taking classes. In August 1988, he was accepted into Second City's touring company, where he would get to perform for audiences every night.

He'd be working with fellow improvisers Paul Dinello, Amy Sedaris, and a comedian from Wisconsin named Chris Farley, along with a few others. They'd spend a few months in Chicago working together and developing skits and scenes before going out on the road. From the beginning, he gravitated toward Dinello and Sedaris—who were a couple—and they toward him, though there were a few bumps in the road.

"He showed up with really high hair and an actor's attitude," said Dinello. "I thought he was pretentious and sort of cold."

"I thought Paul was pretty much an illiterate dolt," Colbert shot back. For his part, Colbert tended to drag out his superior air whenever he was around other actors because he'd earned a college degree in theater. "I was very actorly because I had gone to theater school," he said. "And I was very controlled, I was all about the planning. Paul was sort of a wild, chaotic, impulsive energy comedically. Much sillier, much stupider behavior."

"Stephen approaches things intellectually while Amy and I approach things emotionally," said Dinello. "So when we started, he wanted to take the right road, and he wanted to hear what people had to say, to intellectualize stuff and understand it. Amy and I were more the kind of people who would just jump in."

When the three started working together, Colbert announced to the others that he never laughed or broke character onstage. Of course from that moment on, Amy and Paul set out to prove him wrong. "In the improv community, if you slip up an inch, they ride you like a cowboy on a bronco to the gales of riotous laughter of everyone watching you die," said Colbert.

One night, Amy and Stephen were doing a scene onstage where Colbert was pursuing her as a lover. They started to sing a song, and then Amy turned her back to him and put in a set of false, decayed teeth, which wasn't supposed to be in the scene. "All of a sudden in the middle of the song, Amy turns around and grinned at him, and Stephen burst out laughing," said Paul. "He just lost it and he went backstage. He was all upset about it."

Sedaris said that Colbert just needed to be broken in. "He got really mad at himself," she said. "He went back and slammed the door because he was so upset that he broke onstage."

"I was so mad that we finished the song and then I fucking blew offstage and went and locked myself in the bathroom like a teenage girl, and banged my head against the wall with rage," Colbert said. "But something burst that night, and I finally let go of the pretension of not wanting to be a fool. After that, I've just enjoyed being a fool. It was good medicine for me to get off my high horse."

"I finally let go of the pretension of not wanting to be a fool."

"As soon as he realized he could [relax on stage], he got more playful and became sillier and sillier," Sedaris added.

But there was still no love lost between Stephen and Paul; they could barely tolerate each other. A breakthrough came when McDonald's hired Second City to do a custom-made Christmas show for their employees, and Dinello and Colbert were assigned to write it. Stuck together, they fought it at first, then relaxed, and soon they started to genuinely like being with each other.

"And then we fell in love with each other," Dinello said.

"God, they were inseparable," said Sedaris. In fact, all three couldn't stand to be apart from one another for longer than necessary.

"They were the magic trio," said Dave Razowsky, who performed with them at Second City. In fact, they often referred to themselves as the Three Idiots.

"Colbert was always the Southern gentleman, and always very smart," said Fran Adams, who was an ensemble member with Second City from 1988 to 1994. "Stephen, Amy, and Paul were a trilogy. If you could get Stephen by himself, he would be totally different, but he was very much under their influence. And Stephen and Paul was okay, but Stephen, Paul and Amy weren't a positive energy to the rest of the crew. They were positive to each other, but never to the rest."

"There were definitely cliques in Second City," said Nia Vardalos, who toured with Colbert for a couple of years and would go on to write and star in *My Big Fat Greek Wedding*. "It really was high school all over again."

Stephen didn't care. He'd found a new tribe.

Despite the fact that he loved doing comedy and was in tight with Dinello and Sedaris, Stephen still believed that his destiny was to be a serious dramatic actor. In fact, he'd abruptly quit Second City several times when he was with the company.

He continued to audition for dramatic roles in and around Chicago, and even performed in a few experimental theater productions. "You know, the kind of stuff where there were eight people in the audience," he explained.

Amy and Paul convinced him to come back each time, and neither one understood Colbert's attraction to dramatic acting.

"Imagine getting paid to do what you love, where before, you were gladly performing in bars for free," said Dinello. "And not only getting paid, but sharing the stage with the funniest people in the city and in front of sold-out audiences. It was like going to the greatest college in the world. A place where you could learn, you were encouraged to fail, you got paid, and the beer was free."

"It was like going to the greatest college in the world. A place where you could learn, you were encouraged to fail, you got paid, and the beer was free."

It took several years and much begging and pleading from his friends, but finally Colbert realized that his true destiny was as a comedian, not as a serious actor. "I wasn't enjoying it that much when I did straight, avant garde, experimental theater," he said. "I found that when I did comedy and blew a line, there was laughter backstage. And that was so much healthier than if I blew a line in drama. I like these comedy people better than the dramatic people. I surrendered my need for importance."

"People kept paying me to do comedy, and I kept having a wonderful time, so I finally just gave in to it," he said.

Around the same time, he had another stunning revelation. One frigid winter day in Chicago, Colbert was walking down the street when out of nowhere a Gideon appeared and gave him a Bible. "It was so cold, I had to crack the pages open," he remembered. When he opened the Bible, it flipped open to a recommended list of verses and chapters for different emotions. For instance, if you were feeling anxious, you were supposed to turn to the book of Matthew, chapter 5, and read the "Sermon on the Mount." " 'Who among you by worrying can change a hair on his head?' " he quoted. "It spoke to me."

From that day on, he slowly began to return to the faith of his youth. He was greatly relieved. "There were maybe five years when I couldn't think of why I should believe," he said. "But the desire to believe was always there. The fact that thread was never cut was helpful."

Stephen finally felt that he had a future as an actor—a comedic actor, but an actor nonetheless.

Working for Second City helped make him feel that he was part of something bigger than just performing. "It gave me a sense of being part of a tradition and that I had something to measure myself against," he said. "It also gave me hope that I wasn't kidding myself, that I might have some facility for what I was doing, and there might be a future and a place for me in the world."

Hearing hundreds of audience members laugh and applaud for you obviously didn't hurt either, though that didn't necessarily come to fruition every single night. "Second City would really spoil you because you got such a great response every night," said Dinello. "So if one night it wasn't uproarious, you'd be like, 'Oh, this audience blows.'"

It's not like they hadn't been warned. "Learn to love the bomb," Del Close had advised his students, though it took Stephen years before he realized what he was talking about. "I didn't know what he meant for a long time. He said, 'I don't mean, just sort of get over it and realize that tomorrow the show will be better, but *love* it.'"

Dinello describes one night at Second City when the audience primarily consisted of high school students. "Colbert and I were out there improvising and we did this folk song," he remembered. "And the whole audience quietly got up and started filing out. We're like, 'What the hell's going on?' So we changed the song to, 'They're leaving, we can say 'fuck' now,' and we did this whole song and it had about eighty 'fucks' in it. They asked for their money back, so Second City had to give back two hundred tickets' worth of money."

Colbert learned to love the bomb. "That's when I knew I didn't want to do anything else," he said. "That was also frightening, because I thought, 'OK, I'm totally committed now. I don't think there's anything else I could do.' And I had a little crisis of confidence once I knew there was nothing else in the world I wanted to do."

Once he totally surrendered himself to Second City, Colbert flourished. And though every actor was encouraged to experiment with a variety of characters, Stephen discovered that he kept coming back to one character in particular.

"Second City allows actors an insane playground to try out everything good about themselves and everything bad about themselves to allow them to really find their voice," said Mick Napier, a director. "You try so many different scenes in the improv sets that you learn everything you need to know about yourself. Colbert learned that it works really well when he has this high-status character that's a little bit quirky and a little bit weird."

To Dinello, this came as no surprise. "Stephen always had the ability to play high-status idiots, because he's so well-spoken and the intelligence oozes from every pore," he said. "He also had the ability to fuck with people and still keep a straight face."

Despite the close fit, Colbert still resisted the character that came most naturally to him. "I tended to get locked into the high-status game—the teacher, the doctor, the lawyer," he said.

So he continued to experiment with other personas onstage and during rehearsals. Despite the laughter and applause that his button-down conservative character received, he thought it was somewhat boring, and craved a more exciting character. "I wish I was an old black woman!" he once said. "They have so much character. There's no flavor to me. Who would be interested in me as a person?"

He finally got to be an old black woman in a skit from the Second City production of "Are You Now, or Have You Ever Been Mellow?" in 1994. The scene began with Colbert and Steve Carell—who was a year ahead of Colbert at Second City—playing two men who visit Colbert's hometown. Instead of calling him by his name, Wentworth, Colbert's neighbors called him Shirley instead. When Carell asked for an explanation, Colbert replied that people in his hometown thought he really *was* an old black woman. Carell then started to channel his own inner "old black woman," which the locals also accepted.

Colbert also discovered that life at Second City spilled out into the real world. "If you improvise a lot onstage, you end up doing it in your life," he said. "The basic tenet of improv is 'Always agree, always go along, never deny, don't block.' "

One night, Colbert and Dinello headed out to a bar to relax after a long day of rehearsals. Stephen had a few business cards from his talent agent—who also ran a modeling agency—in his pocket. The two watched a few younger women who were dressed to the nines and dancing by themselves.

Colbert thought the girls were way out of his league. Besides, that night, he just happened to be wearing a pair of ratty red sweatpants. Paul bet him they wouldn't talk to him; Stephen said they would. So he approached them and gave his agent's card to one of the women. "Hi," he said, "I'm from this agency and I just want to talk to you about your look." It worked. They talked for a while, and he walked back to Dinello, who was amused by the whole thing. "There," said Colbert, "I did it. I had a conversation with her. In sweatpants."

Colbert was beginning to sense the power of his talent. And by now, he was totally sold on the short form of improv that was the rule at Second City. He described one golden rule that carried him through: the *yes-and*.

"The *yes-and* means that when you go onstage to improvise a scene with no script, you have no idea what's going to happen, maybe with someone you've never met before," he explained. "And to build a scene onstage, you have to accept what the other improviser initiates on stage. If he says you're doctors, then you're doctors. Then you add to that: 'We're doctors and we're trapped in an ice cave.' That's the *-and*. You have to keep your eyes open and be aware of what the other performer is offering you, and improvise a scene or a one-act play." However, it can then quickly turn into a tightrope for both performers, because neither one controls the situation. "It's more of a mutual discovery than a solo adventure, and what happens in a scene is often as much a surprise to you as it is to the audience."

He also started to see that his fellow performers appreciated his work, and that one of his particular strengths was his ability to help others blossom onstage. "I'm proud of my ability to understand what somebody else is trying to do and help them achieve it, because part of the aesthetic of improvisation is service," he said. "And that's very valuable in your life, as well as in your work."

Despite the constant emotional challenges of doing improv both in rehearsal and in front of an audience, Second City was once a drug haven in the 1960s and 1970s. According to Colbert, when he was there, Second City was squeaky clean. "People actually go there to dry out," he said, but once he wanted to see what it would be like to improvise while high.

It didn't work. "I just got so fascinated with the other people on stage that I didn't say a word for a half hour," he said. "I just thought they were wonderful."

At Second City, performers who spent at least two years in the touring companies fully expected to be invited to join the main-stage company. The idea was that you paid your dues by running all over the country—even the world—and eventually you'd be rewarded with a spot on the main stage, which was more prestigious.

"In the touring company, you do the best of Second City, but I think we were the first touring company that actually started doing our own original material, so we always had a scene of our own in the show," said Sedaris. "That was a first."

There are several touring companies at any one time, with different degrees of desirability, as far as the performers are concerned. Some of the touring companies get better gigs and bookings than others. While some companies get to tour Europe, others get stuck on the community college circuit. And even though the actors are constantly performing and honing their craft, waiting to be called up to the main stage generates an anxiety and anticipation not unlike a minor league baseball player waiting to be asked to join a major league team.

"It's not easy to be a lady-in-waiting there," said Colbert. "You get to be on the road, which is great, but waiting for your work is an exhausting experience, even waiting for a touring company. They keep you hungry."

By any account, the daily schedule was no less intense for Colbert than it had been at Northwestern: Performers practiced and researched during the day, and then went onstage at night. "If an improvisation works we try to remember why it worked and what was funny. Then we rehearse it and try again," he said. "Basically, we just play. That's our job, we play.

"We were all working as hard as we could," he added, explaining that since performers were promoted from one part of Second City to another—first the classes, then a touring company, then maybe another touring company—by the time a performer made it to main stage, instead of feeling like celebrating, an actor more likely would acknowledge what seemed like a logical conclusion to a long, drawn-out process and get back to work. Colbert explained: "It felt more like, 'It seems fairly logical that I'm here [because] I didn't completely suck compared to my co-workers, so I guess I belong here.' No one was leaping up in the air and going, 'I made it!' " Because, after all, not every actor made it to the main stage.

Even so, Colbert, Dinello, and Sedaris weren't a perfect fit once they got to the main stage. "A lot of [earlier] people were sort of conservative," said Sedaris. "It seemed like everyone was from Ohio. And we were definitely more physical [in our comedy]."

Indeed, while many of the performers at Second City—whether they were students, in a touring company, or in main stage—liked to draw on current events and politics for their routines, Colbert, Dinello, and Sedaris preferred to focus on channeling strange and unusual characters, from a hallucinating mail sorter to a serial killer at a laundromat.

To Second City producer Kelly Leonard, Sedaris in particular stood out with her "huge, obscene, crazy characters: hicks, grannies, even a doomed squirrel."

The three had no argument with her conclusion. "Second City is like the island for broken toys," said Dinello. "Dirty, broken toys and a collection of outcasts. We were misfits even there."

"Second City is like the island for broken toys."

In one scene from the 1992 show "Ku Klux Klambake," Colbert was a mailroom clerk who thought that his co-worker, played by Dinello, was really Jesus Christ. "Between Colbert's zealotry and Dinello's embarrassment, the pair form a wonderful team," wrote one reviewer.

In another skit from "Destiny and How to Avoid It," later in 1992, Dinello played an insensitive physician who meets a patient's family. Again, the trio was true to form: "These folks are some of the best wackos this side of *Twin Peaks*," said the reviewer. Sedaris played "a momma who looks like *The Beverly Hillbillies*' Granny on speed" while Colbert played the patient's uncle, who was "dressed in a gym outfit and obsessed with groin pulls."

Despite the fact that some fellow performers looked askance at the Three Idiots' brand of humor, not all did. In fact, the contacts performers made at Second City could be invaluable to a fledgling career. For instance, Second City is where Colbert first met Steve Carell. He occasionally served as Carell's understudy, which at Second City meant that when Carell was out of town, Colbert took his part. They'd also occasionally perform together.

"He's an incredible guy to perform with, and he always gives absolutely everything he has," said Colbert. "I've never seen him phone anything in, and he'll try anything." But unlike his friendship with Dinello and Sedaris, the two Steves never hung out with each other outside the theater.

Just as Colbert was playing around with a variety of different characters and personas, trying to find one that fit best, Carell was doing the same thing. In one early scene they worked on together, Carell played an adult man who was still a virgin.

"It was absolutely [Carell's] idea," said Colbert. "The character was a guy who was Steve's age at the time and he was a virgin, but he couldn't reveal it to his friends because he's too embarrassed." In the scene, Colbert, Carell, and a couple of other actors are hanging out, describing the best sex of their lives. Said Colbert, "Steve's examples were always a little suspect, like 'You know how breasts are so powdery? Like they feel like a bunch of grapes?' "

Once the others caught on to the fact that he was still a virgin, they proceeded to teach him what sex felt like, with one telling Carell to grab his butt and another telling him to put his finger in his navel.

"I was so happy when I saw that he was going to make that into a movie, because it gives me hope that all the scenes we never could quite make work at Second City someday might see the light of day," Colbert later said.

Obviously, the lesson Sedaris had taught him with the fake teeth had stuck with Colbert. "By the time we got on mainstage, he had no problem showing up for a scene without his pants on," said Dinello. "He did a three-sixty and completely tossed the rules away."

"They completely won," said Colbert. "I'm forever grateful that they broke me."

Even though he was thriving as an actor, Colbert's southern sensibilities were challenged on a regular basis at Second City. Actors on the road were known to cope with often-spartan living conditions, but the main downtown theater in Piper's Alley, a tucked-away alley of businesses and storefronts, was even worse: it had a restaurant, the Steak Joynt, that was infested with rats. Scores of stories abound, and the conditions just worsened when the restaurant closed down. As Craig Taylor, troupe member, put it, "The rats had to go somewhere."

And they did, heading straight to the backstage area at Second City, where they set up their new home in the costume wardrobe, which, according to Colbert, consisted of about "thirty years of clothing piled on the floor backstage."

"The smell was just unbelievable," said Colbert. "You'd finish the night and you'd be tired and you had a clown hat on or something, and just threw it on the floor some nights. And the next night a shirt went on top of it, so there were these great compost heaps of things." He'd avoid the pile as long as he could, but then he would remember that he needed a priest collar for a scene that night and it was buried in the pile of rats and clothes. "I'd dig through it just as quickly as I could, shake it out, spray Lysol on it, and put it on," he remembered.

Nia Vardalos had the same memories. "Once I pulled out a costume, and I was trying to decide whether it was too garish, and as I pulled it out, a rat came with it, so I shoved it back and went, 'Okay, I'm just going to go with this skirt,'" she said.

Life at Second City and in Chicago wasn't all work all the time. Though it could be difficult and all-consuming, Colbert still found time for a social life. And he returned to Charleston on a regular basis to visit his family.

In the spring of 1990, he had been dating a woman in Chicago for a couple of years, and she had recently started to pressure him for more of a commitment, telling him that if he didn't propose, she would end the relationship. Stephen felt he wasn't ready to make that leap, yet he needed a sounding board. So he returned to Charleston, where he could talk it over with his mother. Besides, the Spoleto season was about to begin, and he was looking forward to attending some of the performances, which always included at least a couple of world premieres.

"I told him if you don't know, it's not right," Lorna told her son.

Lorna bought tickets for the opera *Hydrogen Jukebox*, with music by Philip Glass and libretto by the poet Allen Ginsberg, and she and Stephen headed to the Dock Street Theatre to see the show.

During the intermission, he and Lorna headed into the lobby, and that's when he saw her.

"I'll never forget it. I walk in and I see this woman across the lobby and I thought, 'That one. Right there.' At that moment, I thought, 'That's crazy. You're crazy, Colbert.' But it turned out I was right."

The woman who caught his eye was Evelyn Brabham McGee, born on July 23, 1963, to Joseph Halstead McGee and Evelyn Moore McGee in downtown Charleston. Joseph McGee was one of Charleston's most distinguished lawyers, and he even served in the South Carolina House of Representatives. Evie McGee, as she was known, grew up in downtown Charleston with her older sister Madeleine, just a few blocks away from 39 East Battery, where Lorna still lived. Evie had attended Ashley Hall, a distinguished all-girls college preparatory school in downtown Charleston.

Stephen crossed the lobby, and they started talking. As it turned out, she'd been aware of him—Charleston can be a very small town because everyone knows everyone else, even if just in passing—but their paths hadn't crossed until now.

In fact, they had several common interests. They both liked theater. She had appeared in a Charleston Stage production in 1978, where she played Rascally Rabbit in the play *CarolinAntics*. They were also both passionate about poetry, specifically the work of e. e. cummings.

"He spent the whole evening talking to her," said Lorna. "I didn't see him again."

A few days later, Stephen returned to Chicago, and he and Evie started a long-distance relationship that mostly consisted of writing letters and an occasional phone call. In the letters, he often sent her poems by cummings. They didn't see each other until Colbert returned to Charleston for Christmas, and though that's when they had their first date, he pretty much already knew that she was the one for him.

It wasn't long before they started making plans for Evie to move to Chicago so they could be together. She took a job as director of development at the Remains Theatre, an avant-garde theater company, and they settled into apartment 15-A at 2738 Pine Grove Avenue, in the Lincoln Park neighborhood.

In fact, Evie was a big reason why Colbert was thrilled when he was invited to join the mainstage at Second City: It meant that he wasn't constantly on the road, and he and Evie could start to forge a life—and a family—of their own.

But after a few years, it was time to move on from his job. He'd always be grateful to Second City; he cut his teeth on comedy, indeed, with the help of teachers and fellow performers, and he finally found his path in life. He felt that he'd gotten everything he could from Second City and that it was time to head to the next level.

"I was there for five years, and it was everything to me," said Colbert. "I gave up doing other theater, and I went. 'If I'm going to be good at this, I have to do nothing else,' and I thought, 'Okay, I'll find out what this has to offer me.' And it had a great deal to offer me—and still does to anybody who wants to take their stupid seriously."

Besides, he had a greater opportunity waiting for him in New York: a part in a new TV show.

So he and Evie made plans to move to New York, but first they took a little detour back to Charleston, where they were married at the Second Presbyterian Church on October 9, 1993.

CHAPTER 6

THE CABLE CHANNEL COMEDY Central was launched by HBO in the fall of 1989, back in the days when cable TV meant fringe programming and viewership was only a small fraction of that of the three major networks.

HBO executives initially programmed Comedy Central with a mixture of stand-up comedians, talk shows, and original shows. Classic comedies and sitcoms also aired, some in their entirety, but some were chopped up into abbreviated clips for a series called *Short Attention Span Theater*, where hosts—or VJs—offered up pithy commentary; one early host was a comedian by the name of Jon Stewart.

After five years on the air, executives at Comedy Central wanted to add more original programming to the mix, so they started to scout around New York for ideas and talent. Amy and Paul had already moved to New York and started to perform locally, doing stand-up and quirky little sketches in off-off-off-Broadway theaters. They brought Amy's brother David along to help out with some of the writing, and he wrote a play called *Stitches*, which they performed at La Mama Experimental Theatre Club in January 1994. The story line was straight out of Sedaris and Dinello's absurdist comedy at Second City: A popular high school girl meets up with tragedy when she has a water-skiing accident and her face is torn off by a propeller. A cosmetic surgeon fixes her face, but it's still deformed; TV producers are so enthralled by her spirit, they offer her a TV show with the name of *Stitches*. She becomes famous, and soon crazed fans are disfiguring their own faces.

Comedy Central producers took notice and invited the two Sedarises, Dinello, and Mitch Rouse, another Second City alum, to create a half-hour show that was patterned after a typical Second City show. The three convinced the network to bring Colbert on board to help out, along with Jodi Lennon, also from Second City. The network ordered six episodes for a trial run, and the crew soon got busy. Tim Hill directed the first batch of episodes; he'd later go on to write for *SpongeBob SquarePants*.

As was the case at Second City, they stayed away from current events and other contemporary references that could date the humor. The first rule of thumb was similar to before: "We try to amuse ourselves," said Colbert.

Since it was his first experience writing for TV, Colbert marveled that they had little or no contact with either the network or the producers. "They left us alone for four months at a time to write," he said. "Then we would come back and use whatever we had come up with. We had a lot of freedom."

The restrictions came later. In the mid-1990s, budgets for brand-new cable shows tended to be pretty low, since the major networks still ruled the roost and many large advertisers like Procter & Gamble and Ford Motor Company thought the cable channels were unproven. So after they finished writing the scripts for the skits and handed them into Comedy Central executives for approval, they often had to go back to the drawing board, but not because the scenes were too risqué—instead, it was because of the props.

"We had no budget whatsoever," said Colbert. "We once wrote a scene with a jackhammer, and the producers said to us, 'That's great, I don't have a jackhammer, do you? No? Then it looks like we're not going to use a jackhammer.' "

Exit 57 was taped in front of a live audience, but it was far from the brand of improv the performers knew back in Chicago. For one, instead of refining a scene until it works, each skit got only two takes. Then, when they watched the show after the fact, they realized that the small screen translates the comedy in a different way than it does for a live theater audience.

Television surprised Stephen in another way. "You shoot something, you're done, and you move on," he said. "I remember thinking, 'I don't get to do that again?' When I was doing material on stage, I would literally do a scene 250 times over the course of a year and got that thing as sharp as a tack before it was over. In TV, there's so little opportunity to discover something new, and sometimes I would love to know what people are laughing at. That's the one thing I miss since with *Exit 57*, we're just guessing."

In any case, *Exit 57* debuted in January 1995. Scenes from the first few episodes were typical of the friends' warped humor, ranging from a video reenactment of a song, "My Wife Dumped Me for a Guy Named Jesus," sung by Dinello, to a group of dentists—part of a self-proclaimed dental guerrilla group—who attack a man in the park so they could give him a dental cleaning.

The actors "never beat a dead joke into the ground," said one reviewer. "Jodi Lennon and Amy Sedaris have managed to compact all the white trash from Maine to New Mexico into one household with the recurring characters of Amber and Bobbie, who make Roseanne Conner's household look like an upscale bastion of good taste."

Another wrote that "*Exit 57* is an unusual fork in the entertainment highway. It's not Generation X humor, since several of the players are in their thirties. Even the show's publicists have a hard time labeling the show; a recent press release trumpeted the show as one 'critics choose to ignore.'"

A cult audience started to build, and ratings for the first run of episodes were good enough that Comedy Central ordered a second batch. Mick Napier, who worked with Colbert, Sedaris, and Dinello at Second City, came on board to direct shows that continued with the same often-surreal brand of humor. In one show, Colbert played a surgeon in the operating room while other physicians look on. When the patient dies on the table, Colbert starts making balloon animals from the organs.

In September 1995, the same month that the second season went on the air, Stephen and Evie's first child, a daughter named Madeleine, after her maternal grandmother, was born. He thought he was on his way.

But word came that *Exit 57* would be cancelled, leaving Colbert to look for a new job. In all, twelve episodes aired over the course of two seasons before Comedy Central pulled the plug, despite the fact that the show earned several CableACE nominations in 1995 in the categories of writing, performance, and best comedy series.

Colbert returned to the audition circuit that he had despised while in Chicago. Only now, he was in New York and had a family to support. While there were more opportunities for hungry actors, the competition was a lot more cutthroat. One of the first auditions he went on was for a new show that starred the former *Saturday Night Live* comedian Dana Carvey.

In 1995, Carvey was hot. He had spent seven years at *SNL*, and Hollywood was calling. He and costar Mike Myers had filmed the *Wayne's World* movie, which was based on their successful *SNL* skit and came out in 1992, and a sequel appeared the following year.

ABC offered Carvey his own sketch-comedy TV show, scheduled to debut in the spring of 1996. He started hiring cast members and writers, including many former *SNL* and Second City members, among them Steve Carell. Colbert's agent sent him on the audition—he and Carvey had never met—and he nailed it.

"I actually held up my own newly born daughter and used her as a puppet. I was completely desperate."

For the audition, "I actually held up my own newly born daughter and used her as a puppet," said Colbert. "I was completely desperate."

The Dana Carvey Show debuted on March 12, 1996, and though the skits were designed to be highly topical, spoofing politicians and others in the public eye, what got the most attention was the fact that each thirty-minute episode would have just one sponsor, like the TV shows of the 1950s and 1960s, including the *Colgate Comedy Hour* and *General Electric Theater.* Patterned after these classic shows, the product would not only appear in the title of the show but also be incorporated into some of the show's skits.

PepsiCo signed on for the deal, and "The Taco Bell Dana Carvey Show" was the first of six scheduled shows for the conglomerate's brand.

Colbert participated in several skits and served as the voice of one half of the cartoon team in the short *The Ambiguously Gay Duo*, a riff on superhero buddies like Batman and Robin, in which it always seemed like there was more going on between the two that never made it to prime time. Robert Smigel and J. J. Sedelmaier created the cartoon, in which Colbert was the voice of Ace and Steve Carell played Gary.

Smigel had written for *Saturday Night Live* and also served as the master puppeteer of Triumph the Insult Comic Dog, which debuted on *Late Night with Conan O'Brien* in 1997. Even though network censors didn't ask to see the scripts for *The Ambiguously Gay Duo*, they wanted to see the illustrations for the cartoon as well as the colors, before approving the skit.

"I was parodying the whole nipple-ization of Batman costumes in the movies, and they were packed pretty well 'down there,'" said Smigel. "So we had to submit the drawings, which was painful enough. For the color of the car I just wrote 'peach.' I couldn't bring myself to write 'flesh.'"

Colbert offered advice and feedback on the scripts and also revised them. Smigel liked his input so much that he then asked Colbert to help write them too.

The Dana Carvey Show also featured a regular segment where Colbert played a news anchor who reported the fake news from *The Onion*, a satirical newspaper that was just beginning to become known nationally. Isaac Hayes and Abe Vigoda, among others, made cameo appearances on the show, and even though Carvey was well known for doing spot-on impersonations, in a few segments Colbert trumped him by playing George Harrison and Geraldo Rivera.

He felt fortunate that he once again had a regular job. "I think it's very funny, and I feel very lucky," said Colbert. "Sketch comedy is what I want to do. How many people get to do that on a prime-time network show?"

In one skit, Colbert played a character who was conducting insane experiments on a life-size fake horse. "One of the nicest moments in the entire production was watching the horse being thrown out of a plane, its parachute not open, and having it explode when it hit the ground," he said. When that happened, "I thought, I *love* this business."

When developing the format for Colbert's newscasts on the show, Carvey drew on his *SNL* days and suggested that Colbert play it right at the camera. "If you have an opportunity to give it right to the audience, there's a special connection that you make by looking at the camera," said Colbert.

However, after the first show aired, Taco Bell pulled its advertising commitments for the rest of the season. The reason: The very first skit had Carvey imitating President Bill Clinton, who was nursing puppies, a kitten, and a baby on multiple nipples in order to show that he was empathetic and concerned about all mankind and the animal world. And the skit where several Taco Bell clerks sang a song where they referred to Carvey as their "whore" failed to please the corporate sponsor as well, despite the fact that Carvey also dragged out his tried-and-true Church Lady character for one sketch.

Reviews were mixed. "The show displays an edge rarely seen in prime time," wrote one reviewer. "The first sketch set the tone, veering between the stale and the strained," said another. "Both the title's mockery and the effort to be topical were wasted. There was a dancing taco and a dancing bell. The debut already looked tired and old."

Even though Taco Bell withdrew their support—along with Pizza Hut, another company under the PepsiCo umbrella—other corporate branches stayed in, including Mug Root Beer and Mountain Dew. But without Pizza Hut on board, they had to scramble for another sponsor for the sixth show, and they managed to convince a local Chinese restaurant group—Szechuan Dynasty—to sign on.

One more show was broadcast—albeit sponsorless—but ratings were dismal, and, not surprisingly, no other sponsors had come forward to offer their advertising dollars. Despite the fact that ABC had contracted for ten shows, they pulled the plug after seven aired, though eight were made.

"It was probably the most bizarre variety show in the history of American television," said Carvey. "I'm not even saying good or bad, just bizarre."

"It's definitely disappointing," said Smigel. "Fortunately, I've had numerous other failed projects to help dilute the impact of this particular one."

"It was probably the most bizarre variety show in the history of American television."

Almost exactly a year after *Exit 57* was cancelled, Colbert found himself in the same precarious position: without a steady job. He was able to piece together a few gigs, including coming on board as a very part-time writer at *Saturday Night Live* when the producers asked Smigel to bring *The Ambiguously Gay Duo* to the show. But it wasn't enough to support himself, a wife, and a child.

He desperately needed a job. Around the time that *The Dana Carvey Show* was cancelled, the news department at the ABC network was looking to fill a correspondent slot on *Good Morning America.* They wanted a man with a straitlaced appearance who could also make a barely caffeinated viewer laugh out loud. A producer in the entertainment department recommended Colbert, and the head of ABC News set up a meeting. Stephen brought his one-year-old daughter Madeleine with him, and during the interviews he went over to the corner of the office and "depotted plants the whole time." He still got the gig.

They hired him for the job, and Colbert got his hopes up once again.

But after doing just two reports, only one aired, and though he pitched twenty more story ideas to the executive producers, they turned every one of them down.

He was out of work again. He scrambled and went on countless auditions, but nothing turned up. For the first time in his life, he started to seriously doubt his career path.

"I was desperate. I had a wife, a new baby, New York rent, and less and less hair to pull out. I would have done a cooking show with a chimp," he said. "I thought I made a huge mistake in what I decided to do for a living."

"I thought I made a huge mistake in what I decided to do for a living."

While other actors would panic and throw in the towel, Colbert dug in his heels and kept going. "It was too late, I couldn't turn back," he said. "It wasn't like I was going to go to law school. The die was cast."

One morning, his agent sent him on an audition for a show on Comedy Central called *The Daily Show*. Though he hated the whole audition process—it made him feel like a trained seal—he agreed to go. After all, there was nothing else on the horizon.

But he didn't get his hopes up, even though *The Daily Show* had been on the air for a year when Colbert auditioned. For one, after winning spots on two previous TV shows that he thought would last, the shows ended up getting cancelled before the contract was up. For another, it sounded like he would run into the same problems he had at ABC. "I thought the show was a terrible idea," he said. "I really didn't want to do [*The Daily Show*] because I hated *Good Morning America*, and I figured it was going to be the same type of show."

But his agent also represented Madeline Smithberg, the executive producer at *The Daily Show*, and he convinced Stephen that it was going to be a totally different concept, and that in fact she'd even be interested in the stories that *Good Morning America* had turned down.

Before he went on the audition, Colbert's agent sent Smithberg a tape of a skit Colbert had done on *The Dana Carvey Show*, "Waiters Who Are Nauseated by Food." Smithberg loved it. "I get a lot of tapes, and most of them are not that great, and this thing just cracked me up," she said.

Colbert went on the audition and talked with Smith and a few other producers and directors. Just as his agent had predicted, they loved his stories. "I pitched them the stories that ABC wouldn't do, and they looked at my resume and said I was genetically engineered to be a correspondent for this show, and that they'd hire me," said Colbert.

The Daily Show hired him on a temporary basis so both sides could see if it was a good fit or not; he was basically assigned to do field reports on an as-needed basis. But he still didn't think it would last. "To me, it was totally a day job. I never expected to stay here because I did sketch comedy and I wrote, and I really didn't think that this show was going to go anyplace," he said. "I did not believe in the show, I did not watch the show, and they paid dirt. It was literally just a paycheck to show up."

Craig Kilborn was the first host of *The Daily Show*. He'd cut his teeth as a sports anchor, first at a Fox station in Monterey, California, and then as an anchor on ESPN's *SportsCenter*. Comedy Central ordered *The Daily Show* into production to replace Bill Maher's show *Politically Incorrect*, which had switched networks to ABC.

When *The Daily Show* debuted on July 22, 1996, it was structured like any local newscast you could switch on anywhere in the country. Kilborn served as the news anchor and read a few national news stories, which were followed by in-studio segments and field pieces from a correspondent or two. Since *The Daily Show* billed itself as a fake news show from the beginning, the correspondents' stories followed suit. "They were all human interest-y and character-driven stories, like squirrels on waterskis, Bigfoot sightings, and alien abductions, but we treated it all like hard news," said Colbert. "We took a ridiculous thing and we elevated it." In the first few years of the show, correspondents never joined Kilborn behind the desk.

They got away with a lot in the early days, simply because nobody knew who they were. When Colbert, a producer, and a cameraman went out in the field, he'd introduce himself by saying he was from *The Daily Show*, and people automatically thought he was from CNN. But some probed a little deeper. "If they asked what kind of show it was, I'd tell them it's an alternative news show," he said. "If they asked what channel we were on, I'd say it's on channel 45 in Manhattan but I don't know what channel it's on here. But if they asked which network, then I had to answer Comedy Central, and they'd take the mike off and leave."

Before the end of the first year, he knew it was where he belonged. "And then I found out that it was full of these incredibly nice, talented people, and I couldn't wait to get there in the morning," he said. "Once I got there and realized this was a great group working really hard, I learned to love the people I was working with."

In addition, Colbert was initially surprised at the amount of input he had to develop and shape the content of his reports, since he thought that the show's writers would primarily be responsible for that. It wasn't long until he learned that this cooperative process helped him develop his character as a fake correspondent on a fake news show.

"It helps individuate us, because we establish our own voices by being involved early on in the writing process," he said. "Otherwise, we're trying to [project] other people's imagined ideas of how we might say it. If we're involved, then we can begin to establish our own asshole personas."

Despite Colbert's love for his work and his colleagues on the show, there was a definite tension on the set, specifically between Kilborn and the cocreator and head writer Lizz Winstead. Even though Winstead had been heavily involved in the initial development of the concept of *The Daily Show*, she was not involved in the final decision about the host.

"I spent eight months developing and staffing a show and seeking a tone with producers and writers, but somebody else [hired] him," she said. "There were bound to be problems since I viewed the show as content-driven while he viewed it as host-driven."

Eighteen months after the debut of *The Daily Show*, things only got worse. In a 1997 *Esquire* magazine interview Kilborn made a few negative comments about the women who worked at the show, which included calling them "bitches." He also said that he thought Winstead wanted to do a Monica Lewinsky on him. When the magazine came out, the network suspended Kilborn for one week. Winstead quit shortly afterward.

Even with Winstead gone, the atmosphere on the show remained toxic. Several reviewers thought both Kilborn and the correspondents were working overtime to be nasty. "The take-no-prisoners attitude of this headline-oriented, half-hour sarcasm-and-shtick program [is] a slick combination of *Saturday Night Live*'s Weekend Update segment, moronic frat-house interplay, political humor, and surrealistic nonsense," said one.

A *New York Times* reviewer concurred. "In the world inhabited and delineated by *The Daily Show*, everyone is an idiot. It's like making fun of the people in line at Epcot: too easy, but darned satisfying when you're cranky. And the central characters seem to have no idea that they'll be savaged when the piece is edited."

Years later, Colbert agreed. "You wanted to take your soul off, put it on a wire hanger, and leave it in the closet before you got on the plane to do one of these pieces," he said. "We had deep, soul-searching discussions on flights out to do stories, saying, 'We don't want to club any baby seals, I don't want to hold this person down and kick him in the teeth comedically.' But sometimes it would happen, because you had to come back with something funny."

"'We don't want to club any baby seals, I don't want to hold this person down and kick him in the teeth comedically.' But sometimes it would happen."

Despite the poisonous atmosphere behind the scenes, *The Daily Show* was consistently one of Comedy Central's top hits.

For the most part, Colbert stayed out of the fray. "I was so new there that I was kept completely out of any sort of political machinations," he said. Even so, what did he think of Kilborn?

"He was really good at reading the teleprompter," he said.

Even though he liked working at *The Daily Show*, his tendency to be on shows that were quickly canceled made him believe that the show would be yanked from the schedule. Plus, it wasn't as financially lucrative as he'd hoped. So he continued to pursue other opportunities, go on auditions for other shows and roles, and work with his friends Sedaris and Dinello on other ideas for off-the-wall shows. *Exit 57* may have been a bit too off-kilter—or ahead of its time—to succeed in 1996, but sooner or later, they hoped they'd hit with something.

And even if they didn't, at least they'd have a blast and make one another laugh while doing it. The Three Idiots prided themselves on the fact that they felt so comfortable with one another that they could shoot one another down and not take it personally. "We can say 'That's not funny, that's just stupid. Why'd you do that?' to each other," said Sedaris. "We can just be brutally honest." When asked how the three have been able to remain close friends after more than a decade, Colbert responded in typical fashion: "I don't know," he said. "Why do people stay in abusive relationships? They must be giving you something, right?"

Shortly after Colbert signed on at *The Daily Show*, he, Amy, and Paul met with Comedy Central executives and pitched a half-hour sitcom that satirized the after-school specials that ran on ABC in the 1970s. The *ABC Afterschool Specials* were half-hour episodes aimed at teenagers with a moralistic story in which the main character faced a social problem of some kind, either at school or home. With titles such as "Please Don't Hit Me, Mom" and "My Dad Lives in a Downtown Hotel," each episode was designed to present the teenage character with a problem, which would be wrapped up by the time the half hour was over, although some were more documentary in style and some were even animated.

Colbert, Sedaris, and Dinello had grown up watching the specials, and they put their own unique twist on their proposal. One day, when rummaging through the used video bin at a local video store, Paul found an old documentary from the 1970s called *The Trip Back*, about a woman named Florrie Fisher. Fisher was a former drug addict and prostitute who spent a number of years in jail, and after she wrote a bestselling autobiography called *The Lonely Trip Back*, she started to visit high schools to give motivational speeches to essentially scare kids straight; the documentary shows one of her talks. After Paul watched it, he showed it to Amy and said, "This is the character you should do."

The pitch: Amy would star as Jerri Blank, a forty-six-year-old former self-proclaimed "user, boozer, and loser" who ran away from Flatpoint High School when she was a freshman but who returns after her latest release from jail and rehab stint.

The network said they'd get back to them.

Like Colbert, the others, who had been busy pursuing acting and comedy careers since leaving Second City, knew better than to hold their breath.

After the departure of Lizz Winstead, the atmosphere behind the scenes at *The Daily Show* worsened. In the fall of 1998, Comedy Central announced that Kilborn would leave *The Daily Show* and take over for host Tom Snyder on *The Late Late Show* at CBS. His last *Daily Show* appearance was on December 17, 1998, and over the Christmas holidays, the staff scrambled to prepare for the new host.

The replacement host would be Jon Stewart, a little-known comedian who had hosted *You Wrote It, You Watch It*, *The Jon Stewart Show*, two short-lived programs on MTV, as well as *Short Attention Span Theater* on Comedy Central. He had also played small parts in several films, including *Big Daddy* and *Playing by Heart*. Stewart had been the voice of a patient on the animated Comedy Central show *Dr. Katz, Professional Therapist*. In addition to being *The Daily Show* host, he'd also share a coexecutive producer credit.

Stewart was ecstatic about the job, which he viewed as "sitting around with funny people, banging out jokes, and creating a television show. I have no hobbies, no outside interests," he said. "I'm fine with spending fourteen hours a day putting a show together with tape and string."

At the same time, though he signed a four-year contract with Comedy Central to do the show, like Colbert, he was realistic enough to realize that the chances for the show's longevity were not in his favor. "Whenever you take over something that is popular and has a fanatical following, you're never going to please everyone," he said. "The trick is to have enough wherewithal to follow through with what you want to do with it and give it time to evolve."

After the debut of his self-titled talk show on MTV in 1993, both critics and fans began to refer to Stewart as the "voice of Generation X." Indeed, after the animated show *Beavis and Butt-Head*, Stewart's show had the highest ratings of any show on the cable channel. Its popularity led MTV to offer it up for broader syndication, which eventually was its undoing, since it was scheduled against late-night shows by Jay Leno and David Letterman in some markets. So while Stewart was thrilled to serve as host of *The Daily Show*, he didn't want to get his hopes up.

Indeed, after the cancellation of *The Jon Stewart Show*, he took some time off to recover. "You go down to the Jersey shore, you lick your wounds for two weeks, and you come back kicking," he said. "You can't just fold up the tents. You've got to refocus yourself and get back in it."

The truth was that critics didn't expect much from his new gig. In fact, one even viewed *The Daily Show* position as a step down for Stewart; "He once seemed destined for more," said the reviewer.

To start, he was the antithesis of Kilborn, who had a vain streak a mile wide; in between segments, he would compulsively fix his hair and makeup. When asked if he'd do likewise, Stewart said absolutely not, cracking, "There are no mirrors." But he did offer up one significant change: "The tone will obviously be a lot more Yiddish," he said. "I think at some point, I'd love to have a little bit of diversity." He added, "But as I keep saying, there is a certain mindset that won't develop until I get there."

His neurotic streak reared up when asked what he'd think if the show succeeded beyond his wildest dreams. "I'm doing everything I can to sabotage my career," he said. "It's a little thing called fear of success, but really, a regular talk show can become your life. For ten years, it's your life. That is what you are and what you do." At the same time, he welcomed the challenge. "[*The Daily Show*] is a different kind of hosting than I'm accustomed to, it's a little less free-form, but we'll find out what I can do well and start tailoring it to that."

"A regular talk show can become your life."

When Kilborn left, two other *Daily Show* regulars decided to exit as well: Brian Unger and A. Whitney Brown. Since Stewart's style was more of a mensch than the nasty guy that Kilborn played, Stewart believed that his more optimistic outlook would have a top-down effect, spreading to the writers. But at the same time, he didn't want to rule anything out. "Hopefully the only things off-limits are [crummy] jokes, but being a stand-up comedian, I know that's not always the case," he said. "You know it when you have to take a shower afterward."

For his part, Colbert didn't plan to change a thing. Even after appearing on *The Daily Show* for more than eighteen months, doing an average of 120 reports a year, Colbert was starting to see what worked and what he could ditch for what was becoming his trademark character. His correspondent character was coming into his own, and his reports had become one of the more popular features on the show.

"When I started doing this guy, the idea was to do field pieces about something pretty stupid but make it seem important," he said. "The key to accomplishing that was to be self-important and to raise self-importance into a matter of national significance."

"[My character] is not unintelligent, he's just idiotic," he continued. "It's garbage in, garbage out. He's uninformed, and perfectly happy about that. What's most important to him is what feels right, not what's true."

CHAPTER 7

When Jon Stewart debuted as the new host of *The Daily Show*, on January 11, 1999, the critics were pleased.

"Happily, it was no trial to watch," wrote one reviewer. "It's a welcome return."

While cast and crew maintained that the change in tone and content would be gradual, the truth was that with such a huge change and attitude at the top, it took only days for the audience to notice.

For one, since Stewart was clearly more interested in politics than Kilborn, the show started running more political stories the very first week.

Colbert had always considered himself to be apolitical, but he experienced a radical shift, and the hiring of Stewart actually helped shift the focus of his stories. "[The show] switched from local news, summer kicker stories, and celebrity jokes, to more of a political point of view," he said. "Since Jon has a political point of view, he wanted us to have one, too," said Colbert. "I've always been a news junkie but I never wrote political satire before *The Daily Show*, Then I found I enjoyed it more than I had imagined."

Yet Stewart didn't hit people over the head with it, instead suggesting to producers and writers that they try to shape correspondents' stories so that they had more of a connection to the news; after all, from the start, *The Daily Show* was billed as a news show, albeit a fake one. One of the complaints that correspondents had when Kilborn was host was that the dichotomy between the news stories and correspondent reports was pretty radical. "He'd do a fairly clever story about the Clinton administration and then we'd run a field report on a guy who was a Bigfoot hunter," said Colbert. Once Stewart came on board, the transitions became smoother and more organic. "Our field pieces were coming out of the news, and not in opposition to them," he said.

Once Stewart had settled into his job and the staffers became comfortable with their new direction, it was time to hire a couple of new correspondents since A. Whitney Brown and Brian Unger, who'd left with Kilborn, weren't immediately replaced. Producers wanted to be sure to match any new correspondents with the new direction of the show. They asked around the studio for suggestions, and Colbert suggested Steve Carell, whom he'd worked with at Second City and on *The Dana Carvey Show*. In fact, it was his skit—"Waiters Who Are Nauseated by Food"—they did together at *The Dana Carvey Show* that had helped Colbert get his *Daily Show* gig. "There's nothing he can't make funny," said Colbert.

It wasn't too long before that Colbert had been scrambling for work, auditioning for any job that came down the pike. Now, ironically, he faced the opposite dilemma, of having *too* much work on his plate. Just a couple of weeks before Stewart hosted his first show, Comedy Central called Colbert, but on another matter.

In December 1998, the cable channel gave the go-ahead for the spoof on after-school specials that Amy, Paul, and Stephen had pitched, ordering ten episodes of *The Way After School Special*, with the first to debut in April 1999.

Colbert was thrilled. After all, he and Evie had recently welcomed Peter, their second child, into their family.

And the series would be shot locally, in New Jersey. Flatpoint High School exteriors were done at Verona High School in Verona, while interiors were shot at Felician College Library in Rutherford; the Willowbrook Mall in Wayne was featured in another episode. Perhaps the most poignant time for Stephen was when the cast traveled to Iona Preparatory School in New Rochelle, New York, to shoot some exteriors; after all, that was where his father attended high school.

The network obviously had high hopes for the show, as they planned to schedule it right after *South Park*, the animated series that had been a hit since its debut in the summer of 1997.

They had to get cracking. The Three Idiots had just four months to pull everything together.

"It's *My So-Called Life* on acid," was how Colbert described the show.

Because of the limited amount of time, Colbert pulled back on his *Daily Show* appearances while he, Sedaris, and Dinello cranked out ten scripts and got a few episodes in the can.

They hit the ground running—first changing the name of the series to *Strangers with Candy*. Nothing about the way they worked together had changed. Their working style was similar to the previous times they'd collaborated.

For one, Amy never learned how to type, and she didn't own a computer or a cell phone. She also rarely watched TV, so she had little with which to compare the episodes they were writing. Perhaps it came as no surprise that the three Second City veterans turned to improvisation in order to write. But before they could even get to that point, they wasted a lot of time. As is the case with many writers, there's a lot of procrastination involved.

One day, for instance, the three agreed to meet at Paul's apartment at one in the afternoon. Amy showed up promptly, but Paul arrived a half hour later, and Stephen didn't make it until two. "Then Stephen decides he wants to get something to eat, and Paul has to walk his dog," said Amy. "Then we go inside and their cell phones go off, and then we start talking about anything but what we're there to talk about. Then, maybe around four o'clock, we'll start to think about what we're supposed to write."

And the way they start is by improvising. "We all have different duties," said Amy. "I lay on the couch and throw out ideas. Then we get on our feet and improvise, we'll laugh really hard, and Paul and Stephen write down what we're laughing really hard about. Later, Paul's the one who puts it into any kind of a script form" said Amy. "Stephen remembers everything he's ever read. And Dinello can build a story arc."

According to Amy, "If we don't laugh, it doesn't go on paper. It's always

Colbert, along with co-stars—and long-time friends—Amy Sedaris and Paul Dinello, pushed the boundaries with *Strangers with Candy. (Courtesy Photofest)*

about cracking people up in the group." Paul and Stephen often referred to their work as chopping wood, doing the preparation in advance, while Amy preferred to fly by the seat of her pants. "They like to know where the scene is going, where I like to discover it on camera. I don't want to have to say these particular lines. Let me be in the moment and see what lines happen. I'm an idea person. I'm confident with the ideas, then they organize the chaos I come up with. I'm really the hostess of the group."

As they dug into developing the first batch of episodes and then filming the first few segments, she remembered that *Exit 57* tended to attract a fringe audience who viewed their skits and characters in a cult-status kind of way. So as they progressed with writing scripts for *Strangers* and pushing the envelope in as many ways as they could, she started to wonder, "Who's gonna watch this?"

Once they developed Jerri Blank's character, they turned to the supporting cast. For his character, the history teacher Chuck Noblet, Colbert turned to his years at Porter-Gaud for inspiration. "He's just what I perceived as the ice-cold attitude of my teachers who hated their jobs, didn't give a damn about anything, and who wanted to do anything other than teach," said Colbert.

Dinello also based his art teacher character, Geoffrey Jellineck, on a former high school teacher. "He used to dress like a student and go to parties and thought he was one of us, but we used to just laugh at him behind his back," he said. "It made us all really uncomfortable, but he thought it was the coolest thing in the world that a teacher would hang out with the kids and try to be like one of them."

They also designed the relationship between Noblet and Jellineck to be a not-so-closeted gay relationship. "They'd been doing those kinds of characters, straight guys who always had the desire to be with each other, at Second City for years," said Amy. "[After all], who'd want to be with Noblet at all? I don't understand what Jellineck gets from Noblet."

For the principal, they turned to another Second City alum, Greg Hollimon, to play Onyx Blackman, a narcissistic, power-hungry principal. But perhaps the biggest stroke of genius came when casting Jerri Blank's father.

"In the after-school specials, the father was always useless," said Amy. "He was curled up on the couch with his back to the camera, or it was always, 'Don't wake up your father,' or 'He's at the office, he's been working really hard.' He was always nonexistent, and we decided to take that to the extreme." So they portrayed Guy Blank—played by Roberto Gari—as totally frozen as the result of a stroke and only shown to the camera in a reaction shot, eyes wide, mouth open, arms askew.

Colbert was thrilled to be working full-time on a show that required him to conjure up stories from the darker recesses of his personality. Though he had ramped down his schedule at *The Daily Show*—doing twenty pieces a year instead of 120—he was afraid of the possibility of being out of work again, so he took whatever came along, including an appearance on an episode of *Whose Line Is It Anyway?* with Drew Carey, which aired on February 24, 1999, when the Three Idiots were putting the finishing touches on the first couple of *Strangers* episodes.

Strangers with Candy debuted on April 7, 1999, on Comedy Central, and reviews were mixed. "Whereas *South Park* became a huge hit by pushing the humor barrier in an often-repugnant way, *Strangers* is a bit more mature and far more clever, but no less twisted," wrote one.

The puns were often laid on thick. For instance, in one episode, the butcher who makes home deliveries to the Blank family is also having an affair with Jerri's stepmother, Sara. His name is Stew, while his kids are named Chuck and Patty.

Almost immediately, the show developed a loyal audience. "Our demographic is an oddly wide one," said Colbert. "We get young teenagers to people in their sixties stopping us and telling us how much they enjoyed *Strangers*. I think our core audience is a lot of damaged people," he continued. "Damaged people are very interesting. The way they behave to cover up their damage is usually very entertaining."

Colbert was listed as a coproducer of the show. He was able to draw on some of his earlier aspirations toward *Hamlet;* in the third episode, he gives a brief monologue based on *Raisin in the Sun* before launching into a break-dancing sequence that continues while the end credits run. In fact, a staged or impromptu dance party by the entire cast—in most cases—became the standard while the end credits ran. "It started as a happy accident," said Colbert.

"One thing we liked about after-school specials was that no matter how bad things got, like if someone's mother has liver cancer, it's all solved in twenty-two minutes and then there's a big dance party," said Dinello.

"I like to watch people dance, it says so much about them," Amy added.

"I like to watch people dance, it says so much about them."

The one exception to the group dance came at the end of the "Blank Stare, Part Two" episode, where Jerri joins a religious cult. Colbert dances solo during the end dance segment while singing a capella "The King of

Glory Comes," a Christian song that Stephen undoubtedly sang countless times over years of attending Sunday school.

From the very beginning, everyone who was working on *Strangers* was surprised at how little input Comedy Central had on the show. "We get to work together and say whatever we want," Dinello said.

Colbert agreed. "We are stunned at what we get away with," he said. "We are walking further and further out on the ledge, waiting for someone to call us back from the window, and no one ever does."

In one episode, Jerri says, "I'm gonna make your pinky all stinky," and she was surprised that it didn't get cut. And in other episodes, a character says "faggot" and "pussy." "We could say one of them, and then after four more episodes we could say the other one," Amy explained. "But there were a few words we couldn't say. For instance, I couldn't say 'Filthy Jew Diary,' but I *could* say, 'Dirty Jew Diary.' They were never consistent."

The only thing the network rejected outright was one episode that featured a midget albino in the story line. And in the "Behind Blank Eyes" episode, where Jerri makes friends with a blind boy who wants to join the football team, they had to omit the part of a mentally handicapped lawyer.

"We had a total sense of freedom," she said. "There were no grown-ups there to slap our hands." And before they signed off on the script, Amy wanted to make sure the script worked, so she'd give it what she called the "high test." "We'd write it and straighten everything out, but then I'd take it home, smoke some pot, and read it and take some notes."

Colbert's wife, Evie, dusted off her acting chops and played small parts in several episodes, including the original pilot episode "Retardation, A Celebration," where she played Nurse Chestnut; and then in the ninth episode of the first season, she played the mother of young Chuck in "To Be Young Gifted and Blank."

Comedy Central renewed the show for a second season.

They were working all the time, and the demands of putting together ten shows in such a short period of time meant they were always playing catch-up. "We were always behind in our writing, and most of the time we were writing it during rehearsal," Sedaris said. Her tendency to make things up as she went along and her improvisational background went against the grain of a weekly sitcom. "We rehearsed so much, it took the fun out of it," she complained. "Do it again? What do you mean, do it again? I wish everything could be like, 'You got one shot, that's it.' "

But at the same time, she loved doing the show. "I don't know if we'll ever have that amount of freedom and fun again," she said.

While some fans loved the show, even Colbert had his doubts about the characters. "Boy, you forget how wrong these characters think," he said. "There's hardly a word, a thought, or an action that isn't somehow a direct contravention of proper human behavior. And they're *insanely* selfish people . . . Somebody watching the show the other night said to me, 'Whoever were Stephen Colbert's authority figures have some answering to do,' but I think that goes for the people who like the show, too."

Stephen received some bad news on August 14, 1999. Even though he had recently added another member to his family, his tribe lost one of its own when his brother Billy died at the age of forty-nine.

After two seasons, Comedy Central gave the go-ahead for a third. But as *Strangers* ramped back up, there was some uncertainty about whether there would be a fourth. As a cult show on a cable channel, the ratings were never that high, and even though no one expected the show to garner the same kind of ratings as *South Park*, its future was up in the air. Since Comedy Central tended to give a series a run of three years, Colbert and the others had a feeling that the third would be the last, but when they tried to confirm the case, they couldn't get an answer. The executives who initially green-lighted the project back in 1998 had left the network.

As the season progressed, the new producer in charge at Comedy Central still wouldn't confirm or deny a fourth season. "I think it was a thorn in her side that it wasn't her show," said Colbert. "She brought the *Man Show* [to Comedy Central] and she wanted her own shows on the network."

A rumor eventually surfaced that *Strangers* was going to be replaced by a new show called *Strip Mall*, and so, when they started to write the script for the last show of the season, they decided to make the plotline that the school board was going to turn the school into a strip mall, but the board wouldn't confirm or deny. "Since [Comedy Central] told us, 'No decision has been made,' the school board told Onyx Blackman the same thing: 'No decision has been made,'" said Colbert.

Strangers with Candy ended its run after thirty episodes. The final episode aired on October 2, 2000.

At the same time, Colbert felt palpable relief that the show's end was in sight.

"It involved everyone, it was unprecedented, and no one died."

Amy disagreed. "I think we could have done more, and with each season it was getting better and better," she said. "I think if we had done another season it would have been really great. We come from sketch comedy, not twenty-two-minute comedy, so [even after thirty episodes] we were still trying to figure it out."

In the end, Colbert was sanguine about the experience.

After *Strangers* went off the air, Colbert went back to going full-speed ahead at *The Daily Show*.

As the show headed into the brunt of the 2000 election season, he hit the ground running. When Jon Stewart came on board, Colbert credited him with marking the start of his political awakening, and even when things were going full tilt on *Strangers* he was already helping to craft the political slant on *The Daily Show*, when the yearlong series "Indecision 2000" launched during the primary season.

"There was no better story for us than the 2000 election because it involved everyone, it was unprecedented, and no one died," said Colbert. "The night that Gore conceded, we were finally able to use the material we were writing for 32 days. It was so much fun to release all that comedy

> **"Stewart 'infected me with his spirit of satire.'"**

that had built up for that time. I couldn't imagine having more fun. We all felt that way."

Stewart "infected me with his spirit of satire," said Colbert. "I learned to talk passionately about things [I] cared about and be fair to a position that [I didn't] agree with. I realized that I had stumbled into a perfect job for me."

He had been playing Stephen Colbert the character on *The Daily Show* for over three years—he debuted as a correspondent on June 26, 1997—and he'd had plenty of time to refine it. He drew from a number of newsmen and anchors to create the amalgam that was his character.

"Stone Phillips has the greatest neck in journalism," he said. "And he's got the most amazingly severe head tilt at the end of tragic statements, like 'There were no . . . survivors,' and he tilts his head just a bit on *survivors* as if to say, 'It's true. It's sad. There were none.'" Colbert also liked the name Stone Phillips because he thought it sounded reassuring to viewers. "Stone, Shale, Bedrock, Gypsum," he joked, adding, "If it was spelled *Stone Fill-Up* then it would be a porn star name."

> **"Stone Phillips has the greatest neck in journalism."**

He also turned to Geraldo Rivera, because he thought the veteran investigative reporter had a great sense of mission. "He always looks and sounds like he's gonna change the world with this one report," he said. "He's got that early seventies hip trench coat busting-this-thing-wide-open look going on. "I read once that when he goes jogging in Central Park, he's like a battleship on patrol."

Colbert also used Brian Williams of the *NBC Nightly News* and CNN's Anderson Cooper to help shape his character. "I'm not entirely sure what Williams is saying, because I don't turn up the volume, but I think he's just adorable," he said. "Anderson Cooper is actually much sexier than Williams, but Brian is in a position of power and you know how attractive that is."

But his biggest influence was undoubtedly Bill O'Reilly, the acerbic conservative host of *The O'Reilly Factor*, one of the highest-rated shows on the Fox News Channel. Colbert soon began to fawningly refer to him as Papa Bear during his *Daily Show* reports and described his character as "a Bill O'Reilly–like commentator, a very well-intentioned, poorly-informed, high-status idiot."

"O'Reilly's the easiest one to reference, because he's the most popular," Colbert explained. "He's the one everyone understands, and he also does it best. He's an incredibly aggressive performer. But the character can be tough, because it's hard for me to maintain the level of self-assurance that someone like O'Reilly has all the time. I'd love to be able to believe that for short periods of time, but I'm afraid if I did that completely well, I'd never be able to turn it off. But how great would it be to feel that great about yourself?

"Like everyone else, he wants to be loved, he just doesn't value curiosity or knowledge," he noted, adding an essential point that is often overlooked. "[O'Reilly] plays the victim," said Colbert. "He trumpets his power while in the same breath declaring his victimhood."

After settling on his list of role models, he gave it his own twist. "On *The Daily Show*, I'm essentially a very high-status character, but my weakness is that I'm stupid," he explained.

His appearance also helped paint a picture of the character, though it was a look that both Colbert and his character favored. "I am a button-down iconoclast in khaki pants, blue blazer, and brass buttons—just no pleats," he said. "I have a healthy disrespect for authority, but this is just how I happen to be comfortable. But I think my look gives me a subversive quality."

"Stephen has a dark, sharp-edged sensibility," said Laura Krafft, a writer who would later work on *The Colbert Report*. "But it's palatable because of his all-American looks. I'm not sure it would work if he looked threatening."

Though the life of his character is "unexamined," Colbert drew on the detailed character preparation that he first learned at Northwestern—indeed, even earlier during his *Dungeons & Dragons* days—and started fleshing out a background and an official biography to help get a handle on the character in the early years. According to Colbert, he has a dog named Gipper and graduated from Dartmouth College in 1986, where he also dated the conservative political commentator Laura Ingraham, who graduated a year before him.

In fact, the *Dartmouth Alumni Magazine* later ran a profile of Colbert—the character—where it detailed that he worked on the infamously conservative college paper *The Dartmouth Review* and joined a party-hearty frat on campus.

However, when Colbert was first developing his starched correspondent character, one of the things he planned to do was to give him a name. But he never got around to it. "I did not intend to do this character in my own name," he said. "He kinda snuck up on me."

As *The Daily Show* progressed, it continued to become an odd hybrid of comedy, news, and straightforward delivery, depending on whom you talked to.

"The last thing I think about is performing," said Stewart. "It's all about the managing, editing and moving toward showtime. Stephen is rendering a character in real time. Typically, he's improvising with people who don't know they're in an improv scene."

Steve Carell added that their improvisational backgrounds definitely helped. "Essentially, you're doing these pieces and you're improvising with someone who doesn't know he's your improv partner," he said, adding that most of the time, people are clueless as to the true intent of the interview. "They have no idea," said Carell. "We just screw with them, and they watch it later and cry."

Colbert took a gentler approach. He discovered that he liked playing the fool, that it was a natural fit for him. But being a nice guy at heart and coming away from the often-nasty tones employed under Craig Kilborn's time, he wanted to give fair warning to his guests and profile subjects. "I don't care what they think of me, but I care about hurting their feelings," he said. So before the cameras roll, he methodically gives a version of the following speech to each guest. "My character is an idiot. So disabuse me of my ignorance." Sometimes they listen, but more often they don't.

"My character is an idiot. So disabuse me of my ignorance."

"They sometimes don't understand where we're going with the conversation," he said. "I talk to them for hours and you're seeing the three or four questions that are important to my segment. They don't necessarily perceive a three-minute edit out of a three-hour conversation. I don't make a big deal out of being funny, and then we do our best to bring 'em back alive in editing."

Everyone reacts differently. Sometimes a guest will fail to point out the errors he or she deliberately makes on camera—primarily because the guest doesn't want to appear foolish or ornery on TV—but often they do challenge Colbert. And when the interview subject does challenge him, he tends to switch gears, either agreeing with the interviewee—therefore throwing them off their track—or going on the offensive.

One example: He interviewed David Rothman, PhD at Columbia University for the segment "I'm with Stupid," which aired on July 9, 2003. Colbert called the professor a bio-ethnicist, and he nicely corrected Colbert's error, advising him it was "bioethicist."

When *The Daily Show* invited State Senator Philip Jimeno of Maryland to come on the show, he agreed, even though he hadn't watched it before, because it offered him a national audience. "I was thinking it would be somebody like Joan Lunden," he said.

But after he shook hands and sat down with Colbert, he soon discovered it was nothing like *Good Morning America*. Colbert grilled Jimeno about legislation he'd sponsored that would safeguard shooting ranges from noise complaints. Two seemingly opposite groups had come out to support the bill: an environmental group and the National Rifle Association. When Colbert commented it sounded like strange bedfellows, Jimeno thought it didn't seem like a typical interview, and the line of questioning just got stranger.

Toward the end, Jimeno said he had to leave, and Colbert said that was okay, even though he had to ask some of the questions again on camera. When a staffer gave Jimeno a release to sign, he asked what would happen if he didn't sign the paper.

"We'll use it anyway," she told him.

In 2003, Colbert traveled to Alabama to cover the story of Roy Moore, then chief justice of the Alabama Supreme Court, who stood up to a federal judge who ordered him to remove a Ten Commandments monument that was on display at the state courthouse. Colbert interviewed the local head of the Christian Coalition for his take on the matter. "The whole time, he kept taking phone calls about tax cuts, and he made a few mistakes on tape that could have been very damning to him, but he got me to promise that I wouldn't say what they were," said Colbert. "It was painful not to run them because it would have been funny, but embarrassing for him, so we didn't. I would have liked to satirically rough him up, because I thought he was bullying people with his religion, but I promised."

"We've always wanted to be less dependent on the Hollywood cycle of standard talk show guests," said Ben Karlin, who joined *The Daily Show* as a writer in 1999 after spending a few years writing at *The Onion*, and though it was tough to convince name-brand guests to come on the show for a couple of years, it finally turned around. Again, he credited the campaign season. "The show made a name for itself during the elections as a place where politicians or journalists would want to come and talk."

Some were absolute fans. After Wolf Blitzer taped a segment for the show, Jon asked if he could hang out for a bit. Blitzer quickly agreed.

"How could I say no?" he asked. "This is the most important show ever."

"We rarely do ad hominem attacks," said Stewart. "In general, it's based in frustration over reality."

"We claim no respectability," added Colbert. "There's no status I would not surrender for a joke, so we don't have to defend anything."

At the same time, even though the overall tone of *The Daily Show* is satirical, "The show is our own personal beliefs," said Stewart. "That's the only reason why we go to work everyday. You try not to let it become didactic, you always remember it's a comedy show more than a political satire, but we very much infuse it with who we are."

Though he had no straightforward news reporting experience, Stewart thought he approached his work in the same spirit, sometimes better. "I think what we do is relatively well thought-out," he said. "And while there are times we step over a line when things are happening fast and furious, the truth is as fake journalists, we exercise far more restraint than the journalists I see." He cited how the media handled the aftermath of the Columbine shootings, where TV crews essentially mobbed students and their families. "I had never seen anything like that," he noted. "We didn't make one joke about it, so as far as our comedy being in the depths, I think we've got a long way to go toward the bottom until we take on the actual ethics of real journalism."

"There's no status I would not surrender for a joke, so we don't have to defend anything."

Colbert agreed. "I'm a comedian," he said. "I don't consider myself to be a newsman at all. If people learn something about the news from watching my show, that's incidental. It's better to watch the show and already know about the news."

But signs were clear that this was already happening, that regular *Daily Show* viewers were beginning to rely on the show as their sole source of news. Colbert had mixed feelings about the early reports.

"It sounds a little bit apocryphal to me, but we do repackage the news, so I suppose that we are a valid source as long as people can understand when we're goofing and when we mean it," he said. "I think you have to have some handle on what's happening in the world to get our jokes, because we only do the most cursory explanation of what the issue is in order to set up our punch lines. We don't talk in depth about any stories. I suppose you could watch our show and sort of get a sense of what's going on in the world, but you'd also be missing half of our joke."

"The most common thing that real reporters say to me is, 'I wish I could say what you say,'" Colbert disclosed. "What I don't understand is why can't they say what I say, even in their own way? Does that mean they want to be able to name certain bald contradictions or hypocrisies that politicians have?"

Ana Marie Cox, formerly known as the political blogger Wonkette, said that Colbert shouldn't worry about real news versus fake news, "Because they think the real news is also fake.

When deciding which stories to cover—after all, with a twenty-four-hour news cycle, there are always plenty of stories out there that just beg to be satirized—there are additional issues to tackle, among them responsibility to the story and the culture. "We try to cover stories that are interesting to people and, more importantly, relevant," said Karlin. "I think we'd be a lot more into finding something that's inherently funny and quirky, but then we have to educate the audience a lot more. Instead, we'd rather talk about what's on people's minds or what's particularly absurd of this moment or of this time."

But not everything is up for grabs. Some topics are absolutely off-limits. After September 11, 2001, Stewart closed down *The Daily Show* for a week and came back a week later with an emotional elegy that was almost nine minutes long.

"Obviously real tragedy is off-limits," said Colbert. "No one wants to do comedy about that. But I would say there's almost nothing that can't be mocked on a certain level as long as it doesn't involve loss of life or deep human tragedy. I don't think we ever looked at something and said that's too ridiculous to make more ridiculous. Contrary to what people may say, there's no upper limit to stupidity. We can make everything stupider."

"Contrary to what people may say, there's no upper limit to stupidity. We can make everything stupider."

Case in point: Colbert cited a story he was particularly fond of called "Death and Taxes," which aired in March of 1999. The town of Saratoga Springs, New York, distributed W-2s to city employees for the previous year, but because of an error with the dot-matrix printer, the forms declared that everyone was deceased—all 350. "So we went up there and covered it as if there had been a disaster where three hundred people had died, to report on the grief and the rage," said Colbert. "What I liked about it was that it highlighted the reporter as single-minded idiot. The reporter desperately needs the story to be what he thinks it is. The story is written before you leave; you're just going there to verify what you already want it to be. In this case, the reporter gets there and it is not what he thought it was but he won't let it go, especially that the people there are filled with rage, and I actually eventually got people to say that they were sad and that they were filled with rage. And it was a great triumph for me as a fake reporter to get them to buy into my idiocy.

"I liked that piece because no one in town looks like a fool. *I* look like a fool," he continued. "We're not shooting fish in a barrel like with alien enthusiasts or Bigfoot hunters; this really is spoofing the self-important, hyperbolic, vulture-like quality of tragedy news."

Bob Wiltfong, a *Daily Show* correspondent from 2004 to 2005, was watching closely. "Colbert nailed the tone of a *Daily Show* correspondent," he said. "He was the standard that everyone else was trying to live up to. When I auditioned for the show, I had been working in local TV news as a real correspondent for ten years before I tried to get a job as a fake one. But to prepare for the audition, I watched Colbert's clips from *The Daily Show*."

It was clear that Colbert had already broken out of the pack of correspondents on the show.

The whole tone of the show had shifted in the year since Stewart first came on board as host. Whereas previously stories about Bigfoot and taxidermied squirrels would have automatically been green-lit, now the future of such pieces was uncertain. "As soon as the presidential campaign started up in 2000, you could see the show begin to change," said Colbert. In fact, at the end of the 2000 campaign season, Colbert—newly politicized—offered up a bet to the other correspondents and producers. "I put a hundred dollars on the table and said to the field producers, if you can get us a Bigfoot story, I'll give you the hundred-dollar bill," he said. "I knew none of that shit was going to get past Jon anymore. Everything had to be grounded in reality, in something that's happening in the world, so we could use our field pieces as an addition to the satirical take that's happening at the desk."

"Some of the correspondents on *The Daily Show* write more than others, some are more traditional performers, but in almost all cases input is pretty welcome," said Karlin. "Anything that can help make it in their own voice. Colbert is the most experienced writer, so he writes or rewrites a lot of his own stuff."

Colbert still loved to write, and he found that writing for himself was easier than writing for an ensemble of improvisers. "Writing for *The Daily Show* is wonderful because as a correspondent you have to come up with a particular take on a specific issue," he said. "There is an actual event in reality that you're spoofing or talking about, you come up with a wrong-headed view of it, and explore it through the lens of your newsman. It's easier to turn out a lot of material that way."

He also found writing for each night's "newscast" to be more freeing than writing for the stage. "You can't feel precious about your words because there's always going to be another story tomorrow," he said. "We've got to get this damn thing on by five o'clock so it has to be written by three, and the story just broke this morning. It's Kleenex comedy: if I fuck up, then I fuck up, there's always another Kleenex in the box. It doesn't mean that we don't try our hardest, or that it can't be really hard to do this work, but of all the writing I've done, this is the most immediately enjoyable."

But by 2000, Colbert's role at the show had already started to shift from when he first started and was mostly out on the road to do his field reports. When Jon came on board as host, everyone pitched in wherever they were needed. "I'm more involved with the show now because the show is really what happens in the studio," he said. But he complained that he actually had less time to do everything than before. "I might get a call from the head writer at eleven A.M. asking me to come up with three minutes on the weapons of mass destruction hunt for that same night, and that will take me the rest of the day."

But viewers were noticing. In fact, for *The Daily Show*'s "Indecision 2000" election night special, almost as many younger viewers tuned into Comedy Central as those who were watching the results come in over at Fox News. *The Daily Show* measured 435,000 viewers aged eighteen to thirty-four compared with 459,000 in the same category at Fox. Since Stewart took over as anchor, *The Daily Show* averaged two million viewers a night, which was huge for cable and significantly higher than Kilborn's numbers, which typically hovered around one million.

In fact, the 2000 campaign season was when *The Daily Show* began to gain critical mass among viewers, and traditional media came calling. During the days leading up to the election, news shows on the networks—like *The Today Show*—were running brief segments from the previous night's show on a regular basis. "It's like they've handed over the reins of commentary and reporting to comedians because we're the only ones who can make sense of it," said Madeleine Smithberg. However, she and other staffers had mixed feelings about their newfound standing. "Our currency is one of insanity. Stop giving us credibility! We don't know what to do with it, it's messing up our shtick."

"We do technology so well so it looks like we're in places that [we're not]."

But that credibility continued to grow. Colbert had long clamored to attend a White House press briefing, and despite ongoing requests, the Clinton administration nixed the idea.

That is, until the president's last day of office, when the administration decided to give Colbert a break. In his segments, Stewart always introduced Colbert as the senior fill-in-the-blank analyst, which could range from the environment to the theater, depending on the subject of the story.

At the press conference, Colbert introduced himself to the White House press secretary, Jake Siewert, as the senior White House correspondent for *The Daily Show* and asked for a one-on-one with the departing president.

"He will not be available for a one-on-one with *The Daily Show*," said Siewert.

"Could you at least ask?" Colbert shot back. The room exploded in laughter.

"We could check."

"Make sure he knows it's Stephen *Colbert*, not Steven Carell, okay? That's *C-o-l-b-e-r-t*. He'll see me."

He didn't meet with President Clinton that day, but his experience sparked an idea that would inspire future correspondent field reports and help immeasurably with fake news reports to come: the birth of the green screen. "While we were there, we did [shoots] of locations at the White House, so now we can go back and be at the White House whenever we want," he said. "We do technology so well so it looks like we're in places that [we're not]."

One of the things front and center that day on the minds of everyone at *The Daily Show* was how the incoming president and his administration would affect future coverage. "I remember people asking me, how are you ever going to find presidential humor now that Bill Clinton is out of office?" said Silverman.

As they would soon find out, of course, they had absolutely nothing to worry about. Besides, they would soon be celebrating: in the spring of 2001, *The Daily Show* won a Peabody Award for "Indecision 2000," the broadcasting equivalent of the Pulitzer Prize. Ironically, it was the only news show that was honored that year.

CHAPTER 8

"As a professional comedian, there's a lot of love you get from an audience's laughter and applause," said Bob Wiltfong, who spent a year at *The Daily Show* as a freelance correspondent. "It's my theory that people get into comedy because there's something missing in their own personal life, and they need that void to be filled through laughter and acceptance on stage.

"Some of the most miserable people I've ever met are comedy people," he noted, adding that Colbert was one of the rare exceptions. "It made for an interesting dynamic at *The Daily Show*, which had some of the smartest, funniest people I've known, all moving toward one common goal, but the flip side was that there were a lot of miserable curmudgeonly people working there. In general, comedy just isn't an environment that lends itself toward happiness."

"It's like a dysfunctional family," said the comedian Lewis Black.

Even though it's their job to be funny, the correspondents at *The Daily Show* were under constant pressure not only to meet regular deadlines but also to try and figure out where they were in the pecking order compared with the other correspondents. It eventually took its toll, whether they were writers or on-air talent. After all, the only step up from being a correspondent is host. Many correspondents were in a state of perpetual worry, never really knowing if Comedy Central would renew their contract for another year. "We never really got any guidance on that, which made us all walk around on pins and needles," said Wiltfong, adding that Colbert probably felt like that at some point in his early days, that his chances were rare to host his own show on Comedy Central.

Wiltfong shared an office with his fellow correspondent Samantha Bee. "She struggled with being the only woman on the show in what is a male-dominated industry to begin with," he said. "She felt like the low person on the totem pole, and that's not a good thing to feel as a performer. Once Stephen was giving her a pep talk, and he told her if all else fails, the one thing she had going for her that no one else had was that she was the only woman," said Wiltfong. "He was very nurturing."

"What you see on air with both those guys is pretty much what they're like off air."

He also studied the different ways in which Jon and Stephen approached their jobs. "What you see on air with both those guys is pretty much what they're like off air," he said. "In order for Jon to do some of the comedy on *The Daily Show* for so many years and for it to be high quality, it has to come from a place of anger, because then it's truly biting and gets at the truth. In real life he's not a ball of laughs, because he's pretty upset about what's going on in the world.

"Colbert is the total opposite of Jon," he continued. "He's very upbeat and personable. He'll call out something and say, 'Can you believe this is going on?' while Jon is more like, 'These assholes, look what they're doing, let's rake these guys over the coals and make it smart and funny because these guys are doing stupid stuff.' "

The two comics, of course, had their own take on things.

"Jon deconstructs the news; he's ironic and detached, while I falsely construct the news and I'm ironically attached," said Colbert. "In fact, I'm not detached at all; I'm passionate about what I'm talking about. I illustrate the hypocrisy of a news item as a *character*. So while Jon's just being Jon on the show, conversely, that's me *not* being me, that's me being that Stephen Colbert guy."

When it comes to politics, comedians tend to be iconoclasts and anti–status quo. "Jon is admirably balanced," Colbert continued. "Every time I work with him on something, he tries to perceive the true intention of the person speaking, left or right, regardless of whether it was something he believed in or not. He wants to *honestly* mock."

In the end, however, they're both after the same thing: "Basically, it's a bunch of guys exchanging ideas, laughing about stuff, and getting excited about smart, funny ideas," said Wiltfong.

The comedian Lewis Black lays claim as the regular who's been with *The Daily Show* the longest; his segment "Back in Black with Lewis Black" first aired in 1996 and is still running today. He and Colbert sometimes chatted with each other at the studio, but they rarely worked together. "I'm much more talented than he is, so it was hard for him to deal with me," Black joked, adding that while the two comedians didn't collaborate on any scenes, they did occasionally give each other feedback and bounce material off each other.

"I was there only once or twice a week while he was there all the time," said Black. "He was originally positioned to serve as knee-jerk contrarian to whatever Jon said, and his evolution was brilliant. He essentially took an improv character and turned him into a personality."

Black also said that he carefully studied Colbert's field reports and interviews. "It never ceased to amaze me that he would take an interview and ask a question and never end up where I expected it to go," he said.

The Daily Show offices and studio were at 513 West 54th Street, on the west side of Manhattan. The environment could best be described as utilitarian office setting with a comedic, almost frat-boy feel to it. A visitor once described it as "a narrow, carpeted hallway with a series of small offices that could be singles and doubles in a freshman dorm." The doors to each office are typically covered with a variety of small bulletin boards, games, dolls, and cartoon characters, along with a smattering of newspaper stories.

"For all the stress and pressure involved in making the show every day, it is a very happy place to work," said the *Daily Show* writer John Oliver. "We have dogs running around the office, free lunch, and no one takes what they do too seriously. It's like a much less trendy Google Headquarters." Competition was fierce to get a job on *The Daily Show*, but perhaps it was even more breakneck among college students to land an internship on the show. After all, they were the *Show*'s most loyal audience. Thousands of applications poured in for the six internships offered each summer on the show.

For the lucky few who did make it to New York, it didn't take long to learn that Colbert was a genuinely nice guy. While many celebrities would normally look down on interns, Colbert didn't, and indeed, for this and other reasons, he stood out.

As a broadcast-journalism major at the Edward R. Murrow School of Communication at Washington University, John Obrien won an internship to the show in the summer of 2002. Most interns came from a comedy background; Obrien thought that his application stood out because of his journalism major. Though he was thrilled at winning the position, he was also warned that his days would be filled with lots of menial gofer tasks like making copies, messengering tapes, and running all over Manhattan getting props for the show. Indeed, on his first day, even though he was unfamiliar with New York, a production coordinator asked him to go to Spanish Harlem to buy a bright orange tank top in size 7-XL at a hole-in-the-wall convenience store. He was also informed that he would have very little contact—if any—with Stewart or the correspondents.

One day during his first week, Obrien was wandering around the office to get a feel for the place, and he bumped into Colbert in the hall outside his office. "I nodded, he nodded back, but then I kept on going," he said. But then he had a change of heart and went back to Colbert's office and introduced himself. "I told him I was from Seattle, and figured that would be it and then I'd be on my way," he said. "Instead, Colbert started to tell me about a shoot he did in Seattle, and then asked me way more questions than I was asking him," said Obrien. "He kept the conversation going for quite awhile."

Another time, Obrien was sent to rescue Colbert when he was running late because he was driving to the studio but was stuck in traffic. "I met Colbert in his car and he ran to the studio, and I parked the car at a local garage," he said. "When I got back, I handed him the keys and he held out his hand. I didn't know what he wanted, so I shook his hand. He shook it, laughed, and asked for the valet ticket." Obrien ran back to get the ticket, and from then on, whenever Colbert saw him in the hallway he jumped toward him and proceeded to do the forearm bash that Mark McGwire and Jose Canseco favored.

At the time, there were about forty people working at *The Daily Show*, and Obrien described the working environment as incredibly relaxed. "It wasn't a pressure cooker at all," he said. "People brought their dogs to work, there were frequent office parties, and overall, it was very loose," he said.

Colbert shared an office with Carell on the top floor, filled with a huge U-shaped desk, and they sat with their backs to each other as they worked. They kept a neat office, with a few pictures and bobbleheads scattered around the place.

Seth Zimmerman interned with Obrien at *The Daily Show* in the summer of 2002, and he remembers watching Colbert and Carell review a script for their "Even Stevphen" debate, where each correspondent takes an opposing side of a timely and often controversial subject. Sometimes they'd rehearse it in the interview room, other times they'd go over it backstage.

"It was cool to see the two of them go over an Even Stevphen scene because they made it look like they'd been doing this forever," said Zimmerman. "They seemed so natural but also so iconic. They were always hitting a button of some kind, and they'd always laugh. Once they got on camera, of course, they'd be totally professional, but beforehand they'd both turn it on and off at will as they tinkered with the sketch. Backstage, right before they went out, they'd toss a football back and forth."

Everyday, the interns rotated within several departments, ranging from general production to accounting to working with the writers. Mandy Ganis was a *Daily Show* intern in the summer of 2003.

"We were all working in such small quarters, so we got to see everyone all the time and talk with everyone," she said. "They weren't big names yet; they were friendly and laid back."

The humor on the show naturally extended throughout the rest of the office, including the intra-corporate documents, a weekly newsletter, and the bible for each new intern: *The Intern's Guide to "The Daily Show."* The book gave them everything they needed to know during their tenure and was written with typical *Daily Show* humor. A job description for each staff member was listed, along with the location of his or her office. For instance, Jon Stewart's office was located on the second floor, and this was his job description: "Hosts, writes, consults, manages the Bennigans off of exit 7 on the Jersey Turnpike." Colbert's was "Correspondent, Resident of Middle Earth, also a human musical."

Ganis soon learned that when it came to the administrative staff, writers, and on-air talent at the show, the most valuable intern was whoever was handling general production that day. The primary job was to buy food to stock the entire office, including the green room, the control room, the writers' lounge, and the kitchen. The list was preprinted and lengthy, with around fifty different items to inventory.

The list included the following:

- Three boxes of cookies for the control room
- Three bags of candy for the green room
- Soy milk—vanilla if they have it
- Seven blocks of Philadelphia cream cheese
- Three Fuji apples
- Three boxes of Kleenex (unscented)
- Lucky Charms ***EVERY DAY***

The intern in charge of the shopping was supposed to first check to see if anything needed replacing before heading off to D'Agostino, a supermarket around the block. If, for instance, there were only two Fuji apples in the house, the intern would buy one more that day.

"Interns are in charge of getting the food for the writers because everyone's so busy they don't have any time to do anything but work," said Joe Legaz, who interned at *The Daily Show* over the summer of 2003. "Once, the intern coordinator was telling us about the contents of the candy bowl, and Colbert went by and said in a stern voice, 'Don't screw up the candy.' "

Food responsibilities were not limited to the general production intern. For instance, for the intern assigned to the writers' lounge, the first order of business was "to bring the writers' bagel basket up at 9:30 and bring it back down to the kitchen between 10:30 and 10:45."

And regardless of the cereal stash, the intern was required to bring back at least one box of Lucky Charms. If not, there'd be hell to pay.

They definitely had their priorities straight.

Colbert filled in for Jon as the guest host of *The Daily Show* for the first time on January 24, 2001.

Like Colbert, Stewart was also fitting in outside work when he could, though he preferred movies. He had already played small parts in *Big Daddy* and *The Faculty*, but when NBC approached him for a sitcom development deal in 2003, where he'd also serve as executive producer, he agreed with one condition: that Colbert be the star and co-writer.

The two began work on the script for the pilot. The premise of the sitcom revolved around a man in a small town in South Carolina who is thinking about moving elsewhere but is continually pulled back home. "It's about people who sacrifice what they think they may want for what they know that they love," Colbert said. "It's exactly the sort of thing I've wanted to do for a long time. It will draw on my experiences growing up in South Carolina, which I've always wanted to share with people who don't understand about where I come from."

Given his experience working in TV and knowing the slim odds of getting a project from the idea stage to a show on a prime-time network schedule, Colbert understood that the show would probably never get made; he set the odds at ten to one against making the sitcom.

"I'm very happy to be doing it," he said. "I'm excited, but I just don't want to get too excited."

"This is a coup for NBC to be in partnership with such clever and creative writer-performers as Jon and Stephen," Jeff Zucker, the president of NBC Entertainment, said at the time. "I can't wait to see the finished product."

In the end, Colbert's suspicions were spot on; the sitcom never got beyond the initial script for the pilot.

Although Jon and Stephen spent a lot of time working and laughing at the studio, their friendship was mostly limited to the office. "In theory, I think Jon would be excellent company," said Colbert. "But I have nothing to back it up." And he didn't hang out with Carell after hours either, though they shared an office.

"The biggest mistake that people make is thinking that Jon and Stephen sit down before every show and say, okay, how are we going to change the world, or some bullshit like that," said Ben Karlin. "They both really just want to get a laugh."

"Colbert would be comfortable not only in any discipline, but in any era," said Stewart. "If you transplanted him to the 1600s and suddenly he was involved in the medieval arts, or even dentistry, he would be fine. I consider him, oddly enough, like the Internet."

Colbert volleyed back his admiration. "Jon's very generous and treats me like a peer," he said. "I think I still think of him as an older brother; he comes before I do, and he's bigger. He's taught me a lot, how not to worry about what goes on outside the building and just get our work done every day."

As the mutual love fest continued, some at the show noticed that the two began to shut others out. As he had previously done with Sedaris and Dinello, Colbert had found another tribe he felt comfortable with. Maybe too comfortable, based on how others perceived it.

"One negative aspect of working with Colbert from the perspective of the other correspondents was that he was very tight with Jon," said Bob Wiltfong. "Jon and Stephen were always very friendly and chummy with each other. On set or during rehearsals they were the best of friends, but it was an unusual occurrence when other correspondents engaged Jon in conversation."

On election night in 2004, all the correspondents were in the studio for the live broadcast. During the rehearsal, the correspondents sat in a corner while Stephen and Jon sat at the desk bullshitting with each other, making no attempt at conversation with the others. "It always seemed like a world we couldn't get into, and it struck me as curious," said Wiltfong. "I didn't know why that dynamic existed and I wasn't the only one. Ed Helms and I talked about it, too. But Jon just doesn't let many people in and Stephen was one of the few."

Part of the problem, unvoiced among some, was that the close relationship between Stewart and Colbert—along with an increase in guest host appearances—meant that it was clear who was going to be next to move up the ladder. "There was a bit of grumbling among fellow comedians that you don't want to see another comedian succeed because it means less laughter and stage time for you," said Wiltfong. "That's part of the business."

Another part of the business that couldn't be avoided—especially with the often-passive-aggressive ambush quality of conducting guest interviews—was lawsuits.

Colbert was sued for a story that ran in the fall of 1998 about a senior-living development called Leisure World in Orange County, California. The residents—all eighteen thousand of them—wanted to splinter off from the city of Laguna Woods and form their own town. The fight started because the surrounding towns didn't agree.

The concept of Colbert's story was to do a piece called "Grandfatherland." Colbert interviewed Bert Hack, an official at Leisure World, who was campaigning for the separation. In the story, Colbert drew parallels between Hack and Hitler. "We had him up on a hill and asked him to tell us about the town," he said. "I used a few straight-arm gestures, and so did Hack."

Once the story ran, Hack filed suit in Los Angeles Superior Court against Comedy Central Network, Aardvark Productions, Colbert, and a producer and editor at the show. In the suit, Hack charged them with defamation, fraud, concealment, intentional infliction of emotional distress, and violation of right of privacy.

But that wasn't really the issue. Instead, Hack sued because he maintained that Colbert and the other staffers said they were from CNN, not Comedy Central.

"He said we claimed we were from CNN," said Colbert. "We didn't say that, but we didn't necessarily say we were from Comedy Central, either. We didn't know he was a retired lawyer, which is the most dangerous kind of lawyer because they have all sorts of time to crawl up your ass. And he did." As Colbert described it, here's how he initially answered Hack's questions:

"We didn't know he was a retired lawyer, which is the most dangerous kind of lawyer."

"Where are you from?"

"A small cable news show out of New York."

"What channel?"

"45, 47, I don't know if you get it here."

Hack must have said okay and not probed further.

"If they ask which network, then we say Comedy Central and start packing our bags," said Colbert. "Hack sued, but as part of the settlement, we agreed to never show "Grandfatherland" again."

After that, Comedy Central set strict guidelines in place for correspondents and writers to follow. "We all know to avoid certain topics as well as jokes that could start a lawsuit," Colbert said, "and every day, a script of the show goes to our legal adviser to be okayed before the taping. For instance, the Church of Scientology is not the subject of jokes on

The Daily Show. And we do not put beloved children's characters into adult situations. And when working off a sound bite, no matter how mean the man-on-the-street sounds, we can't follow him up by saying something like, 'This man then left to check on the body in his trunk.' "

Before long, the Three Idiots were at it again.

Amy Sedaris wanted to write a book about a worm. Editors at Hyperion had been following Amy's career—since *Strangers* went off the air in 2000, she had appeared in a few movies, including *Maid in Manhattan* with Jennifer Lopez, and she had been featured sporadically as a publicist on *Sex and the City*—and in 2002, they called her in for a meeting to see if she had any book ideas.

She and Dinello had once developed a Second City sketch about a worm, which was based on an ongoing story about an orange ceramic worm she and her brother David adopted when they were kids. "We named him Montgomery, and we used to make up stories about him," she said. The worm's long gone, but she always thought it would make a great children's book. The plot: "More or less, it's about a worm trying to figure out what kind of worm he is, so he goes on these adventures," she said.

"It's all about reaching for the lowest star."

"Somehow the worm gets split in half, and the head goes one way and the tail goes the other, but they'd go on different journeys and meet up at the end. Maybe he lives in a donkey's ass for a night. It's all about reaching for the lowest star," she said. "He wasn't particularly ambitious, but the point was, that's okay. A lot of people aren't ambitious. He just goes through life."

The kicker: The story ends when Montgomery realizes that he's a tequila worm and an alcoholic.

Dinello warned her that the subject matter seemed a bit dark for a children's book, but Amy wanted to try it out anyway.

They went to the meeting and faced a roomful of business-clad executives. After Amy finished her description of the book, there was dead silence. As Dinello described it, they were looking at "gape-mouthed stares."

Finally, one of them spoke.

What else do you have?

Out of nowhere, Sedaris said, "When I was growing up, my family used to decorate the top of the piano and call it Wigfield."

The editors perked up.

"I had been making things up about Wigfield since I was a kid," said Sedaris. "To me, Wigfield was something like a mall that sold wigs and hair and bakery goods." She then proceeded to describe the town and the residents of her childhood imagination, and Paul jumped in. "I riffed on an idea that we would create character monologues opposite photographs of us in character with wacky captions," he said.

"With maybe some recipes," said Amy.

Soon the two of them were improvising.

The editors agreed that it sounded like a book and Amy and Paul got busy. But something was missing: Colbert. Once they described the project to him, Stephen agreed to help out with the book despite his heavy workload with *The Daily Show*. "I work all the time mainly out of fear that the day will come when I can't think of anything funny," he said.

Colbert helped refine the idea. He had visited Jefferson, West Virginia, population three hundred, for a *Daily Show* story that had aired in January 2001. "It was one of those times when I did a piece for *The Daily Show* and thought I could do forty minutes on these people, instead of just three and a half," he said. The town was basically nothing more than a tax shelter for strip clubs, adult bookstores, and used-auto-parts stores. The recently elected mayor—an ex-stripper who worked at a place called Ho' Boys Used Tires—wanted to dissolve the town. Not everyone in town agreed—particularly the business owners—and several different factions each declared that they were in charge.

"The town council had appointed a sheriff, and the mayor had appointed a chief of police, and the two men would try to run each other off the road and wreck each other to see who would be chief of police," said Colbert. "Plus, Jefferson was next to the world headquarters of Union Carbide. It was like Bhopal in Appalachia, just a horrible, horrible place."

They took some of the elements of Jefferson and folded them into the book *Wigfield*. The basic story line is about a small town in danger of being wiped off the face of the earth since the government plans to demolish a dam and flood the town so that some salmon can be saved. A journalist visits the town to interview what he expects will be a local population intent on saving their peaceful small town, but what he finds instead is chaos, feuds, and townsfolk who turn out to be the opposite of what he expects . . . kind of like Jefferson, West Virginia.

They got to work. First up: character development. The main character is a journalist, Russell Hokes. "Since none of us had written a book at that point, it made sense to create a narrator who had never written a book," said Dinello. "Really, I don't think he's even read a book, and that really freed us up because we no longer had to pay attention to any of the rules of grammar."

As they did when writing scripts for *Strangers*, they sat in Dinello's apartment tossing ideas around, Amy lying on the couch while Stephen and Paul improvised, and they wrote a few scenes. They met a few more times and cranked out more scenes, totaling around 2,500 words. "We thought we were pretty close to being done, so I asked Paul to check the contract to see how many words we had to write," said Colbert. "He checked, the contract said fifty thousand, and I thought he was joking."

"We needed a higher word count," Dinello said. "We panicked."

They were blocked. So instead of continuing to write, they decided to do the photographs first. That way, they'd be able to act out the characters and play dress up, and maybe they'd get inspired. The top designer Todd Oldham was a good friend of Amy's, and he signed on as photographer for the book. They traveled to his Pennsylvania studio, and between Oldham's photographs and the Three Idiots' costumes, makeup, and improvisations, they became unblocked. Each one played a number of different characters in the story: Sedaris played forty-eight-year-old Mae Ella Padgett, who claimed she was the oldest citizen in town, and also played a stripper named Cinnamon; Colbert played a stripper named Raven—"thanks to a lot of duct tape here, a lot of tucking here and a lot of thrusting there"—and an Indian doctor named Raja Chuhas; while Dinello channeled the theater director Julian Childs and the taxidermist Lenare Degroat.

The photo sessions did the trick. "Being in costume and playing with the characters really inspired us," Dinello said. "That really helped the word count." And even when they got stuck with the manuscript, they turned to their main character: "Russell Hokes' lesson of all this is that if you need to really pad out a book, use synonyms a lot and don't be afraid to let a metaphor just spin completely out of control," said Colbert. "You can fill up half a page that way."

When *Wigfield: The Can-Do Town That Just May Not* was published in May of 2003, the first-time authors went on tour to Boston, Atlanta, Chicago, New York, and Washington, D.C., and did a series of book signings, readings, and performances to promote the book.

As Sedaris described it, "The show is part play, part slide show, part book reading, part improvisation," and the authors "wanted to show Todd's photos in color, so we put it together and put the show on the road." An oversized photograph of each character was projected on the screen behind the actors.

After the performance, they held a reception so they could sign books and talk to their fans. It was the first time that Colbert had met his fans close up—there was never any budget or time to do public appearances when *Strangers with Candy* was on the air—and in the three years since the show had been off the air, Colbert's stature as an entertainer had multiplied as a result of *The Daily Show*. He was surprised that his fans were so numerous but also that they were, well, so odd.

"They're very nice people, but sometimes the fans would scare us."

"They're very nice people, but sometimes the fans would scare us," he said. "I could tell by looking out at the line at the book signings who was a *Strangers* fan and who was a *Daily Show* fan. *Strangers* fans tended to be the ones with the shaved eyebrows. I think I understand what people mean by the phrase 'cult show' because there is that kind of cult look in some of the people's eyes, which is *great* for us. For me, I could go, '*Strangers*, *Daily Show*, *Strangers*, *Daily Show*.' Or, '*Strangers*, *Daily Show*, anything else Amy has done.' Maybe it wasn't a resounding endorsement of the people who raised these people, that they would respond so positively to something so anti-authoritarian as *Strangers with Candy*."

Right on the heels of the publication of *Wigfield*, there was more good news. In June came the announcement that the Three Idiots had been hired to write the screenplay for the movie version of *Strangers with Candy*. "This will be an even more twisted version of the television show," promised the producer, Mark Roberts. "Longtime series fans will enjoy the film, and newcomers won't be left out."

By the time the announcement had been made, however, they'd already been hard at work on the script and hit a few snags.

"It's going really slowly," Amy admitted. "But don't [say] that because it'll make the producers nervous. Say you've read the screenplay and that it's really good, but it needs more action verbs."

For one, they'd all been working on different projects since *Strangers* went off the air. Even though they once spent most of their waking hours for almost two years living inside the skin of these characters, they'd been away from them for three years. Plus, whereas before all they needed to do was come up with one simple story line—like Jerri joins a religious cult or contracts a sexually transmitted disease—in order to develop a movie around the characters, they had to think about how to expand the story to fit not only ninety minutes but also a much larger screen.

"The intention was to make each other laugh while we were writing the show, and that's never changed," said Colbert. But as they discovered when writing *Wigfield*, the three would likely have to figure out how to do something that they hadn't done before.

Up to this point, they always managed to pull a rabbit out of the hat, and this time was no different. They handed in the finished script, and the movie went into production. But what surprised them even more is that any of their projects got the green light in the first place.

"We have this little saying, which is 'fooled them again,'" said Dinello. "If we manage to sell something, or someone is pleased with what we have done, all we can think of is how we deluded them. How could they possibly like our ideas? Why are they laughing? Didn't they hear those words?"

Just when it didn't seem possible that Colbert could squeeze anything else into his schedule, something came along that he couldn't pass up.

In the spring of 2003, he started to appear in TV commercials for General Motors in a recurring role as a mad investigator intent on finding the *real* Mr. Goodwrench. The campaign had Colbert and a sidekick traveling from one dealership to another in hot pursuit.

In each thirty-second spot, he ambushed both customers and employees outside the dealership to ask, "Mr. Goodwrench—who *is* this one and only GM expert?"

The campaign is actually the reincarnation of a similar Mr. Goodwrench campaign from the 1970s, and General Motors decided to go with the new campaign, in part to appeal to the younger fan base that Colbert attracted. The company was wise to let Colbert do what he does best: just be Colbert.

"The thing about Stephen Colbert is that he's an idiot," said Daniel Hennessy, the creative director at the ad agency that created the ads. "Even though he comes across as smart, he can't figure it out that we know who is Mr. Goodwrench."

In one commercial Colbert grills three different mechanics to find out which one is the *real* Mr. Goodwrench. When they say they all are, Colbert gets disgusted and barks into a megaphone for the *real* Mr. Goodwrench to step forward. In another spot, Colbert essentially re-creates his *Daily Show* character to ask random people on the street if they think Mr. Goodwrench does root canals along with regular car maintenance. In a third, he asks a police officer to issue an all-points bulletin for Mr. Goodwrench, because if he really does have over a million hours of training annually, then he is clearly violating labor laws and should be hauled in immediately.

GM decided to dovetail its investment in Colbert by also participating as a sponsor on *The Daily Show* Web site.

Though he appreciated the exposure and the revenue that the commercial series provided, Colbert never really felt comfortable with the gig. "I don't think I can sell out any more than Mr. Goodwrench," he said. "I reached an apogee of pimping."

At least when he made an appearance on *Crank Yankers*, a Comedy Central show where characters similar to Muppets act out real prank calls made by a rotating cast, including Jimmy Kimmel, Kevin Nealon, and Sarah Silverman, he didn't feel like he was selling out.

In his skit for the show, Colbert called a phone-sex service ostensibly for a friend who was deaf.

"Slow down a second," he said at one point, "I'm not a very fast typist."

Though Stephen and Evie lived in New York City when they first moved there from Chicago, once they had Madeleine, they moved to Westchester County, thinking it was more family-friendly. After a few years, however, they decided that it was not only too expensive but also not a good fit for them—for one, they felt that it didn't offer enough diversity. They also still had to be within easy proximity to Manhattan for Stephen's commute. So in the summer of 2000, they settled into Montclair, New Jersey, a bedroom community of Manhattan, about fifteen miles away from the Comedy Central studios. Madeleine was five, Peter was two, and their third child, John, was born in 2002.

At home, Stephen found that what worked to make audiences laugh would sometimes work at home, but often not.

"My kids don't think I'm funny, but they think I'm silly," he said. "I do silly things like fall down and run into things. I talk to inanimate objects."

He also tries to train them in the way of humor, for good and for bad. "For a solid year, Madeleine and I made up jokes on the spot before she went to bed. One of her favorites was, 'What did the cow say?' 'What?' 'Ruff.' 'Why?' 'He had a dog in his mouth.' "

At the same time, he used his comedic background to help make bad things seem not as bad. "It's hard to laugh and cry at the same time," he said. "If my son scrapes his knee, I'll say, You seem to have scraped your ear very badly."

But he doesn't use the same sarcastic and ironic tones that elicit laughter from *Daily Show* viewers. "Kids don't get irony or sarcasm because it just sounds mean to them," he said.

Compared with most parents, Stephen and Evie have a pretty restrictive TV-viewing policy for their kids. "During the week, the kids are allowed a half-hour a day, but on the weekends, when Mom and Dad try to sleep in, all bets are off," he said. "I've instituted a new rule that when commercials come on, my daughter has to press the mute button. Otherwise, Peter falls into a trance: *I want that. I want that. I hear, and I obey.* We also have TiVo, which Evie and I love because we can regulate their watching. We decide with the kids what to record, like *Sagwa* and *MythQuest.* I'll also record adult shows they might like, such as *Modern Marvels* on the History Channel."

But he doesn't want them to watch him on *The Colbert Report.* "I want them to know me as Dad," he said. "While I'm insincere on the show, my character is very sincere. I look like their dad, I sound like their dad, I shout more than their dad, but I say things I don't mean, and a child isn't going to know that's a character. Then they're going to think I don't mean it when I say I'm proud of them or I love them, and I'm going to tuck them into bed one night and say I love you, and they'll say, that's very good, Dad, that's very dry."

Evie is an at-home mom and is more familiar with the everyday lay of the land than Stephen is. When she leaves him alone with the kids, it doesn't take long for him to be reminded of his inadequacies, as well as the fact that the shoe can be on the other foot. "Comedy often relies on decreasing the status of one person, like a rich guy in a top hat slipping on a banana peel, and sometimes my kids do that to me," he said. "Once, Evie took the afternoon off, and I had them all crying five minutes after she left. I couldn't believe how wildly out of control things got so quickly. I was yelling at them, and my daughter asked why. I said that I was trying to teach them how to behave. She said, 'This is how you teach children? By making them cry?' I was so outmatched by this six-year-old. She had thrown the banana peel my way. I had to laugh."

In terms of his parenting musts, he has several that he lives by; it almost sounds like he's delivering a monologue on TV: "Never underestimate kids' tenacity," he advises. "Raising a child is like wrestling a small but relentless opponent." Next: "You can't beat children in a logic battle, their simple minds are better at it. Go with what adults are good at: Tyrannical Authority." And finally: "Any child's meal—breakfast, lunch, or dinner—can be improved by the addition of a toaster waffle. Want to get your kids to eat vegetables? Accept that waffles are vegetables."

Though he loved being a father, having kids brought up some earlier angsts. While some folks would be afraid of flying for the rest of their lives after losing a father and two brothers to a plane crash, Colbert took a more pragmatic view.

"The way I've always looked at it is what are the odds of it ever happening again?" he asked rhetorically. "We've paid our dues in that direction, and flying does not scare me." Though there was a brief time when it made him just a little bit nervous. "It didn't scare me until I had my own kids, then I thought what could I do?"

September 11, 2001, was the twenty-seventh anniversary of the plane crash that killed his father and two brothers. Stephen's sister Lulu happened to be in downtown Manhattan.

"We heard a bang, and the building just shook," she said.

A few minutes later, she looked out the window to see people leaping from the World Trade Center to their deaths.

"It was one of those moments that are so surreal in your mind," she said.

After she made her way north through dusty streets where she didn't know whether she'd live or die, she made it to the Port Authority Bus Terminal and got on a bus heading south to Charleston, where, along with her brothers and sisters, she had to learn to live with the second September 11 tragedy of her life.

One day in the fall of 2003, when working on scripts for *The Daily Show*, the producers and writers discovered that one show was running a bit short.

Why not run a fake ad for a fake show starring a fake news correspondent?

They ran it by Colbert, and it sounded good to him. The writers came up with a promo for the imaginary *Colbert Report*, despite the fact that the show didn't exist.

"I tried to ape whoever was the loudest and rightest in prime-time cable news," he said. They did around four of these promos, which ran through 2003 and 2004, and thought nothing more of it.

CHAPTER 9

As *THE DAILY SHOW* began to head into its second full presidential campaign season, with the highlight being the 2004 Republican and Democratic National Conventions, the tide was turning. Politicians were starting to realize that making an appearance on *The Daily Show* was an effective and easy way to reach America's younger voters.

The trend harkened back to earlier presidential campaigns, most notably in 1992, when Governor Bill Clinton appeared on *The Arsenio Hall Show* to serenade viewers with his saxophone. But it dates back even further to 1968, when the candidate Richard M. Nixon appeared on *Rowan and Martin's Laugh-In* and told the audience to "sock it to me," the mantra of the show.

The Daily Show's travel budget was in somewhat better shape in 2004 than it had been during the last election cycle, when Colbert had to ask an online news reporter if he could tag along on the reporter's press pass. Though the green screens were still used more often than not, when Colbert and crew did travel, they shot as much footage as they could on location to provide them with weeks of footage and backdrops.

"We shoot video [backgrounds] of locations wherever we go in the United States and sometimes in Europe, and we just roll them behind the reporters later to create the illusion," said Colbert. "I don't know why every news program doesn't do it, because we fool people all the time."

Just before the Iowa caucus in 2004, the campaigns for Governor Howard Dean and Senator John Kerry called *The Daily Show* and said they wanted to be interviewed on the show; Dean was ahead of Kerry in the polls. Colbert loved the idea. "We'll do it like Paris Hilton and Nicole Richie on *The Simple Life*, two rich East Coast Ivy League men who try to slum on the farm to connect with the farmers," he said.

When Colbert and crew showed up for the shoot, both candidates were apparently missing in action. Kerry had suddenly shot ahead of Dean in the polls by eight points, and instead of traveling on the campaign bus crammed full of reporters, he started to travel by helicopter and forgot all about the interview, while the Dean staffers were in full panic mode and didn't want to talk to Colbert. Dean's campaign tried to make amends by promising to check if Dean would be available in a few days, but Colbert would have none of it.

"We reminded them that we're fake press and are only here for two days in order to create the illusion that we're going to be here for the entire campaign," he explained. "I said if they didn't give us an interview today, there's absolutely nothing for us to put on the air. We'll shoot lock-offs of locations and do it in front of a green screen, but no interview and we're leaving at 3:00. So, yes, we travel with the press, but only to the point where we can create the illusion that we're press. We never forget that we're not."

Once the conventions started, Colbert was absolutely in his element. He was particularly looking forward to the Republican National Convention in New York, which ran from August 30 through September 2. "Republicans are far more interesting because the president's going to be a little bit more on the defensive, which will lead to hopefully some interesting nights at the convention," he said. "And with all the protesters, it's going to be very interesting."

"The conventions are like industrial films," he continued. "They're sales rallies where politicians say things people have already heard to people who already believe them."

He also compared doing political interviews outside the *Daily Show* studio with his Second City days, when he could map out a particular story line up to a certain point, but never knew where he'd end up. "We don't really know what's going to happen until it does, and it's hard to say what's going to be interesting," he said. "The hypocrisy at both conventions is easy pickings."

But once he got to the convention, he found that the increased visibility and popularity of *The Daily Show* had endeared him to Democrats but had the opposite effect with the GOP. "I couldn't get people at the Republican National Convention to talk to me," he said. "It was like banging my head against a brick wall." But he didn't necessarily blame it on his image and reputation.

"Republicans tend to have huge contempt for reporters in general, whether they knew who I was or not," he said. "I had to compliment a woman on her blouse to get her to talk to me—and that woman turned out to be a sister of a friend of mine."

"Republicans tend to have huge contempt for reporters in general, whether they knew who I was or not."

Then again, after attending the Democratic convention in Boston in late July, there was nowhere to go but down; shooting the convention had been the highlight of his *Daily Show* career so far. On the last day of the convention, Colbert and the crew had been shooting all day and were just going to crash, but they had four passes for Kerry's acceptance speech that night, and Colbert rallied the troops, gathered together a camera crew, and headed over.

"At first, they wouldn't let us in because there were too many people in the hall," he said. "There were twenty thousand seats, but they gave out forty thousand tickets, and everyone came. We couldn't stand still at any point inside or the fire marshals would kick us out, so we literally had to keep moving. We shot for the next five hours, and it was the worst night of shooting we've ever done, and yet something came out of it because we turned it around in twenty-four hours, and it probably was the work I was most proud of up to that point." The resulting segment aired on August 3, 2004, and included homages to Willie Nelson and

Madeleine Albright. Colbert put his usual spin on things by describing Teresa Heinz: "That bitch is loaded."

Except for *one* thing. Since he and Stewart started working together on *The Daily Show*, one of his biggest and constant challenges was to say something that would make Stewart laugh on camera. "I knew the piece was good if he couldn't look at me when we were at the desk together," Colbert said.

He got yet another chance at the Democratic convention. Barack Obama was just starting to get noticed by the national media, and he'd given the keynote speech at the convention. Colbert reported a story on the fact that Obama was the son of a goat farmer, and after the story, when he and Stewart were giving its summary, Colbert said that he was the son of an Appalachian turd miner and the grandson of a goat-ball licker. "Jon couldn't look at me for the entire thing," said Colbert.

"I don't think you get any better than 'goat-ball licker,' not the joke, just not laughing [when delivering it]. We were shrieking, beating the desk during rehearsal. Jon said, 'You're kidding yourself that you're gonna be able to get through this.' I said, 'Jon, if you hold it together, I'll hold it together.' And then I knew halfway through, whatever dark thoughts about my childhood I had to summon up and later deal with, I wasn't gonna laugh."

In the wake of the conventions—indeed, even while they were still going on—*The Daily Show* got noticed in a big way. Perhaps the greatest irony was that Colbert's previous short-lived employer, *Good Morning America*, invited him to appear on the show to offer additional commentary during the conventions.

The buzz was getting louder: On September 19, 2004, right in the middle of the election coverage, *The Daily Show* won two Emmy Awards for Outstanding Writing for a Variety, Music, or Comedy Program as well as for Outstanding Variety, Music, or Comedy Series. Immediately afterward, a litany of political household names agreed to appear on the show, among them Pat Buchanan, John Edwards, President Clinton, and John McCain. And yes, Kerry finally went on the show.

Approximately 1.1 million people viewed each episode of *The Daily Show*, an increase of 20 percent for 2004 alone. But what was even more amazing was that the show achieved a 0.74 rating for the third quarter; *The O'Reilly Factor* was slightly ahead at 0.76.

Best of all, in the first nine months of 2004, Comedy Central added fifty new advertisers. "*The Daily Show* is a good piece of that," said Hank Close, Comedy Central's executive vice president of advertising sales. "It's a very, very strong driver of our revenue."

"It's in advertisers' sweet spot," said Brad Adgate, senior vice president of corporate research at Horizon Media. "Young people are the least likely to read a newspaper or watch TV news, and *The Daily Show* is one show that really has found a niche."

When some TV shows become successful, occasionally advertisers will request that the producers clamp down on including anything in the show that could be viewed as controversial or negative toward the product. While the former *Daily Show* correspondent Bob Wiltfong had seen that this was often the case in his days spent in traditional TV news, he said he never saw any signs of this happening at *The Daily Show*. "The show was so successful, they didn't dare touch it," he said. "As a former TV correspondent, I felt like there was less concern about what advertisers thought while we were in the editing room or writing, and there was never any talk of whether Comedy Central would lose advertising revenue if we made this joke. 'Do we need to take off the gloves with this guy but not with that guy because of his connections with Viacom?' No, that never happened, while when I was working on a real TV news show, it did occasionally come up: 'Run this, and we'll lose this advertiser.' But never at *The Daily Show*, and I was surprised. I thought, this is the way *real* journalism should be."

"This is the way *real* journalism should be."

However, perhaps the most surprising bit of information to come out of the studies is that though the show—and Comedy Central—was long known as an efficient way for advertisers to reach the 18–34 demographic, after the conventions ended and the election season heated up, the age of the average viewer actually began to *increase.* According to *Advertising Age*, the median age of the average *Daily Show* viewer for the third quarter of 2004 was 35.7; in comparison, the median age for news shows on the three major networks was a whopping sixty-plus. The age of the average *O'Reilly Factor* viewer was pegged at fifty-eight.

Election night 2004 arrived, and it was a real nail-biter, at least on the set of *The Daily Show.* The night echoed the drawn-out 2000 election, and Colbert put his usual spin on things, showing up wearing pajamas, announcing that he was in it for the long haul. "No predictions from me this time," he announced. "I'm waiting until every vote is counted, recounted, notarized, and then personally embossed. I've got some canned goods back here, a cot, and I am prepared to miss my children's developmental milestones."

What would life be like on a postelection *Daily Show*? "After this, nothing but Carmen Electra and Bigfoot jokes," said Colbert. "And I'm going to be cashing in on some of this new street cred of mine to get some of the ladies, if you know what I'm saying."

The Daily Show won a Peabody for its 2004 presidential campaign coverage, "Indecision 2004."

Colbert's increased visibility and the rise in ratings and popularity of *The Daily Show* meant that people took notice, and soon other shows and networks came calling, or at least sniffing around. Stewart's predecessor, Craig Kilborn, had left the *Late Late Show* in the summer of 2004, after almost five years, and CBS was trying out a few guest hosts—like Drew Carey—as they scouted around for a new permanent host. They wanted Colbert, but he turned them down.

He had something else in mind. And so did the powers-that-be at Comedy Central. Though *The Daily Show* was definitely a fun place to work, it was also known for making stars out of its correspondents. And after a certain amount of time, either the correspondent left or was just not asked back.

After the success of his costarring role as Evan Baxter in the 2003 Jim Carrey movie *Bruce Almighty*, Steve Carell was already getting more movie and TV offers from Hollywood. He left *The Daily Show* in the spring of 2004 to begin work on the American version of *The Office*, based on a popular BBC series, and *The 40-Year-Old Virgin*, a movie that would be released in 2005. After Carell's departure, Colbert became the next in line, but it was clear that Stewart wasn't going anywhere fast.

"At that time, Colbert was a total rock star among correspondents," said Bob Wiltfong. "When any of his stories ran, there was a huge reaction from the audience. The feeling among the rest of us was, Why is this guy still on the show?"

Besides, Colbert was getting restless. "I couldn't imagine how much longer I could do it," he said. "I still liked it, and I didn't want to *not* like it."

"If your name's not Jon Stewart, there's only so many places you can go on *The Daily Show*," said the executive producer, Ben Karlin. "Steve Carell and Steve Colbert were the first two we identified as giant talents with breakout potential, but we didn't have the mechanism in place when Steve Carell started getting offers, so he left. With Stephen, we didn't want to have him go off and become a huge star without working with him.

"He'd been there a long time," said Karlin. "He was never going to be the host—it was Jon's show. But we didn't want to lose him, so we tried to figure out what else could someone like Stephen do."

They soon came up with a solution, with a little help from one of Colbert's greatest inspirations.

In the fall of 2004, Andrea Mackris, a producer at *The O'Reilly Factor*, sued her boss, Bill O'Reilly, accusing him of sexual harassment. But hours before she filed suit, O'Reilly preemptively filed a lawsuit, which accused her of extortion. The countersuits played out in public—Mackris sought 60 million dollars in damages—for two weeks before she received an undisclosed settlement.

But for Colbert, Stewart, and Ben Karlin, the sex scandal opened up a whole new realm of possibilities for Colbert's character.

"Bill O'Reilly's purported sex scandal meant that there was more to be done with the character-driven news than had been done already," said Colbert. "It hinted at a personal life that you never got to hear about, that you never got to see. Besides, I don't know why someone hasn't copied *The Daily Show* yet. I, personally, was eager to rip us off."

"I don't know why someone hasn't copied *The Daily Show* yet. I, personally, was eager to rip us off."

They also looked back to those fake promos for the fake *Colbert Report* that had aired several times on *The Daily Show*.

The idea seemed ready-made.

Executives at Comedy Central were looking to extend *The Daily Show* franchise, as were Stewart and Karlin for their production company, Busboy Productions. Building a show around Colbert's character seemed doable.

The O'Reilly Factor with Stephen Colbert is how they pitched it.

Once they started to flesh out the show, Colbert said, "But I can't be an asshole."

"You're not an asshole," said Stewart. "You're an idiot. There's a difference."

Colbert agreed. "The audience wouldn't forgive Jon for saying things most comedians would want to say," he said. "But we can say almost anything, because it's coming out of the mouth of this character."

"The challenge of these things is how to evolve and keep it fresh and keep people from being bored with your voice," said Stewart. "We were lucky to have the guy as long as we had him. In fact, one year we kept him because we hid his keys."

The deal was made and announced in the spring of 2005: Stephen Colbert would host his own show starting in the fall.

"It's as if my character on *The Daily Show* got promoted," said Colbert. "I always wanted to do more with this character. At the same time, the character will not change. He's the exact same guy from *The Daily Show*, he's just been promoted into the host's chair."

Said Stewart: "Stephen has such encyclopedic knowledge and I figured using himself as the foundation of a character like that, there was no question he could do this every day. He was just ready. He wears that character so perfectly," he said. "Colbert is irreplaceable, but we'll be happy to save the money."

Just as Colbert made his announcement, Comedy Central received news of a big blow: the comedian Dave Chappelle—at the time Comedy Central's biggest star after Jon Stewart and *The Daily Show*—was AWOL.

Though the third season of *Chappelle's Show* was supposed to start on May 31, the show was postponed. Details were scarce. Rumor had it that Chappelle had admitted himself into a sanitarium in South Africa, but no one confirmed anything. Comedy Central supposedly had a 50 million–dollar deal with Chappelle for two seasons, because sales of his DVD were so stellar; season two alone moved 2.8 million copies, which at the time was the highest-selling DVD of a TV series. Plus, in 2005, *Chappelle's Show* ranked second behind *South Park* as Comedy Central's most watched show; *The Daily Show* placed at 5 in the ratings.

"It doesn't break them financially, but it's a big setback for them from a programming strategy standpoint because you build on your hits," said the cable television analyst Larry Gerbrandt. "Hits are so rare in this business."

Then the movie *Bewitched* came out in June 2005, a twist on the 1960s sitcom featuring a fetching suburban housewife—who just happened to be a witch—and her bumbling ad-executive husband. Colbert played Stu Robison, a Hollywood writer, while his old buddy Steve Carell played Uncle Arthur, the part that Paul Lynde made famous in the original sitcom.

The reviewers were not kind. "Nora Ephron's attempt to reconceive the standard TV-to-bigscreen adaptation goes bizarrely haywire here, spinning out of control like a runaway broomstick," said one, while another was masterfully brutal: "Oh, let's just cut to the chase here: What the hell is Will Ferrell doing to his career? *Bewitched* is *Being John Malkovich for Morons*. And Stephen Colbert appears in a small role that wastes his time."

Colbert ignored the poor reviews and forged ahead. The first thing he and Stewart decided to do was to move *The Daily Show* to 733 11th Avenue. Colbert and *The Colbert Report* staffers would take over the offices and studio at 513 West 54th Street.

Already, interest in Colbert's new show was keen. *The Colbert Report* was given the 11:30 P.M. slot, right after *The Daily Show*. The producers decided that one way to play off of each comic's strengths and to keep viewers watching would be a nightly "toss," where Jon checks in with Colbert at the end of *The Daily Show* to get coming attractions for *The Colbert Report* and, it was hoped, keep viewers watching.

"It'll be like O'Reilly segueing into Hannity, Hannity into Greta, Larry King into Aaron Brown, but the focus will be me, lots of me," Colbert said. "Occasionally, we'll turn the camera elsewhere, but only for pacing."

He also viewed his own show as a way to further refine his character. "I loved [the CNN reporter] Aaron Brown when he was on the air because he had a folksy love of language where he would ruminate the news at you, which I miss. And Anderson Cooper, too, because he's so sexy, he's so crisp," he said. "Plus, the correspondent that I play now is very self-inflated, and he's the story as much as his story is. The fact that he cares about something is what makes it worth being on the air, not that it's necessarily news. It's about the person himself."

As well as that person's warped worldview. To develop segments for the new show, Colbert drew on his high school debate experience by declaring that he planned to explore themes in the form of debate topics. For instance: "Seat belts: Are they worth the loss of liberty of the upper torso?" he pondered. By introducing a regular segment called "Formidable Opponent," Colbert could up the ante on the narcissism of his character by having him debate himself.

He planned to fill each show with his own analysis, which, by his take, wasn't that different from what news programs were doing already. "News analysis used to be one sentence at the end of the story. Now analysis can go on forever. You don't need new news to have new analysis. The needs of the news business have turned it into a word factory," he said. "With the twenty-four-hour news cycle, there's not any more news now than there was in my childhood. The cycle requires to be filled; you tell the story, a little sliver at the top of the hour. Then you have someone talk about that little bit of news, and that analysis can be spun out endlessly because it could be true, it could be bullshit, you could have passionate dramatic opinions on both sides and build a narrative structure, all for a story that doesn't have one. News thrives on this; it mistakes opinion for news, and opinion ends up being argument, and shouting doesn't make it any clearer.

"I could just take their transcripts and read it with a different inflection, and I think that would be fine. This show literally does write itself because someone else has written it for me," he added.

"This show literally does write itself because someone else has written it for me."

Most unusual, Comedy Central decided that, unlike other new shows under consideration, they didn't need to see a pilot episode in order to green-light the show; the entire premise was based on Colbert's character. "We wanted *The Colbert Report* to look at everything through the eyes of this character, which was the inverse of *The Daily Show*," said Karlin. "What does this person believe in? What is the consistency, and is there some joy to be found in the inconsistency? And how are we going to squeeze more funny out of the news in a way that doesn't seem redundant?"

"I see *The Daily Show* as a 30-minute preamble to *The Colbert Report*," Colbert added. "It's like an appetizer before you get to the main course.

We just feel like there are games to be played there that we don't play on *The Daily Show*, and we think we can turn that into a half-hour."

After Comedy Central announced that it would launch *The Colbert Report* in the fall, Stephen took off with his family for Charleston. While Evie and the kids spent time with his family and friends during the extended summer holiday, Stephen signed on to crew with his friends on one of twenty-one boats for the annual Charleston-to-Bermuda sailboat race, across one thousand miles of open ocean and straight through the Bermuda Triangle.

He agreed to the trip despite the fact that he doesn't consider himself to be a sailor.

"My friends got me a slot on one of the ships, and they said, 'You get the right safety gear and we'll get you there and make sure you don't drown,'" he said. The trip took a week, and he joked that he was amazed that Evie said he could go. "My rule is, your wife says you can go away for a week, you go, even if it's life-threatening."

He joined Team Tao. Each member was responsible for a specific task on the forty-five-foot boat; Colbert was named cook, chaplain, and chief morale officer. Seasickness wasn't an issue, according to him. "We found the rum pretty early," he said. "It was supposed to be a dry cruise, but everybody thought of their locker as the exception."

He didn't have much downtime, however. "We lost our power and our communication," he said. "We lost our toilets on the second day. We lost our sails at one point. And it was a wonderful experience."

This despite the fact that Team Tao came in dead last. The trip took seven days; it was only supposed to take four days.

"I think we reached the limit of just how close we could get," he said. "You lose your toilets on day two and you've got five more days together. That's crusty seamanship. One more day and I think we would've gone cannibal."

When Colbert returned home, he immediately started work on his new show and began to divvy up responsibilities. *The Colbert Report* would air four nights a week, and the first one would go on the air in October. Some of his *Daily Show* co-workers would do double duty: as executive producer, Ben Karlin would help run *The Colbert Report* in addition to *The Daily Show*, and he and Colbert hired the former *Daily Show* and *Late Night with Conan O'Brien* writer Allison Silverman as well as the former *Onion* editor Richard Dahm as head writers.

In a way, Allison Silverman is the female version of Stephen Colbert, with a couple of variations on the theme. For one, she cut her comedic teeth tracing the path that Colbert had already taken. After graduating from Yale University, she headed for Second City and ImprovOlympic, where she spent several years training and learning about comedy writing. Unlike Colbert, however, she discovered she liked writing comedy more than performing and took a few jobs—including writing for *Who Wants to Be a Millionaire*—before she signed on for a couple of years with *The Daily Show* in 2000. She worked for *Late Night with Conan O'Brien* before leaving to join Colbert.

And just as Stephen had been teased by his elementary school classmates for being Catholic, Silverman was teased because she was Jewish and grew up in Gainesville, Florida, which is more Bible Belt than Miami. "I remember being told I would eventually be going to hell because I was a Jew," she said.

However, some doubted the premise of the show. Even Doug Herzog, the president of Comedy Central, who had granted the show an initial eight-week commitment of thirty-two episodes, worried if Colbert's character was enough to carry a half-hour show four nights a week.

But Silverman had no such reservations. "I very much trusted Stephen's abilities, because I felt that even if it was a failure, it would have been a smart failure," she said. "I left a secure job, a job I enjoyed on *Late Night with Conan O'Brien* to do *The Colbert Report*. Even if it was only thirty-two episodes, I knew I had to do it. I felt wherever Colbert was leading it, it would be something good."

Even Colbert had his doubts. "I was hesitant to do *The Colbert Report* because Jon's a great guy to work for, and we had so much fun," he said. "I was worried that I'd be tossing away everything I'd worked for all those years, that I was a fraud, and it was only the context of *The Daily Show* that made me funny. I was terrified."

The first episode of *The Colbert Report* went on the air on October 17, 2005.

"[We viewed] that first show as our thesis statement: What you wish to be true is all that matters, regardless of the facts," said Karlin. "Of course, at the time, we thought we were being farcical."

Perhaps no one segment on the debut helped set the tone of the show more than "The Word," which Colbert viewed as a spoof on "Talking Points Memo" on *The O'Reilly Factor.* Though it now seems like a touch of brilliance, the truth is that Colbert and writers and producers were still tinkering with scripts and scenes up until taping.

They had the segment ready, but Colbert didn't feel it was quite there yet. As they did a final run-through before taping, he hit the brakes.

"["The Word"] isn't stupid enough," he said. "We're not talking about truth, we're talking about something that *seems* like truth. The truth we want to exist."

And that's when it hit him. "Truthiness." *That* was "The Word." It was perfect, because it concisely summed up the gist of Colbert's character: If you believe it enough, despite evidence to the contrary, then it's true.

"They don't need to back up anything they say," he said. "Bill O'Reilly has this quote, 'How come you don't believe it when I just said it?' And that's the way it is, once he says it, it's gospel. It's admirable. I watch him with my mouth open. How does he do it? I wish I could completely take the filter off my mouth like that," he said.

The set of *The Colbert Report* was specifically designed to tie in with the narcissistic personality of Colbert's character. Known as "the eagle's nest," the centerpiece of the stage is his massive desk, shaped like a C for Colbert. He explained that everything on the set is a direct reference to *The Last Supper* by Leonardo da Vinci. "All the architecture of that room points at Jesus' head," he said. "The entire room is a halo. On the set, I wanted all the lines on the set to converge on my head. And so if you look at the design, it all does, it all points at my head. There's a sort of sun-god burst quality about the set around me."

A massive portrait of Colbert hangs on the wall above a fireplace, and "The Colbert Report" appears in a number of places around the set, including on the desk and walls.

"There are no televisions behind me, like Brian Williams has, or even Jon Stewart," he continued. "At certain angles, there are monitors behind Jon that have the world going on, which implies that that's where the news is, and that's where the information is, and the person in front of it is the conduit through which this information is given to you. But on my set, I told them I didn't want anything behind me, because it all comes from me. I'm not channeling anything. I *am* the source."

There's a separate alcove off to the side where Colbert interviews guests, and in keeping with his character's personality, whenever a guest is introduced to the audience, the camera stays on Colbert while he runs around his own desk before he heads over to sit down with the guest. Silverman came up with the concept. "For me, it felt like a strong statement of ego, that Stephen would be jealous of even that tiniest moment when his guests would be in the spotlight," she said. "So he diverts all of the attention to himself."

Unlike other talk and comedy shows, which can take awhile to find their legs, *The Colbert Report* seemed to have been shot out of a cannon from the very first show, despite taking some big risks from the beginning. For instance, on the first show, Stephen cracked a joke about James Brady, the gun-control proponent, who at the time was protesting a bill pending in Florida that would allow citizens to use a gun in self-defense. Colbert didn't understand why Brady wouldn't support the bill wholeheartedly, given that if he had had a gun during the assassination attempt on the life of the then-president Ronald Reagan in 1981, he could have shot back. Colbert named him as the top threat to America in the "ThreatDown" segment. He then invited Brady to appear on the show. Brady sent a fax, though he never appeared on the show.

Though there was outrage in some circles, the reaction to the show from critics and the audience was generally enthusiastic.

Said one reviewer: "*The Colbert Report* has gotten off to an impressive start with a topnotch premiere followed by a respectable second outing that underscores just how challenging it will be to sustain this half-hour high-wire act four nights a week."

The Colbert Report debuted with a 1 household rating, which represented 1.13 million viewers.

"It became so clear so quickly that it was going to work that it was kind of astounding," said the Comedy Central president Doug Herzog. "When the show debuted, I remember thinking that it had been birthed fully baked. That's so rare. I don't know if I've ever seen it before. The whole thing fits him like a glove. It's really a virtuoso performance."

"*The Colbert Report* depends on Stephen's ability to process information as this other person," said Stewart. "I've seen talk-show hosts who can't do that for real, and then you watch Colbert and it's like the first time you use broadband: 'How the fuck did that happen?' He's rendering in real time. He's basically doing his show in a second language."

After only eight shows, Comedy Central renewed *The Colbert Report* for an entire year.

However, there was one casualty from Colbert's new show. Shortly after the debut of *The Colbert Report*, General Motors announced that it was dumping Colbert from their Mr. Goodwrench ads.

To explain the switch, GM said it wanted to rely less on a comedic message and to instead focus on promoting regular vehicle maintenance. "Maintaining your vehicle is a serious thing, and we thought a more serious message would bring that across," said Michelle Ostrowski, a GM manager.

Though Colbert was disappointed, with the success of *The Colbert Report*, he obviously didn't need the money.

It didn't take long before *The Colbert Report* and *The Daily Show* started to siphon viewers away from the old stalwarts of late night: Letterman and Leno.

"Dave is definitely not the essential viewing that he was even two, three years ago," said Aaron Barnhart, critic for the *Kansas City Star*. "Letterman is now a traditional, old-school television choice. I don't feel a sense of urgency around the show; that has shifted now to Jon Stewart's show [and Comedy Central]. Whether that's fair or not, the fact is that it's happened."

In response, Leno tried to update *The Tonight Show* toward a younger audience by featuring regular appearances from Howie Mandel and Fred Willard, as well as allowing the then-cutting-edge Internet cartoon company JibJab to unveil new cartoons on the show.

First with *The Daily Show*, and then *The Colbert Report*, it was clear the old school was in trouble.

CHAPTER 10

TEN WEEKS AFTER THE debut of *The Colbert Report*, it was evident that the show had made an impact when the American Dialect Society announced that they selected "Truthiness" to be their word of the year.

With the success of the show, the world came calling.

"People are constantly asking me, 'How does it feel to have such an impact?' I just want to be funny," said Colbert. "I'm a comedian, not a political thinker. We're changing the world one factual error at a time. Besides, I'm not playing it nearly as hard as someone like O'Reilly or Hannity does."

His approach to comedy and commentary found favor with a surprising person. "I feel it's a compliment," said Bill O'Reilly. "He does it without being mean-spirited, which is a refreshing change. Ninety percent of them are just vicious and they use their platform to injure people, but it doesn't seem that Colbert does that. The formula of his program is that the [writers and producers] watch the *Factor* and seize upon certain themes that work for him. He ought to be sending me a check every week, because we're basically the research for his writers."

Papa Bear hit on an important point: "People can see under the character," said Silverman. "There's a tension Stephen brings to this that makes him a really great performer. People can see that he's a really decent guy under this thing that he's wearing."

Indeed, when *Late Night with Conan O'Brien* invited him to appear shortly after the debut, Colbert agreed, with one caveat: he'd do it as long as he could still make it to his son's swim practice.

"I think it ultimately boils down to Stephen having that rare star quality of playing a character who is somewhat unlikable in a very likable way," Karlin says.

"He's able to create a universe where something surreal happens that seems ordinary, and all of a sudden the absurd appears not mundane but expected, organic," said Stewart. "He can have a conversation with Richard Holbrooke and Willie Nelson and it all makes perfect sense, and yet it couldn't appear anywhere else without appearing burlesque. Somehow he has managed to create a fake world that has impacted and found standing in the real world."

In fact, from the first show, they started tinkering with the concept and the presentation. The philosophical questions and twists that arose as a result of the show were fascinating.

For instance, when asked if he was caught off guard—even disturbed—by the fact that so many viewers believed outright everything that came out of Colbert the character's mouth, he dismissed the concern. "It does not scare me at all because I don't take myself seriously," he said. "My character wants to do these things. We're making jokes." He also noted that "so many real people declare fictional news and the press agrees."

However, he did worry that he was occasionally going overboard. Though the "Formidable Opponent" segment fits that category, for example, its seeds were planted back in Chicago in the *yes-and* routines that were an integral part of Second City. "We've got a lot of people on our staff with a background in improv, and with Formidable Opponent, you agree to something that's been initiated and you take the next step," said Silverman.

"You don't want to sound like a madman, but ["Formidable Opponent"] always starts out reasonable but escalates into madness," said Colbert. "Stephen is basically split in two people. There's a logical but ineffectual one, and an illogical, completely aggressive one, like Good Kirk and Bad Kirk from *Star Trek.* Stephen 2, as we call the Stephen who's always invited in, is far more aggressive. But with neither one would you watch their show."

While he didn't find it difficult to switch the character on and off—after all, he'd gotten a lot of practice on *The Daily Show*, albeit only for two minutes at a time—he began to employ different levels of the personality. "It's a sliding scale, depending on the situation and who I'm talking to," he said. "Sometimes I'll have someone on talking about genetics, and I'll dial the character down.

"I'm a satirist, so I've got boxing gloves on if the person is worthy of satire, but I'm not an assassin," he added. "When that happens, it's because something happened during the interview that got me going, and I have to immediately encapsulate how I feel as the character or else I'll reveal myself." But during those times when he's gone too far, he's inclined to let it go. Only once did he feel he went too far and wanted to make amends by apologizing. "There's only one person I've ever really wanted to apologize to, and you'd never guess who it was. I will someday. I just have to find the right time to do it. But the character has to do it on the show, not me."

While some comedians allow that mask to fall, Colbert readily admits that he never takes it off. "I try to wear his mask lightly, but never really take it off fully, because it allows me to say things that you would not forgive me for saying," he said. "That's how the character helps me. I can get away with shit. *Most* of the time."

He slipped into his character effortlessly. "At Second City, the old rule is wear your character as lightly as a cap, you can take it on and off as needed, and I do that on the show," he said. "I like jumping over the line between who I am and who the character is, to confuse the audience."

"Probably about 80 percent of the time, Stephen Colbert the character's view is different than the view of Stephen Colbert the person," said Allison Silverman.

"There are times that I agree with my character," he said. "It doesn't matter to me if you know when that is. I'm not here to affect you politically or socially. I'm here to make you laugh. I just use the news as the palette for my jokes."

The longer he spent doing fake news, the more his disdain for real news grew. "The media is a lamprey that latches onto a subject and just sucks and sucks and sucks until your brain and your soul is as dry as a crouton," he said. But perhaps there was another reason. As Amy Sedaris put it, it may just be easier for Colbert to be funny when he's speaking through the character's voice. "I am always surprised that he can get up in such a good mood because he's had so much sadness in his life," she said.

Whatever level he was operating at, his fans loved it, especially since he was actively inviting viewers to be in on the joke, often by taking part in it. The dynamic soon took on a life of its own. "A lot of times, Stephen is asking the audience to play with him," said Silverman. "And it's very fun to play with Stephen Colbert."

The Colbert Nation began as a joke, but when he first addressed viewers directly as his "nation," something clicked.

"They wanted in on the fun," said Colbert. "Our actions plant seeds, and then we'll go, 'Oh look, someone responded to that in a way we hadn't intended.' That was something we didn't expect: we joked about the Colbert Nation and then we said, 'Oh shit, it's real.' That's another aspect of improvisation, that discovery is better than invention. [The viewers] self-organized it. I love that, and you can't force that. But you do have to acknowledge it."

For instance, in the summer of 2006, Colbert heard about an online contest run by the Hungarian government to name a newly constructed bridge spanning the Danube River. Along with some long-dead Hungarian war heroes and kings, the actor Chuck Norris was also in the running with 11 percent of the vote . . . that is, until Colbert got involved.

On the August 9, 2006, episode of *The Colbert Report*, he gave his nation the Web site address and told them to write in his name. A week later, he gave an update on the show and announced there were only 1,774 votes. He provided very specific instructions to viewers about the Web address and what to click on. A day later, almost 440,000 votes were counted. But that wasn't enough. It wasn't until the show set up a special voting link at the official Web site colbertnation.com that the voting went through the roof: in fewer than twenty-four hours, Colbert received almost seventeen million votes.

In response, the Hungarian government changed the rules midstream by unearthing an obscure law specifying that the bridge could only be named after someone who's dead and who was also fluent in Hungarian while he or she was alive. But in an attempt to rectify the situation, the Hungarian ambassador to the United States then appeared on *The Colbert Report* to make amends.

"What makes the show entertaining is that Stephen has essentially made it interactive, where it's not just us sitting and watching the show," said DB Ferguson, who runs NoFactZone.net, a fan site. "You don't hear about *Daily Show* fans going off and naming things after Jon Stewart," he said. "Stephen will say, 'I want this named after me—go, Nation!' And inevitably, the fans will pick that up."

The Colbert Nation was made up of fans, but as Colbert recalled from the *Wigfield* signings he did with Sedaris and Dinello, fans came in a variety of flavors. Most were okay; a few were scary.

"He's new to being the Man," Karlin said a year after the debut of *The Colbert Report*. "He's in that first blush of fame that's thrilling. Jon is over it."

For Colbert, it wasn't a total surprise. "The funny thing is, I knew when we were developing this show that we were doing a show that parodies the cult of personality," he said. "And yet, if the show was successful, it would generate a cult of personality. It had to. That means it's working."

"The funny thing is, I knew when we were developing this show that we were doing a show that parodies the cult of personality. And yet, if the show was successful, it would generate a cult of personality. It had to. That means it's working."

Though he'd always been somewhat known by a small contingent of rabid fans since his *Daily Show* days, being the star of his own show brought a whole new kind of attention his way. "The letters that say 'I'm getting the messages you're sending me through the television screen' are not great," he said, adding that this kind of correspondence takes up a small percentage of the pack.

"People see us having a good time on the show, but they don't expect me to be like the character out in the world," he said. "I think they say 'hi' to me as a person and they'd like me to say 'hi' as that guy, so they understand it's a different person. Or they'll come up and try to scare me as a bear, or something like that."

One thing that surprised him was how many people send him art they've made to honor his character. From paintings to puzzles and masks, fans send him almost everything. The most unusual piece he's received is a full set of armor made from leather that's not only his exact size but also has his family crest on the front in bronze. Though he tries to send thank-you notes and responses, from very early on the volume was just overwhelming, so he's had to take an unorthodox approach to acknowledge his fans. "I don't really know how to return [the gratitude] other than to try to do a good show that night," he said. "We've thrown stuff into the show and we've put it on a bookshelf, and on some of the blogs fans have said they've noticed."

When he's out walking around, whether by himself or with his family, fans often don't notice him. In his hometown of Charleston, he's sat at a table by himself in the bar of the Charleston Place Hotel, and in the dark of the room he looked like just any other businessman. But when people do recognize him, his wife Evie is amused by the attention. "It's not so much that it's invasive," she said. In fact, she will often walk a few steps behind him so she can see how people react and watch people's faces when it hits them, if indeed it does. "I like to see the reactions," she said. "With the college-age boys, sometimes you think they're going to fall over."

"I'll be stopped by people my mother's age, who is in her eighties, and I'll be stopped by people my niece's age, or twelve, my daughter's age," he said. "I love being able to go all over the map."

. . .

Before every episode, the audience is prepped first with a warm-up routine by the comedian Pete Dominick to get them in the mood, and then Colbert goes onstage to say a few words. Regardless of the topic of the show or the guest lineup, he always inquires if anyone in the audience wants to ask him a couple of questions "to humanize me before I say horrible things." He does the same thing before every guest interview, whether on the set or taped, by saying that his character is "an idiot" and to "disabuse me of my ignorance."

Despite his growing fame from *The Daily Show* as well as front-page headlines about his new show, some guests still didn't realize what they were getting themselves into when they agreed to let Colbert interview them.

"My character calls anyone who's been on the show a 'friend of the show,' but on a certain level, we're grateful to anyone who plays along with this, because a lot of people won't," he said. "They don't know what to make of the character. Some people want to be faithful and making fun, and sometimes it works, sometimes it doesn't. I think it makes guests more nervous than they would be on another show. They don't know whether there's gonna be a moment of attack journalism. But I try not to make it that way, I try to make it as comfortable as possible."

Barney Frank, the nation's first openly gay congressman, appeared on one of the first shows in October 27, 2005, in the series called "Better Know a District," where Colbert set out to profile all 435 districts of the United States House of Representatives by interviewing a congressmen from each, one at a time.

It didn't go well. "You're left-handed and you're Jewish," Colbert told Frank at one point in the interview. "But there's something else about you, and this is the elephant in the room that I'm not naming, but as a journalist I feel like I have to." He then paused, and said, "Uh, you're a little overweight," before quickly asking what Frank's wife thought about it.

Despite the fact that Colbert had given his usual spiel about the fact that he was going to interview Frank by a character who was an idiot, the congressman was so taken aback by the unusual line of questioning that he was stodgy and unanimated throughout the interview and didn't smile once.

Frank later referred to the show as sub–Three Stooges. "I like political humor, but I found this really strange," he said. "His basic interview technique was to pretend he didn't know things. That wouldn't be funny in junior high school."

"Barney Frank was the toughest interview because I thought he was enjoying himself," said Colbert. "I was wrong."

"Barney Frank was the toughest interview because I thought he was enjoying himself. I was wrong."

Mark Udall, a Democrat from Colorado's Second District, went on the show a few weeks later, and his experience didn't fare any better. "I've climbed Mount Everest, trekked across Utah's desert lands, and even suffered through amoebic dysentery," Udall said. "I can say unequivocally that interviewing with Stephen Colbert was the worst experience of my life. Now, having said that, I wouldn't necessarily say he is Mount Everest. He's more like Mount St. Helens: lots of hot air, noise, and drama, but hopefully no real threat."

But Linda Sánchez, a Democrat from California's Thirty-ninth District, loved her experience. "Oh my God, it was hysterical," she said. "You have to know it's comedy, and that they're going to edit you so you look foolish," she said.

Although it was left on the cutting-room floor, Sánchez said that Colbert got in a few jokes about her sister Loretta—a congresswoman in California's Forty-seventh district—comparing them to the tennis-playing sisters Venus and Serena Williams. At the end of the interview, Linda Sánchez said that Colbert said, "Thank you, Loretta."

"Thank you, Mr. Stewart," was her retort.

Richard Holbrooke, former U.S. Ambassador to the United Nations, had a blast. "That was the most fun I've ever had on television," he said. "There's this great sense of groundbreaking adventure, this feeling that it's on the cutting edge, that it's the hottest thing in America. And at the center of it all is Colbert himself. I have never seen a television performer about to go on live television who's enjoying himself so much."

And Representative Jim Moran, a Democrat from Virginia's Eighth District, was surprised by the response. "I'm just stunned by the number of my constituents who watch it," he said. "Colbert reached more of a demographic that's difficult to reach, and in a more positive way, than anything I can think of." At the same time, while he thought that Colbert was easier on him than on some other representatives, Moran called his profile generally positive, though he did also refer to it as "consensual rape."

Colbert was surprised that he enjoyed doing the interviews, because he thought it would be his least favorite part of the show. "It was the biggest question mark for me because when I'm interviewing someone in character I'm not an assassin, and I don't want them to feel unwelcome," he said. The challenge was how to adjust the character with a variety of personalities. "With someone like Bill Kristol who is defending himself, I have to dial it all the way up, but with someone from the Human Genome Project I dial it down because he's not a punching bag. But now, it's my favorite part of the show because I'm improvising. I don't know what's going to happen in the interview."

That said, he does do a little bit of preparation for the interviews. "The writers have put more thought into it than I have, so we sit down and talk about my character's viewpoint of the person, and spend fifteen minutes talking about it," he said. Then once the interview*ee* arrives, Colbert is often frustrated by the constraints of the format. "Sometimes I really want my natural curiosity to run wild with the guest, and it kills me that I can't know more about what they're talking about because I'm there to be funny. Sometimes I just want to talk."

For "Better Know a District," Colbert usually shoots interviews back-to-back, traveling to Washington for the day so he can knock out several in a row. "Boy, you have never needed a cup of black coffee more than when you're between congressmen three and four," Colbert said. "They're a ball of fire."

He did have a wish list of districts and congressmen he wanted to feature on the segment, but his holy grail was Nancy Pelosi. Unfortunately, she had other ideas. "She once said that she wouldn't recommend anyone going on the show and my character was really upset," he said. "I've been thinking of having Philip Seymour Hoffman on, he could play her, he's a good enough actor."

"We want people to be in pain and confused. I make up facts left and right."

Though Colbert was, essentially, playing an ultraconservative character who he was spoofing so liberals could laugh, no one group was immune from being his target or from being confused as to whether he was telling the truth or not. "We want people to be in pain and confused," he said. "I make up facts left and right. Liberals will come on the show and say, 'Well, conservatives want this to be a theocracy.' And I'll say, 'Well, why not, the Founding Fathers were all fundamentalist Christians.' And they'll say, 'No, they weren't.' I say, 'Yes, they were, and if I'm wrong, I will *eat* your encyclopedias.' Most people give in at that point. The person folds, because they don't realize I have no problem making things up, because I have no credibility to lose.

"One of the things I love about my character is I can make vast declarations and it doesn't matter if I'm wrong," he said. "I *love* being wrong. So my character can tell you exactly what's going to happen: The Democrats are going to change everything. We're going to have gay parents marrying their own gay babies. Obama's gonna be sworn in on a gay baby. The oath is gonna end, So help me, gay baby."

Whenever someone has called foul, Colbert has pointed to O'Reilly as inspiring him in the realm of fake news, and he has also said that President George W. Bush did exactly the same thing. "Facts matter not at all. Perception is everything, it's certainty. People love the president because he's certain of his choices as a leader, even if the facts that back him up don't seem to exist. It's the fact that he's certain that is very appealing to a certain section of the country," he said. "Some people look for someone to say, 'Listen to me, don't question, and do what I say, and everything will be fine.' "

Colbert tempered his words by saying that there is sometimes a time and place for this, like just after September 11, 2001. "We wanted someone to be daddy, to take decisions away from us," he said. "I had a sense of [America's current leaders] doing bad things in our name to protect us, and that was okay. We weren't thrilled with Bush because we thought he was a good guy at that point; we were thrilled with him because we thought that he probably had hired people who would fuck up our enemies, regardless of how they had to do it. That was for us a very good thing, and I can't argue with the validity of that feeling."

April 2006 was turning out to be a watershed month for Colbert. Just six months after the debut of *The Colbert Report*, the awards and requests for his appearances, plus a few surprises, came pouring in.

In addition to recognizing the word *truthiness* early on, *Time* magazine added him to their annual list of the hundred most influential people in the world. While Colbert joked that "my character is absolutely telling more people," he felt uncomfortable by the honor. "I'm slightly embarrassed by the idea they would put me on the list," he admitted. "I actually tell people I was named one of the 100 people who might be able to sell a magazine."

At the dinner held to honor the hundred on the list, he finally ran into Papa Bear.

"Oh, it had to happen sometime," said O'Reilly.

Colbert said they chatted and that O'Reilly was generally pleasant and actually gave him a few words of advice. "He said, 'Watch your guests.

You have an Olbermann on, you have a Franken on, that's a pattern. Your audience may not think about it, but they have a sense of it.' "

Colbert said, "But you saw how I played with Olbermann, I didn't take him seriously."

"Not everybody watches your show as closely as I do," O'Reilly responded.

"I thought, 'Take me now, Jesus,' " said Colbert. "I was so thrilled."

Next up: a book deal. Colbert signed a deal with Warner Books, the same publisher that produced Jon Stewart's bestselling *America (The Book),* which has sold more than a million hardcover copies since its September 2004 publication. Colbert's literary agent, Dan Strone of Trident Media Group—who not coincidentally was also Stewart's agent—sold the untitled book for an advance of reportedly close to 3 million dollars; the scheduled publication date was fall 2007. "This book will have the same noble goal as my television show: to change the world one factual error at a time," said Colbert.

Then, on April 29, 2006, he appeared as the featured entertainer at the White House Correspondents' Dinner, an annual event that's an institution in Washington, where almost three thousand guests—both politicians and media—eagerly await the announcement of the keynote speaker and host, usually a currently hot entertainer.

When he received the invitation, Colbert was thrilled. "I'm so excited, I'm going to levitate," he said.

He asked several writers from *The Colbert Report* to help him write his speech.

"A group of writers worked on that speech together," said Silverman. "This is the type of material we write every night. It never occurred to me that it would affect the audience so intensely. But what we didn't take into consideration was who the audience was going to be: politicians and press people. When we had rehearsed that speech a few hours before, in front of hotel staff, we never had any sense that there might be a problem."

"The only time I thought we were going a little bit too far came when we were riding the train from New York to Washington," said Colbert.

Colbert and his wife, Evelyn, at the White House Correspondents Dinner on April 29, 2006; Stephen was the keynote speaker. *(Courtesy Reuters/Corbis)*

"My wife was sitting in front of me reading a draft of the script. About every thirty seconds she'd turn around and say, 'Oh, no!' But we knew we had a rare opportunity, and we didn't want to blow it. Whether or not [President Bush] enjoyed it, I got to perform for the president. And I stayed up the whole night before rehearsing the jokes."

In fact, Colbert and the president even chatted for a bit before the speech. "We actually had a very nice conversation beforehand about the subject of irony," he said. "I told him how nice it was that I, who am satirical and whose comedy can be critical of the administration, get to do this."

During the speech, Colbert wasn't aware that anyone was offended. "It's hard to tell what's going on in that room," he said. "When a joke hit, it was a real high to hear those people laugh. When it didn't, about a thousand people laughed, which is still pretty good. I never had any sense that I was upsetting anyone."

"The speech definitely wasn't getting a great response," said Silverman. "But Stephen is a fearless performer and he just kept committing to it and plowing forward. Having once performed myself, I know how difficult an accomplishment that is. It was inspiring."

The speech started off calmly enough, but the political hot-button zingers were mixed in with neutral statements, which made for an odd back-and-forth between insults and banalities. One wonders if the purpose was to defuse the barbs. He almost sounded like a stand-up comic, like Jackie Mason or another insult comic, bringing one pun after another. Then again, he and his writers weren't accustomed to writing a monologue to run sixteen minutes followed by a seven-minute video, which he billed as an audition tape for White House press secretary. It was a lot even for a crew of writers accustomed to cranking out a half-hour show four nights a week.

He began with this: "I believe the government that governs best is the government that governs least. And by these standards, we have set up a fabulous government in Iraq." He followed with this: "I believe in pulling yourself up by your own bootstraps. I believe it is possible. I saw this guy do it once in Cirque du Soleil. It was magical!"

Then he went after the press: "So the White House has personnel changes. And then you write, 'Oh, they're just rearranging the deck chairs on the Titanic.' First of all, that is a terrible metaphor. This administration is not sinking. This administration is soaring! If anything, they are rearranging the deck chairs on the Hindenburg!"

Then he put the Reverend Jesse Jackson in his crosshairs: "Jesse Jackson is here. Haven't heard from the reverend in a little while. I had him on the show. It was a very interesting interview, very challenging interview. You can ask him anything, but he's going to say what he wants at the pace that he wants. It's like boxing a glacier. Enjoy that metaphor, by the way, because your grandchildren will have no idea what a glacier is."

Most infamously, perhaps, was this passage directed at Bush: "I stand by this man. I stand by this man, because he stands for things. Not only for things, he stands on things, things like aircraft carriers and rubble and recently flooded city squares. And that sends a strong message, that no matter what happens to America, she will always rebound with the most powerfully staged photo-ops in the world."

Afterward, Bush told him, "Well done."

"Then he gave me a little Texas wink and a chill went down my spine," said Colbert.

As he made his way back to his seat after the speech, he sensed something wasn't quite right. "I saw that people weren't making eye contact with me, and they were looking away."

"Colbert crossed the line," said an aide to Bush, and another concurred. "Bush has got that look like he's ready to blow. I've been there before," he said.

Within a few weeks, the audio version of Colbert's roast of President Bush had hit number one on iTunes.

"We were surprised at the strength of the response," said Silverman. "The reaction to that speech was a lesson on how many people wanted a voice of criticism at that moment in time."

More like how many didn't. The backlash was swift from some surprising corners, because Colbert didn't just roast the president but included the media in his critique as well, insinuating that they had gotten too cozy with the White House administration during a time when they should be turning over every stone. Here's more:

"And as excited as I am to be here with the president," he said, "I am appalled to be surrounded by the liberal media that is destroying America, with the exception of FOX News. FOX News gives you both sides of every story: the president's side, and the vice president's side." He continued: "But the rest of you, what are you thinking? Reporting on NSA wiretapping or secret prisons in Eastern Europe? Those things are secret for a very important reason: they're super-depressing. And if that's your goal, well, misery accomplished. Over the last five years you people were so good, over tax cuts, WMD intelligence, the effect of global warming. We Americans didn't want to know, and you had the courtesy not to try to find out."

But even there, however, the reaction was odd: reporters who were notorious for criticizing Bush's every move fell into two camps: either they were strangely silent on the speech, or they lashed out at Colbert for his ill-aimed barbs.

One review began this way: "Comedy Central's faux news show host Stephen Colbert stupidly delivered a stingingly satirical speech about President Bush and those who cover him at Saturday's White House Correspondents' Association Dinner."

Another reviewer said that he'd "bombed badly." For his part, Colbert read some of the early reviews and stories, and then decided that it would be best if he ignored the coverage and concentrated on *The Colbert Report*, though he later said, "Do I like catching someone for being a hypocrite? Hell yeah! I'm not saying truth to power, I'm saying 'Fuck you' to power. And in the case of the White House Correspondents' Dinner, I'm pretty sure that power was saying 'Fuck you' right back."

On a lighter note, the next honor was a bit easier to take.

On June 3, 2006, Colbert was awarded an honorary doctorate in fine arts from Knox College in Illinois. "All I did was give a speech, and now everybody has to call me Dr. Colbert," he cracked.

And then came the Emmys.

This was the first year that *The Colbert Report* was in the running, and it racked up several nominations, competing against *The Daily Show* for the best Variety, Music, or Comedy Series and for Outstanding Writing for a Variety, Music, or Comedy Program. Director Jim Hoskinson also received a nod for Outstanding Directing for a Variety, Music, or Comedy Program.

Colbert was nominated for Outstanding Individual Performance in a Variety or Music Program, where, among others, he was up against Barry Manilow for *Barry Manilow: Music and Passion*, a PBS documentary that went behind the scenes of Manilow's long-running Vegas show by the same name. Manilow won.

The Colbert Report didn't win any of their categories, but there were a couple of notable events. When *The Daily Show* won for Outstanding Variety, Music, or Comedy Series, and Stewart went onstage to give his acceptance speech, he said, "I think this year you actually made a terrible mistake, but thank you."

Manilow appeared on *The Colbert Report* a couple months later, and

Colbert accused Manilow of stealing the Emmy out from under him. But they signed a peace treaty and brokered an agreement by which they would share custody of the Emmy, switching it back and forth every six months. Then they sang a duet of "I Write the Songs."

Despite the perks, awards, and public recognition, the stress of producing four new shows a week—or 162 shows a year—was beginning to take its toll.

Four months after *The Colbert Report* debuted, Colbert's hair started to go gray. "He's so busy and he's so sleep-deprived," said his wife Evie.

"Four months after *The Colbert Report* debuted, Colbert's hair started to go gray."

But life was about to get even busier. Rumors started to circulate about a petition for a possible Stewart-Colbert presidential ticket; T-shirts and bumper stickers bearing the words "Stewart-Colbert '08" started to appear first on college campuses, and then spread to the mainstream.

Stewart said that he and Colbert had absolutely no intention of running for public office, but that the mere suggestion of such a ticket was a blunt indication of how people felt about American politics.

"Nothing says 'I am ashamed of my government' more than 'Stewart-Colbert '08,' " he said.

"Nothing says 'I am ashamed of my government' more than 'Stewart-Colbert '08.' "

Others took it one step further. When Colbert marched as grand marshal at the Northwestern homecoming parade in the fall of 2006, some students wore Colbert-Obama '08 T-shirts. He appreciated the gesture, but joked, "I can't tell Jon I'm dropping him to go with Barack."

But Colbert had no intention of standing still, especially as the one-year anniversary of *The Colbert Report* neared. His philanthropic side also began to emerge publicly about this time, and in a big way. He already knew he could mobilize his "nation" to name things after him, so he thought it was possible that he could do the same for nonprofits and charitable organizations. His first test was to auction off his infamous portrait, which hung above the fireplace on the set and showed him standing in front of the same portrait. He decided to put the portrait up on eBay, with the money from the winning bid donated to Save the Children. He had no clue how much the painting would fetch.

As it turned out, the portrait ended up in Charleston when the owners of Sticky Fingers, a chain of barbecue restaurants, had the top bid of $50,605 and decided to display the picture in their Charleston restaurant. A replacement portrait—adding an additional portrait within a portrait—replaced the original on the set.

The *Strangers with Candy* movie came out in July 2006. From the beginning, the film was set up as a prequel to the TV series. It provided a lot of the backstory on Jerri's years before returning to high school. Though fans had been speculating about a possible movie since the series went off the air, as was the case with so many projects that the Three Idiots came up with, their new project, the film, was created while they were working on another project.

"When we were working on the book *Wigfield*, we kept coming up with this funny stuff Jerri Blank would say," said Sedaris. "So Paul and Stephen just put it in a file. By the end of the book, we had all this Jerri Blank stuff and we thought it'd be funny to write a movie."

Best of all, Sedaris, Dinello, and Colbert would be back in their element. "We like playing selfish people," she said. "Selfish people are funny, especially when they're adults. That's our style. That's really it." Just as she had in the TV series, Evie had a small role in the movie, this time as Clair Noblet, the wife of Chuck, the character that Colbert played.

The TV show had developed such a cult status that from the first announcement of the movie, several major stars started clamoring to make cameo appearances in the movie. Some who made it: Philip Seymour Hoffman, Sarah Jessica Parker, and Allison Janney.

Colbert was realistic about the uphill battle they'd face when it came to making a well-loved cult TV series into a full-length movie. "I guess we're going to take the simplicity [of Jerri's life] and string it out into a film length," he said. "After all, the shows were really about how Jerri deals with a simple moral dilemma. Three acts later, she's either learned something or she has something to say. We want to maintain that level of simplicity, but still have a large enough scope that it's worthy of being on film. That's going to be the hardest part. None of the characters have to change, and I don't think the visual language will change that much. I think it's just finding an issue large enough to hold a film."

Once the movie was in the can, Warner Bros. didn't want to release it. "So we bought it back and released it," he said.

As Colbert expected, the reviews were not kind. "*Strangers with Candy* the series was thirty minutes per episode, and *Strangers with Candy* the movie is nearly ninety minutes, and like a lot of short-form sketch comedy adapted to the big screen, it never entirely justifies its existence—other than revisiting a beloved character one last time," said one reviewer.

"The only character, in fact, that touched a chord with this viewer is [Dan] Hedaya, who plays the bedridden, unconscious dad," wrote another reviewer who awarded the film NO stars. "He gets to sleep through the movie."

The year ended seemingly where it started: with *truthiness* once again winning recognition, this time from Merriam-Webster, the dictionary publisher that conducted an online survey asking respondents to vote on the one word that best described the past year.

"We're at a point where what constitutes truth is a question on a lot of people's minds," said the Merriam-Webster president, John Morse. "'Truthiness' is a playful way for us to think about a very important issue."

CHAPTER 11

DESPITE THE FACT THAT it looked easy to put *The Colbert Report* together day in and day out, for Stephen, Allison Silverman, and the other writers on the team, creating the show wasn't as simple as giving a few news stories a fake twist before tossing them into the air and seeing where they landed.

A typical day at *The Colbert Report* is a beautiful thing to behold, but it's not for the meek of heart. From the moment the staff—writers, producers, interns, and other staffers—enter the building, they hit the ground running and never stop until they leave at the end of the day.

"I read a lot of newspapers, watch some TV news, and have a staff of writers and then we chop wood all day long," said Colbert. "We show up angry or exasperated about something, and we try to turn that into jokes six hours later."

For one, the executive producer, Silverman, admitted that on an average day, she worked at least eleven to twelve hours, but that's only the time she spent at the office. Before she arrived at the studio around 9:30, she'd already spent an hour or two reading the morning papers, combing through them for any ideas that might make a good *Colbert Report* story.

The Colbert Report has an experienced research staff that monitors the newswires and Internet news sites for any stories that are bubbling under or look like they're ripe for a Colbert angle. Silverman said the researchers have to be on top of their game and constantly monitor the news feeds, adding, "It can get dangerous if the producers should miss something important."

At the 9:30 writers meeting—which lasts around ninety minutes—Silverman and the other writers bat around a few ideas based on that day's headlines as well as others carried over from the day before. "Then the writers go off to write and we meet with the rest of the staff to let the production and graphics people know what we need," she said. "Around one o'clock, the scripts come in, then we meet with everyone to say, 'All that stuff we told you this morning? It's gone. But we have another idea.' "

"You may throw three hours at an idea and then realize another one was better," Colbert concurred. "On a daily show, you don't necessarily have the luxury of being wrong. If you are, the last three hours of your day will feel like the last hours you'll ever do the job. But, if you're right, you'll feel like you could do it for ten years."

"We're constantly asking ourselves, 'Do we really want to say that, or are we just parodying what other people are saying?' " he said. "We ask, 'Is that really what the story is about all the time?' "

Where do the unused jokes and other cutting-room-floor material go? More often than not, they end up on Twitter, at @StephenAtHome.

The show tapes at 7 P.M., but writers, producers, and Stephen continue to tinker and change things right up until the last minute. "The clock is just a demon ticking away on the wall until 5:15 when I have to be down in the studio," said Colbert. "Then we do a rehearsal, and on a good day we have a half hour to rewrite a twenty-two-minute show. You have to be frugal with other people's writing, but there are times when Allison is a real stickler for facts, where she'll say something didn't exactly happen that way, and I'll say, 'Put the damn joke down, we don't have to get it exactly right, we can make a correction the next night.' Anyway, with my character, it's much more important how he feels about the news than whether or not he's giving you anything real or not.

"Ernie Kovacs said that every good idea he ever had was because it was 3:15, and he had a 3:30 production meeting," Colbert joked. "That sense of, oh, we're in trouble, we've got to make this thing work because I promised myself and others, but I don't know how. That's one of the things that's the most fun for me on the show. Maybe the thing that's eventually going to kill us on the show is that we love trying to do something that we probably shouldn't get away with, or that we shouldn't be able to achieve, and it was because it was so hard that I loved it. I'm a junkie for exhaustion, and I'm a junkie for setting up my expectations too high and then trying to meet them.

"It's a little bit like a forced march to get the show done everyday because [everything] is a prepared moment," he continued. "Not for a guest necessarily, but for me because I have to establish what my character's take is on that person's work or on their writing or what they represent. So we end up writing a twenty-two-minute monologue every night. And I think probably that's an unsustainable level of script output. We're finding different ways to push away from me, but it's a slow process."

During the first few months of *The Colbert Report*, Colbert and the writers were tinkering and revising the scripts right up to the last minute to airtime. But when Comedy Central extended the show for another year after the first two weeks, they were able to relax a little because they could hire a few more people and stockpile scripts over breaks.

"Generally, we have scripts in pretty good shape twenty-four hours ahead of time, but some days we end up doing a soup-to-nuts rewrite," said Colbert. "Sometimes you get pressed by that clock into a point of view that you don't necessarily believe is the best, but that you know will be comedically successful. That is a danger, but we try to continually name that danger. If we don't do it half the time, I feel great."

Silverman said there are challenges writing for Stephen Colbert the character. "It can become confusing, because I'm writing on a lot of different levels," she explained. "I often think of it in terms of driving on the highway in reverse by looking in your rearview mirror. Stephen Colbert is a person who plays himself, so as a writer, I have to consider what I want the character to say. I also have to figure out what the real Stephen is saying, and how the audience will react to it all, and then how the guests will respond. It becomes even more complicated on the 'Formidable Opponent' portion of the show. You have to write both the argument and counterargument, *and* you have to get jokes out of both. It can be overwhelming."

Colbert said he loved to watch Silverman wrestle it out. "Sometimes I'll see her having an ongoing argument with the computer screen, and I realize she's trying to figure out the argument of the Stephen Colbert character," he said.

"Both Stephen and I really enjoy what can be done with language," said Silverman. "His background allows him to twist words in a very effective way. He is extremely well-read, and he has a ferocious memory; he can pull it off."

Even though the atmosphere in the office is still playful and congenial, there's no ignoring the fact that it's a lot harder than it looks. "Comedy writers have to keep upping the ante for themselves," said Colbert. "Whatever the game is, they have to make it more extreme because they get bored with their own writing."

"Comedy writers have to keep upping the ante for themselves."

"It'll always be a challenge," added Silverman. "But I also think to some extent that part of what inspires us is the difficulty of it."

Colbert has the last word on everything; whether it's too offensive or not, it stays or goes depending on what he says. Writers tend to work in pairs. "Both writers write and act out the lines," said Silverman. "There's definitely a need to say Stephen's lines out loud, to hear if they really sound like his character."

The way they decide which stories to cover depends on the story as well as the context. "Sometimes the news drives us, especially when there's a lot of news going on," he said. "Other times, it's what we decide to cover, but it depends on the news cycle and what's being talked about." For instance, health care and insurance consumed the first half of 2009, so *The Colbert Report* had no choice but to cover these topics. "It was unignorable, and it's easier to make jokes because we don't have to educate the audience, but it became monotonous and relentless. Tonight we're doing a story about a sugar shortage, but that's *our* decision as opposed to the news deciding for us, in the case of health care," he said in an interview with Pete Dominick.

At the same time, the writers also have to be careful not to duplicate anything going on at *The Daily Show*. Despite the distinct tone of the two shows, there is bound to be at least some crossover. "The game they're playing is a slightly different one from us, so we don't trip on each other that much," said Stewart. "And let's put it this way: This ain't the Serengeti. There's plenty of food to go around."

Since Ben Karlin was executive producer of both shows, he visited both studios several times a day to check for any duplication.

For example, in the fall of 2006, during the Mark Foley sex scandal, when a Republican congressman from Florida sent explicit notes to a sixteen-year-old male page, Karlin green-lighted stories for both shows.

The Daily Show take: "It's the Jewish Day of Atonement," said Stewart. "I don't know how many days of fasting can get you out of trying to bang sixteen-year-olds. My guess is at least three days. Even after that, probably a month of salads."

Colbert, on the other hand, said that the media had gotten it all wrong about Foley, explaining that "stud" really stands for "Strong Teenager Using Democracy" in text-message shorthand, and that "horny" is short for "Happy On Reaching New Year's."

"Every January 1," he said, "that is the message I send to my buddies at Stephen Colbert's Youth Camp for Young Studs: 'I am incredibly horny.'"

Stewart also reviews scripts for both shows before nailing them into the schedule. "He looks at our scripts, and helps us to see where to find the most fruit," said Colbert. "His instincts are maddeningly good, and I don't recommend going to the mat with him over a comedic idea. We actually talk way more now than we did when we worked together, because I now understand how difficult his job is, to executive produce and then to be the ultimate writing voice of everything that gets said. I need someone's advice, so I call fairly frequently."

Once the audience is seated, the scripts have been tinkered with, and the clock ticks closer to seven, it's do-or-die time: "I don't actually become Stephen Colbert until right before the show," he said. "You can't be Stephen Colbert all day because he'd be a terrible executive producer. He'd shout at everyone the first time anything went wrong because he has no patience for incompetence. Then, right before they call me for the show, I have a special button that I push on my side that releases the gas."

Colbert—the character—also has an off-camera preshow ritual; whether he does it for real or in his head is kind of irrelevant, though in the first couple of years, he did involve the audience by running up and down the aisles, high-fiving everyone. "We decided that my character had to sing the lyrics to the song, 'I Want You to Want Me' by Cheap Trick into the mirror," he said. "It was one of the first decisions we made about the show because, more than anything else, as much as he says he's bringing the truth, he just wants to be liked." He's also said that his character shaves his entire body just before going onstage.

Of course, there are hours of pressure, last-minute frustrations, and countless challenges involved when a staff of ninety puts out a show essentially from scratch four nights a week. The stress would kill off lesser mortals. So why do *Colbert Report* staffers do it?

It's simple. They love love love their boss.

"Stephen Colbert is an incredibly easy person to work for," said Peter Grosz, a writer for the show. "He's amazingly easy to write for because he has an incredibly open mind. He wants to hear all ideas and has a lot of faith and trust in his writers, and expects that anything coming out of your mouth is going to be something worth listening to. Like any other actor, writer, or improviser, there's always something a bit off from the norm. But I wouldn't say that he's got any crazy quirks, like he has to have a pineapple juice before he goes on."

"I think the staff works harder for [Colbert] because of the way he treats us, and because how much they enjoy doing the show," said Pete Dominick, who does the preshow crowd warm-up. "I could name a lot of TV hosts with staffers who regularly try to sabotage the show because the host is a prick."

But Lizz Winstead, who worked with Colbert on *The Daily Show*, says there's a different reason. "If you look at the shows that people like, whether it's Jon Stewart or Bill Maher or Colbert, the people who work on these shows and the reasons shows like these are successful is because anybody working on any of these shows would do it for free anyway," she said. "To do this, it has to come from your core, from your belly, so being able to work on a production is really great. Also, when you get young, interesting writers who are just starting out in the business, they're learning a bunch of really cool skills, like what it means to be in a writing room and have ideas turned down, not because they're not funny, but because they're not written in the tone of the show. It teaches them to write for an entity, not for themselves. And it also gives them tape to put on their reels."

"It's a lot of work, but I'm not complaining because all a performer wants is to perform more," said Colbert. "Like every performer, I just imagine that tomorrow I won't be working and that I'll never work again. I think every time I try to create something—and this time it's no different—I think I'm a complete fraud. How could I create something? I have no ideas. This is ridiculous. Oh, there's been a horrible mistake. I wonder if I could still go to law school."

"Like every performer, I just imagine that tomorrow I won't be working and that I'll never work again."

But regardless of the job at *The Colbert Report*, it is all-consuming whether for Colbert or for a production assistant, and leaves little time for anything else.

"Now we just need to figure out a way to do it that's humane for the people who work on the show," he said during the show's first season, when it wasn't unusual for staffers to sleep in shifts under their desks. "There's no time for anything else.

"The hardest thing about *The Colbert Report* is doing 162 shows a year," he said. "The best thing is working with people you just love. We call it 'The Joy Machine' because without that, it's just a machine, and it will eat you up."

However, joy or not, it does eat up some. "Stephen works really hard, and always did," said Charna Halpern, his ImprovOlympic teacher from Chicago. "He's always been a go-getter, a performer, he loves his work and works harder than anyone I know. But the writers [at *The Colbert Report*] have no life. They work during the day, then they stay at night so they can write the next day's show after they finish the previous night's show. They take turns going home at night. One night, one writer will say, okay, you can go home, and then tomorrow night, I'll go home.

"There is absolutely no downtime," she continued. "I know a writer who quit the show because he couldn't handle the hours."

Colbert concedes that this is the hardest part of the job. "The show is a daily, ravenous beast," he said. "It asks me to use everything I've ever learned about being a writer and performer, and I have no desire to do anything else.

"But I could give everyone a year off, and they'd still come back tired," he added.

CHAPTER 12

Colbert started 2007 off with a bang by appearing on *The O'Reilly Factor*. To make things even more interesting, O'Reilly agreed to appear on *The Colbert Report* on the very same night: January 18.

"I look forward to the evening," Colbert said. "It is an honor to speak face-to-face with a broadcasting legend, and I feel the same way about Mr. O'Reilly. I have a genuine admiration for O'Reilly's ability to do his show."

From the preamble, it sounded like it would be one big lovefest. O'Reilly, for his part, said, "I'm really looking forward to speaking to a man who owes his entire career to me."

But when he appeared on the *The O'Reilly Factor*, Colbert fired the first shot. "I want you to know that I spend so much time in the world that is spinning all the time, that to be in the no-spin zone actually gives me vertigo," he told O'Reilly, who parried back by immediately focusing on the pronunciation of his name.

"I spoke to your third-grade teacher, Miss Crabtree, who said back then you were little Steve Col-*bert.* Is that right?"

"In South Carolina, I was Steve Col-bert," he replied, launching into an us-against-them position. "Bill, you know you've got to play the game that the media elites want you to do. Some places you can draw the line, some places you can't. You and I have taken a lot of positions against the powers that be, and we've paid a heavy price." Then he added: "It's hard for me to be you. I'll tell you that much."

"It is? It *is*?" O'Reilly thundered. "Don't you owe me an enormous amount of money?"

"Well, if I were imitating you, I would," Colbert retorted. "But there's a difference between imitation and emulation. Let me tell you the difference, okay? If you imitate someone, you owe them a royalty check. If you emulate them, you don't. There's a big difference."

O'Reilly kicked into his a best-defense-is-a-good-offense mode. "So who are you? Are you Col-bert or Col-bear?"

Stephen refused to get ruffled, and it was hard to tell whether he was answering in character or as his real self; at times, it seemed as if he was straddling the line between them. "Bill, I'm whoever you want me to be. Col-bert. I'm at the foot of the mat here."

It would be safe to assume that when they switched chairs later on—when O'Reilly appeared on *The Colbert Report*—that things would continue much in the same vein. But O'Reilly was on the defensive throughout much of the interview. He asked Colbert if he had read his new book, *Culture Warriors.*

Colbert said of course, and when he brought out a copy of the book, it had a 30-percent-off sticker covering O'Reilly's face. "This was a huge mistake coming on this show," O'Reilly grumbled.

"This was a huge mistake coming on this show."

Colbert then switched gears to put him at ease by showing the audience a photo of O'Reilly's face superimposed on a male stripper's body. "Maybe you should go undercover as a secular humanist," he suggested.

"This would play in San Francisco," said O'Reilly. "I could get elected mayor of San Francisco like that."

When Colbert suggested that O'Reilly was a bit of a brawler, O'Reilly denied it. "I'm effete," he said. "This is all an act."

Colbert then went in for the kill. He leaned in close to ask, "If you're an act, then what am I?"

In the end, Colbert was glad he'd done it, but he was taken aback at how things turned out, especially on his own show. "I was a little disappointed because—and this was a revelation—I thought he was playing a game," Colbert said. "I thought he was assuming a persona on his show, but when he came on my show, he dropped it. I was disappointed that we couldn't actually come to an emotional or argumentative agreement over things. He saw the mirror that I was presenting and he didn't want to play. I thought that it would be this fugue of O'Reilly's going at each other."

A couple of weeks later, however, Papa Bear was back in full character when he told his audience that his appearance on *The Colbert Report* qualified for his "Most Ridiculous Item of the Day" segment. "After his visit here a couple of weeks ago, Stephen Colbert and his entourage borrowed *The Factor*'s microwave oven," O'Reilly told his audience. "They apparently used it as a prop on their broadcast and then took their sweet time getting it back to us. I'm happy to report the microwave is now back in our green room, but it's a new one, not the one they stole, with Colbert graffiti all over it. Members of Colbert's staff did not attempt to sell our microwave in order to get money to buy drugs. Apparently, that was a vicious rumor started by Jon Stewart, and we are happy to set the record straight."

Since *The Colbert Report* first went on the air, a veritable cottage industry began to spring up on YouTube and on online forums, where fans made it their job to show clips where Colbert broke character, either by laughing unexpectedly or in a media interview with someone like Morley Safer or Charlie Rose, where Colbert spoke as himself.

"As much as I want to make the audience laugh, I really want to make Jon laugh."

Indeed, the most infamous moment came on *The Daily Show*, when Colbert was eating a banana while reporting on a scandal about Prince Charles. "Such a proud moment of professionalism," he said. "You work for years crafting cogent satirical essays and the thing that everybody remembers is me making love to a Chiquita and bursting into laughter. What you can't see off camera is that Jon started laughing first. And I'm weak. As much as I want to make the audience laugh, I really want to make Jon laugh."

Though most of his breaks with character only lasted a few seconds, if that, there was one occasion when Colbert totally broke character for almost an entire segment.

On May 9, 2007, Jane Fonda appeared on *The Colbert Report* to promote her new movie, her second appearance on the show in six months. Her earlier shot was with Gloria Steinem on a segment billed "Cooking with Feminists," where Colbert wore a "Kiss the Cook" apron, and both ladies did indeed do just that. "There's a little Barbarella left," he said.

He invited her back on the show when it came time to promote her new movie, *Georgia Rule*, where she played a grandmother with an unruly granddaughter, played by Lindsay Lohan, who moves in with her. After Colbert introduced Fonda on the show, he didn't even get a chance to sit down before Fonda came over and started running her hands all over him before he even sat down. That's when the trouble started. She climbed on his lap and stayed there the entire time, stroking his hair, blowing in his ear, and kissing him.

For once, Colbert seemed at a loss for words. Not only did he break character, but he seemed truly uncomfortable.

"She brought a game, she was gonna out-character me," he said. "It was fun, but I was completely off my game."

After the taping, a staffer had run out and bought flowers for him to bring home to Evie. When he got home and she saw the flowers, she asked him what happened.

"Well, Jane Fonda," is all he managed to say before she blurted out, "I don't want them!"

Evie was upset, but not for the reason he expected.

Later that night, as they watched the show, Evie was amused by Stephen's overt discomfort. She turned to him and said, "Don't ever let anybody take over your show again!"

He didn't expect this. "But honey, if I'd stayed in character I would have flipped her over and gone at it on the table!" he protested.

"It doesn't matter," said Evie. "You gave her the higher status."

Colbert recalled an old *Tonight Show* where Johnny Carson was interviewing an animal trainer with a squirrel monkey, and the monkey climbed onto Carson's head. Carson froze up but continued to tell jokes. He was afraid if he moved, the monkey would attack him. "Jane Fonda was my squirrel monkey," he said.

"That was the most out of character I've ever gotten," he added. "It became very hard to maintain my character when she put her tongue in my ear."

"It became very hard to maintain my character when she put her tongue in my ear."

Stephen Colbert was everywhere. Even people who didn't watch him were aware of him. It looked like he could do no wrong. He even got his own ice cream flavor when Ben & Jerry's introduced a Stephen

Colbert–inspired flavor, Americone Dream: vanilla ice cream swirled with caramel and fudge-covered pieces of waffle cone.

"They sent me home with unmarked containers of ice cream," he says. "We tasted it. My wife said it was the best ice cream she has ever had. And I don't think it's just because she's married to me, so we gave it a thumbs up." When asked to describe the flavor, he said, "It actually tastes like me. No one will ever find out, because I'm married, but this is what I taste like. Very sweet."

He set up the Stephen Colbert Americone Dream Foundation, in connection with the Coastal Community Foundation of South Carolina and designated that all of his royalties from sales of the ice cream would go into the fund. The first to benefit from the sales were the families of the "Charleston nine," nine firefighters who died in a fire in the city in June 2007.

"Stephen Colbert the character sees himself as a product," he said. "It's market penetration. And the fact that he now physically is a product: You can ingest me and enjoy me externally and internally at the same time."

However, not everyone was enamored of Colbert, and it wasn't just conservatives. Colbert hosted an authors' breakfast forum at 2007 BookExpo America, an annual publishing trade show, which featured the author Khaled Hosseini, who had written the bestseller *The Kite Runner*, a serious literary novel set in Afghanistan. Just as his jokes hadn't gone over with everyone at the White House Correspondents' Dinner, Colbert's humor was a bit too much for some to take at the expo, including Hosseini.

He introduced the author with a brief monologue, starting off by saying that he assumed *The Kite Runner* was a story about a boy who loves kites. "I loved yo-yos, so I can relate," he said. Next, he referred to *A Thousand Splendid Suns* as "another book about global warming."

By this time, even the audience was groaning, but not in a good way. Instead of laughing good-naturedly, Hosseini decided to take Colbert head-on. "You trashed *The Kite Runner*," said Hosseini. "It is un-American to dis *The Kite Runner*."

"I was a little mad at you at the time; I don't remember why," Colbert responded, saying that after making fun of the book his yard was "filled with women's book clubs."

Though some later said they were just joking around at the show, and Colbert invited Hosseini to appear on *The Colbert Report* a year later, it did show there were a few cracks in the façade.

Stephen Colbert, superhero?

With the launch of *Tek Jansen of Alpha Squad 7*, a five-part comic book series published in July 2007, Colbert did indeed turn into yet another character, this one in cartoon form.

Based on the "Alpha Squad 7" animated cartoons that appeared as an occasional segment on *The Colbert Report* since August 2006, each comic book contained two separate tales, both starring Colbert. "We wrote it as if it was Stephen Colbert in space, so he had a robot eagle sidekick and he was going after alien bears," said John Layman, the writer in charge of the main story in each issue. "He's got a radioactive robotic monkey sidekick as well as an evil pet named Meangarr, a giant energy void. And then he has girlfriend after girlfriend after girlfriend."

It wasn't *Dungeons & Dragons*, but Colbert loved it because he had a great deal of input into the story line and the art. "There was quite a bit of back-and-forth because I think Stephen Colbert is a geek," said Layman. "I've had editors who don't pay that close attention."

The second story in each comic was designed as a case file of sorts, where Tek—aka Colbert—goes undercover to solve a crime. The writer Jim Massey encountered the same thorny issues that Allison Silverman did when writing for Stephen Colbert on *The Colbert Report*. "It's a fictional character based on a fictional Tek Jansen book, which is supposedly written by Stephen Colbert, who is actually Stephen Colbert playing a character *named* Stephen Colbert," he said. "So there are four or five layers of fictionalizing going on there. Trying to figure out where, in all those layers, you start building the character is fun."

The illustrator, Scott Chantler, was also surprised that Colbert, along with executive producer Ben Karlin, was so involved in the project. "They gave us a surprising amount of feedback, encouragement, and time, given their other commitments," he said. "They particularly wanted us to understand how the Tek character differs from the Colbert character. This isn't a comic book version of *The Colbert Report*, it's better! It's space opera! Aliens die! Humans live! In a universe so vast, we're like ants! Except for Tek. He's not an ant."

When Chantler first plotted out a few spec drawings of Colbert as Tek, he kept one thing in mind. "I try to draw Tek as if he were the most confident man in the universe," he said. "This is a character who's convinced he's right about everything. I try to put that cockiness and arrogance across in every frame."

While Colbert pretty much held off on commenting on the story line until the tale was complete, he was concerned with the appearance of the cartoons, from the layout to the background to how the characters interacted with one another. "He had a very clear idea of what he wanted the art to look like, in terms of visual style," said Chantler. "He and his team looked at the art first in pencil roughs, then inked versions, then finally the finished, colored pages, and they always gave me notes on what they did and didn't like. The comic is definitely taking a different direction from the animated bits on the show, which was Stephen's idea. He wanted something a bit more serious and dramatic in tone, something that played it as straight as he does on the show."

"This is a godsend!" Colbert said after he broke his left wrist in the summer of 2007. "When something like this happens to me, it's a golden ticket."

He meant that in several ways: First, it provided him with material for the show. Second, he turned it into a money-raising exercise for charity.

During his usual preshow warm-up, Colbert fell on his wrist while dancing and singing to "I Want You to Want Me." Drawing on the popular Livestrong yellow bracelet campaign by the cyclist Lance Armstrong, Colbert decided to start a "wrist awareness" program by selling similar pink rubber bracelets to raise money for the Yellow Ribbon Fund, which helps active military personnel injured in the line of duty while they recuperate and adjust to life back in the United States.

But he didn't stop there. He then auctioned off the cast on eBay after first having a number of celebrities autograph it, including Mike Bloomberg, Katie Couric, Bill O'Reilly, and Nancy Pelosi. The Wriststrong bracelets raised $171,525, while the winning eBay bid for the cast was $17,200.

"If I had known that it would give me the opportunity to help our wounded veterans, I would have shattered my triquetrum a long time ago!" he joked.

But he also showed that he was serious about the troops. How long would he keep the bracelet on his wrist? "Not until the war is over," he replied.

The year continued its feverish pace in October, when Colbert's first book, *I Am America (And So Can You!)* was published. It debuted on the *New York Times* Best-Seller List at number one. Colbert, for one, viewed it as an extension of his show. "It's just like an O'Reilly book or a Hannity book," he said. "You know, twenty subjects on all of the important things: the culture war, religion, hygiene, sports. I just think things and then I say them. Sometimes I don't even think them."

"I just think things and then I say them. Sometimes I don't even think them."

Just as he had done with the Tek Jansen comic books, Colbert had a good deal of input into the design and layout of *I Am America*. "There are sections of the book in the old person's chapter that are in large print because we know that the elderly cannot read anything below thirty-six point type," he explained. "It's also the visual version of yelling at old people. My actual feelings about the elderly are in a much smaller font, just for their own feeling's sake."

For the most part, the reviews were positive. "Colbert's opus feels familiar," wrote one reviewer, though he "crams an awful lot into *I Am*

America, so much that it sometimes feels forced." And his character's imagined nemesis—*The New York Times*—even had good things to say, albeit with a caveat: "*I Am America* certainly has its moments," wrote Janet Maslin, "[but] the full-monty Colbert television brilliance doesn't quite make it to the page."

Though he continued to get offers for movies and other stints, he turned most of them down. His family came first. Madeleine was now twelve years old, while the boys, Peter and John, were, respectively, nine and five. "One of the things I like about TV is you can have a level of normalcy if you want it," said Colbert. "I don't have to move to Los Angeles; I can stay in New York, which I love. I don't have to go on location to shoot a movie. I know what I'm doing five days a week, forty-two weeks of the year. That kind of pattern is rare, I think, in an actor's life, and I am very grateful to have it."

Despite his desire to live an average family life, his ability to do so was about to change. What started out as a joke turned serious—or was it?—and by the time it was over, Colbert would be a little shaken.

In a strange incarnation of art imitating life, just as many politicians—and some celebrities—release a book when they announce that they're running for national office, so too did Colbert, twisting the game by doing so, even though less than a year earlier he had vehemently denied the issue.

With a presidential election year looming and coverage of potential candidates already building on both *The Daily Show* and *The Colbert Report*, the Stewart-Colbert '08 proponents kept up their campaign.

Suddenly, to the delight of his fans, Colbert announced in the fall of 2007 that he would give it a try, running in the presidential primary as a Republican *and* a Democrat. "That way, I can lose twice," he said.

But only in South Carolina, his home state: "I'm running in South Carolina because I believe that it's the greatest state in the union," he said. "I believe I can make a difference there, and I think it's time to focus on South Carolina. Florida tried to jump South Carolina's primary date for both the Republicans and the Democrats. I don't want Iowa and New

Hampshire to be the only people in the United States who get to control who is a bellwether state. And if Iowa and New Hampshire don't like that, they can take some of that Iowa corn and stick it right up their Dixville Notch."

People from a variety of places weighed in. "The great thing about America is as long as he meets the requirements and his check clears, he can be on the ballot," said the South Carolina Republican Party chairman Katon Dawson. "Anybody can run for president. We look forward to him filing."

Joe Werner, the executive director of the South Carolina Democratic Party, agreed: "If Stephen wants to run for president of the United States in South Carolina, that's his right," he said.

"I'm shocked Stephen Colbert would run for president," said Terry Sullivan, the state campaign director for Mitt Romney. "He's clearly overqualified for the job."

"We are happy to see another South Carolina native enter the race," said Teresa Wells, state communications director for the Edwards campaign. "We welcome him and the return of his Southern accent to South Carolina. Our staff would like to challenge his staff to a South Carolina debate: *I Am Barbecue (And So Can You!).*"

He made his formal announcement on *The Colbert Report* on October 16, after which, like every other potential candidate, he swiftly made the rounds of the talk-show circuit. First up: *Meet the Press.*

"I don't want to be president, I want to *run* for president," he said. "There's a difference. I'd be making the statement that I was able to get on the ballot in South Carolina, and if I can do it, so can you."

He then floated the question of who would be his vice president and—seriously or not—revealed that he had already been offered a vice presidential slot on someone else's campaign: Arkansas's governor, Mike Huckabee.

"The Governor offered me the position on my show and when a certain other person named Hannity on a different network asked him who he liked [for vice president] he said he had already made a promise to me," he said. "So if I get the ticket, I probably have to offer it to him just tit for tat."

Borrowing a page from *The Dana Carvey Show*, he christened his campaign. "Hail to the Cheese Stephen Colbert Nacho Cheese Doritos 2008 Presidential Campaign."

Things got serious very fast, starting with the pollsters. Public Opinion Strategies polled one thousand likely voters and showed that Colbert would receive 2.3 percent of the vote in a Democratic primary, coming in ahead of Governor Bill Richardson, Senator Chris Dodd, and Congressman Dennis Kucinich.

The other candidates were not amused. Said Richardson's spokesman, Tom Reynolds, "This is a serious election with serious consequences and we are not going to comment on this ridiculous exercise. The country has seen eight years of a joker in the White House, and look where it got us."

Colbert filed to get on the ballot as a Democratic candidate in South Carolina, paying the $2,500 filing fee just before the noon deadline on November 1, 2007. He opted for only the Democratic primary because he thought the $35,000 cost to add his name to the Republican ballot was too high.

But it didn't take long for the Democratic powers-that-be in South Carolina to have a change of heart. Perhaps it was a campaign speech he gave at the University of South Carolina in Columbia, in which he launched into a discourse on the differences between South Carolina and Georgia. Or perhaps it was because they thought the real Stephen Colbert would be running, not the character or vice versa. In any case, admittedly, it was sometimes hard to tell.

"You all must be thrilled to have me here," he told the crowd. "I love South Carolina almost as much as South Carolina loves me. I have a promise to make to you. If elected, I will crush the state of Georgia. And for good measure, the state of Tennessee."

He then delved into the differences between South Carolina and Georgia peaches; of course, in his eyes, South Carolina's were superior. "They're more numerous, more delicious, and more juiciful, and their fuzziness is unparalleled," he said.

"Over my dead body will Colbert's name be on the ballot," said Waring Howe, a member of the executive council. "He's just trying to use

South Carolina Democrats as suckers so he can further a comedy routine, and it detracts from the serious candidates on the ballot."

Less than two weeks after Colbert made his initial announcement, the executive council of the state Democratic party voted 13-3 to boot Colbert off the ballot.

And just in case Colbert had designs on the Republican ticket, the South Carolina Republican party chairman Katon Dawson said that Colbert "would be better off spending the $35,000 entrance fee to buy a sports car and get a girlfriend."

"They tell you when you're a child that anyone can run for president," said Colbert, his hopes dashed. "But apparently not you, Stephen Colbert."

"They tell you when you're a child that anyone can run for President. But apparently not you, Stephen Colbert."

Though he had earlier joked with Morley Safer in a *60 Minutes* interview that "the only hope that I'll actually do this job right is if I begin to believe my own line of crap," he realized that the line between the real and fake Colberts was thin and had become almost nonexistent during the campaign.

"I came close to believing my own line of crap when I was running for president," he admitted, adding that it was a scary place to be. "Even the *Report* staff was confused, and my publicist asked me, 'Is this a joke or is this real?' "

Perhaps Stewart phrased it best when he told Colbert, "You touched it. You got close enough to touch it, and it got on you." Colbert then revealed how much of a test the whole thing was when he spoke about what had gone on behind the scenes. He'd been talking with a few members of the executive council, who told him he had nothing to worry about and that he should stay in the race, while they had already planned a meeting to figure out how to prevent him from getting on the ballot. "They were lying to me. That was disappointing. I thought I could put myself all the way into [the political process] and not feel [the corruption], but I did. I started to understand why people end up not being so good," he said. "Because they get lied to *a lot*."

In the end, he kept the exercise in perspective in explaining his primary reason for running. "I couldn't have the presidential election *not* be about me," he summed up.

Colbert shrewdly viewed the campaign in the same way he did his Wriststrong campaign and the Ben & Jerry's Americone Dream flavor: as an opportunity to raise money for a charity or nonprofit organization. During the short-lived campaign, Colbert urged viewers to support his presidential campaign by donating money to South Carolina school classrooms through a then little-known organization called DonorsChoose .org, a charity that accepts financial donations that it then gives to schools. In just a few weeks, viewers donated over $66,000 to the program.

"I get asked to do a lot of things that could raise millions of dollars," he said. But he liked the purpose of the group enough that he even joined the board of advisors. The DonorsChoose.org founder, Charles Best, asked him to help moderate a panel to announce the receipt of a 4.1 million–dollar grant from the Bill and Melinda Gates Foundation. Colbert agreed to help, and then some.

"When I asked him to make the announcement, I only asked him to show up and say a few words and read off a couple talking points I'd given him," said Best. "But he was incapable of half-assing his performance. He had to spend time thinking about his remarks and make them hilarious and eloquent. He knew it wouldn't be televised, that only the kids sitting around him would hear him, but it didn't matter. He had to give it the same thinking and dedication as what's seen by millions of people."

The difference in Colbert's endorsement of the group was significant. Before he got involved, DonorsChoose.org had a team of twenty-five employees; that number jumped to fifty-two in the summer of 2009. "And before, we served one million students," said Best. "Now we're up to 2.2 million."

In fact, Colbert is so dedicated to the group that tucked into the parting-gift goody bag that every guest on his show receives is a $100 DonorsChoose.org gift certificate to spend on the site.

During Colbert's "campaign," however, a more serious matter was brewing: whether or not *The Colbert Report* would still be on the air in the near future.

The same day that Colbert was filing to run on the ballot in South Carolina, the contract between the Writers Guild of America and TV producers and studios was set to expire. All of *The Colbert Report* writers were members of the union, which meant that in case of a strike, there would be no show. Negotiations were ongoing, but chances for a resolution appeared to dim, and writers had already voted to strike if their demands were not met.

The main sticking points revolved around digital media—including the Internet and smartphone applications—and higher payments to writers for each DVD that sold with their work in it. At the time, writers earned four cents a DVD, which they wanted to be increased to eight cents.

On the one hand, after such a crammed 2007, Colbert could definitely use a break, and so could his staff.

But like other daily news shows, even though it was a fake news show, *The Colbert Report* still needed new content for each show. While some segments and features could be prepared in advance, a lot of the show was still being cranked out up to the last minute before taping that evening's show.

"We'll be affected by a strike, as will be everybody else," said Tony Fox, a spokesman for Comedy Central. "The two shows that are most impacted are *The Daily Show* and *The Colbert Report* because they air four nights a week."

Reruns were the only option, even though ratings plummeted whenever *The Colbert Report* went into repeats, but, more important, Colbert was a member of the Writers Guild, as was Stewart. "They both write for their shows under the Writers Guild contract," said Michael Winship, president of the Writers Guild East division. "Our position is that they could not do any of the work that they normally do as a Writers Guild member in terms of writing and performing material on the show."

As expected, talks broke down; twelve thousand TV, movie, and radio writers went on strike; and *The Colbert Report* went into repeats the first week of November.

Colbert was named celebrity of the year by the Associated Press in late 2007, but in keeping with the strike, he turned down all interviews. He did, however, make one statement about the honor: "In receiving this award, I am pleased that I was chosen over two great spinners of fantasy: J. K. Rowling and Al Gore."

CHAPTER 13

EVEN THOUGH HE'D RATHER be working, Colbert took the strike as his first chance to take a break in years and reveled in it, though it did take a little getting used to.

"The first thing I did when the strike got called was to start acting like I was newly single," he said. "I started to make a lot of soup and went to buy a hoodie and some yoga pants."

He also grew a beard, which he pledged to shave only when the strike was over. What he felt more acutely, however, was the lack of having an audience to entertain four nights a week. "I love being onstage. I love the relationship with the audience. I love the letting go, the sense of discovery, the improvising," he said. "When I don't get to perform, I'm probably more neurotic. The weeks when I'm writing and not performing—which are supposed to be weeks off for me—are much harder for me than weeks when I write *and* perform, because I get that release, and I get to connect to the audience." Five weeks into the strike, it was clear that he'd be walking around with hair on his face for a while, as both sides had met several times to negotiate without success.

Carson Daly was the first host of a late night talk show to return to the air, albeit reluctantly. "An ultimatum was put in front of me," said Daly. "It was, 'Put a new show on by December 3 or 75 people are fired. What's your answer?' "

Soon, other late-night shows began to cave. The first shows to return to work—without their writers—were *The Late Show with David Letterman* and *The Late Late Show with Craig Ferguson*, both on CBS. Like Daly, both hosts explained that the entire nonwriting staff would be laid off if they continued to stay off the air.

Then, shortly before Christmas, Colbert announced that *The Colbert Report* would return to Comedy Central on January 7, presumably for similar reasons. He and Stewart offered up a joint statement: "We would like to return to work with our writers. If we cannot, we would like to express our ambivalence, but without our writers we are unable to express something as nuanced as ambivalence."

In concession to the striking writers, however, both Colbert and Stewart slightly altered the names of their shows: Stewart's became *A Daily Show with Jon Stewart*, while Colbert merely started pronouncing the Ts at the end of *Colbert* and *Report*. It was unclear how Colbert's show would be presented, given that the writers were such a vital part.

The first show back, on January 7, revealed the difficulty. The introduction lasted only fifteen seconds as Stephen uttered only four words with lots of space between each one. Then he asked the audience to give him a standing ovation, which filled up another two minutes. Comedy Central executives—and Colbert himself—had worried about basing an entire show on a single character before giving the go-ahead to the show back in the spring of 2005, and this revealed why they were so hesitant to do it. For "The Word," he ran clips from past shows to fill the segment, but ironically, he couldn't have a new word, because there were no writers.

Even though he was trained extensively in improvisation, Colbert still found doing the show to be a challenge because he was essentially improvising without a partner. "Doing the show during the strike with no teleprompter was the hardest thing I've ever done," he admitted.

But aside from the work difficulties, it was clear that Colbert was also uncomfortable being back at work while his writers were on strike. He thought back to the hospital-workers strike that his father had faced at MUSC back in 1969. Even though Stephen was only five years old at the time, he remembered his father telling stories about it. He called his older brother Ed to fill in the details, and Ed told him how their father and Andrew Young had worked behind the scenes to end the strike a hundred days after it had started.

Colbert knew he had to have Young on as a guest. His father had said of Young, "Watch him. He's going places." And he did, by becoming a U.S. congressman from Georgia's Fifth District, the mayor of Atlanta, and the U.S. ambassador to the United Nations. When Colbert got him on the phone, the first thing he asked Young was, "Do you remember my father?"

"Very well," Young replied. "Very well."

They spoke a bit about the 1969 hospital-workers strike, and then Colbert invited him to appear on *The Colbert Report.* "I wanted him to come on the show to talk about that experience in light of what I'm going through right now," said Colbert. "I needed something to talk about and this would be a wonderful way for me to talk about it." Young said he'd be happy to.

On January 22, as negotiations dragged on between the union and the producers, Young came on the show. It was a poignant look at Colbert's personal history—which few fans knew about—and included a video montage about the hospital strike.

In fact, his father was never far from his mind or those of his family members. In early 2008, plans moved forward at MUSC to renovate the building where Dr. Colbert had his offices, which currently served as the education center, as well as create an endowed professorial chair named in his honor. Stephen offered to help raise some of the money through public appearances.

Perhaps it was no coincidence that the writers strike ended only a few weeks after Young appeared on *The Colbert Report.* On February 12, the strike was officially over, and the writers returned to work.

Within a few days, everything was back to normal, including the phenomenon known as the Colbert Bump, in which anyone who appears on the show—or even when a particular product is mentioned—almost instantly experiences a boost in popularity, whether it's a rise in the polls, a book gets boosted into the top of Amazon's bestsellers, or someone wins an award or honor of some kind.

The Colbert Bump was cited so much by politicians ranging from Mike Huckabee to the congressional representatives that had appeared on the show for "Better Know a District" that a professor at the University of California at San Diego decided to conduct a study.

James Fowler, associate professor of political science, researched how an appearance on *The Colbert Report* affected campaign donations. He found that Democratic candidates generated a 44 percent increase within thirty days after appearing on the show compared with candidates who hadn't appeared on the show.

But he discovered that there was a curious difference between how Republicans and Democrats experienced the bump. While for Republicans, the bump was only a couple of percentage points, it was much more significant with Democrats. "The Democrats who were willing to go on the show were actually doing much worse prior to coming on the show, which means that they were interested in taking a risk," Fowler explained. "Republicans were actually doing much better than average before they came on the show, which means that they had to feel very secure in their campaigns in order to be willing to risk being made fun of by Stephen Colbert."

In fact, just how far Colbert had come—and how much politicians valued even his tacit endorsement—became clear when Colbert and his staff took *The Colbert Report* on the road and shot on location in Philadelphia for an entire week in April 2008 to coincide with the Pennsylvania primary.

The presidential campaign season was heating up, the bulk of the primaries were behind them, and there were three Democratic candidates still duking it out. On the last day of the show in Pennsylvania, April 17, 2008, there were a few surprises.

First, Hillary Clinton came on the show to demonstrate how she would take charge in a crisis by helping to fix a couple of technical problems on the set. Then John Edwards showed up to do "The Word": *valued voter*. The show ended with Barack Obama doing a live remote from a political rally.

The logistics were a nightmare. Not only were there more Secret Service agents on the set than anyone could count, but coordinating the schedules of all three to appear within a brief time frame for taping was close to impossible.

"We didn't know whether it was all going to come together, and we didn't know for certain until Wednesday whether Clinton would make it, and we didn't know if Obama would make it at all until shortly before he appeared," said Colbert. Edwards had already committed and approved the script. "The show was going up late, and we wanted Obama's appearance to be a surprise, because we didn't want to set up expectations, so I didn't even want it in the script in case it didn't happen."

Even the stage manager was in the dark. "The Obama people were ready to go ten minutes before we got to his section of the act, but I didn't want to do him before John Edwards went out because the show would kind of be over once we had Barack Obama on because it was meant to be the closing moment," said Colbert. "Of course, in television, you can rearrange things later, but I wanted the evening to be a real organic experience for the audience, especially because there were a thousand people in that theater. The whole night was a tightrope walk, but I really wanted that final show to have everybody on it."

He was glad the writers were back, because they had to hit the ground running to create scenarios and scripts that would showcase each candidate's strength. First, they decided that "The Word" would work best for John Edwards. Then they turned to Hillary: what is the message that she wants to convey most of all? That she's competent and able to handle emergencies. "So we created an emergency for her to handle, which just happened to be the rear projection screen going out," he said.

When it came time to figure out which problem to give Obama to solve, however, they were stuck. They bounced several ideas back and forth, but nothing really seemed to fit, and the writers couldn't agree.

The week that *The Colbert Report* was in Philadelphia, Obama's detractors on the campaign trail were making a big deal of the fact that the candidate didn't wear a flag pin on his lapel, implying that he was not a true American. At noon on Thursday, Obama still hadn't committed to appear on the show, but when the lapel-pin issue was mentioned in one of the debates earlier that week, and Obama referred to it as a petty political distraction, Colbert knew he had the message the candidate would offer on the show: that he was there to put petty political distractions on notice, with the help of his "On Notice" board, a regular segment on *The Colbert Report.*

Colbert and his writers quickly wrote a script, and it all came together when Obama appeared on the rear projection screen that Hillary had just "fixed." It was skin of the teeth the entire week, from the uncertainty if any of the candidates would appear to it all fitting together at the last minute, but the entire time Colbert was in his element. "I love being in situations where I feel like I'm in trouble," he said.

"I love being in situations where I feel like I'm in trouble."

In mid-June, he was once again honored when he found out that *The Colbert Report* had won a Peabody Award for its 2007 season. The Peabody is widely considered to be the most prestigious award for excellence in broadcast and electronic journalism. In accepting the award, Colbert gave it his typical spin: "I proudly accept this award and begrudgingly forgive the Peabody Committee for taking three years to recognize greatness," he said. "On a personal note, I'd like to say that I've long been a fan of Mister Peabody, as well as his boy Sherman," he added in a nod to the animated cartoon from the 1960s.

The Peabody was followed by *The Colbert Report*'s first Emmy Award for Outstanding Writing for a Variety, Music, or Comedy Program, beating out *The Daily Show.*

When the four hundredth episode of *The Colbert Report* aired on May 28, 2008, it was clear that the show and Colbert had reached a critical mass more quickly than *The Daily Show*, and some felt that the show—

Colbert and Jon Stewart served as co-presenters at the 2008 Emmy Awards. *(Courtesy Reuters/Corbis)*

and its host—were already more popular than the man who had given Colbert his start, Jon Stewart.

"I think that in terms of buzz and critical momentum, *The Colbert Report* is hotter this year than *The Daily Show*," said James Poniewozik, the television critic at *Time* magazine. "Colbert has really made his show into something like a movement over the past year or two, not just a show, but a kind of two-way participatory media stunt involving his audience."

Despite the fact that Colbert's presidential aspirations had been dashed in the previous year, some still couldn't let go of the idea that he would seek higher office one day, as himself or as his character. Once Barack Obama won the Democratic nomination in the summer of 2008, the media decided to play around with a few improbable races. One pitted Jon Stewart—not mentioning a vice president—against Barack Obama, and 55 percent of respondents favored Stewart. In a race featuring a Stewart-Colbert ticket, however, 64 percent cast their vote for *The Daily Show* host compared with just 36 percent for Obama.

In August, Bing West, the former assistant secretary of defense under President Reagan, appeared on *The Colbert Report* to promote his new book, *The Strongest Tribe: War, Politics, and the Endgame in Iraq.* In the first five years of the second Iraq war, West spent months on the ground with the troops, making some sixteen journeys to the war-torn country. In the last trip before appearing on Colbert's show, General David Petraeus's security detail gave West a signed photograph of them specifically to give to Colbert, which West presented after his appearance on the show. Written on the photo: "Stephen, come on over." Colbert and the other staffers were intrigued by the possibility and started to investigate what it would take to present the show from Baghdad, Iraq, for the benefit of the troops.

"I talk about the war on the show, so I feel a particular debt to the people over there," he said. "I thought it would be a huge mistake to turn down the invitation and I'd be kicking myself for the rest of my life if I didn't do it."

Although Colbert was all for going, he was nervous about asking his staff. After all, the sheer logistics of doing their job in a war zone seemed insurmountable, though by that point, much of the danger had passed.

When Colbert first broke the news, everyone loved the idea. "We became very excited about putting on a show for those guys, but that actually made it hard to figure out editorially," said Allison Silverman. "We knew that the show was popular over there, but at the same time, I knew there were plenty of troops in the audience who hadn't seen it before. We usually assume that the audience in our studio is pretty much like our audience at home, but Iraq would be very different. The studio audience would be quite different from our audience at home, and we'd have to figure out, does this joke go to the people in the room, or does it go to the people who are watching at home?"

The technical challenges of producing a show from a war zone were going to be tough enough, thought the supervising producer, Tanya Bracco, when she first heard the news. She thought they'd send a crew to Iraq, shoot a few segments in between, and then put the whole thing together back in New York.

But that's when Stephen announced that he wanted to produce live shows directly from Baghdad.

That's when Bracco had second thoughts. "What resources do we have?" she asked. "Is it even possible?"

The technical staff contacted a production unit in Kuwait to help out with the job. "When we told them what we wanted to do, which was to basically replicate our show from back home, he told us it was impossible to do," Colbert said.

Colbert tacked the photo to a wall in his office. "I kept it up there as a reminder, 'You can do this. This *is* possible.' "

With the presidential conventions bearing down—in 2008, the Democrats would be in Denver while the Republicans held court in St. Paul, Minnesota—there was the usual buildup in the fall, to cover the race and the debates, and with the introduction of Sarah Palin as the Republican vice presidential candidate, the satirists had a field day. But unexpectedly, *The Colbert Report* stayed away from both conventions, while *The Daily Show* was there in full force.

The Colbert Report ran a variety of stories about Palin that fall, but Jon Stewart perhaps phrased the overall theme of the election season best: "Everyone likes new and shiny. Joe Biden is an absolutely eccentric character, but that's how powerful Palin's story is: it has cast the first African-American presidential nominee, the oldest [non-incumbent] presidential nominee, and a really wild cork vice-presidential candidate completely out of the picture," he explained. "The press is a bunch of six-year-olds playing soccer where nobody has a position, it's just, 'Where's the ball? Where's the ball? Sarah Palin has the ball!' Because they can only cover one thing."

On October 29, Colbert dedicated "The Word" to his official presidential endorsement. Though since his character is an ultraconservative, he had to couch it in a certain way. "Guys like Scott McClellan and Colin Powell and Chris Buckley are all endorsing Barack Obama and getting attention for it, and I thought, there was no way my character would sit on the sidelines while these conservatives were getting attention for crossing the line and endorsing Barack Obama and being part of an historical moment," he explained. "So we thought that maybe there's a way for me to endorse him, but not support him. [My character] wanted to make sure that no one voted for him, but he wanted credit for having endorsed him."

"Nation, I have no choice but to respond to my fellow prominent conservatives who have the gall to endorse Barack Obama," he began, "which brings me to tonight's Word. I endorse Barack Obama.

"I know this is shocking," he continued, "but it's the only solution to what I see as a crisis, namely that these guys are getting attention and I'm not. The media should be talking about *me*, because my endorsement of Obama just now took real courage, the courage to cross party lines from a party that is a staggering mass of flaming agony to the party that looks like it's got a pretty good shot at winning this thing."

A week later, as they had done twice already in 2000 and 2004, Stewart and Colbert—and correspondents from *The Daily Show*—joined forces on election night to present "Election: Indecision 2008: America's Choice." In addition to the election of the first African-American president, another historic first occurred on the set of *The Daily Show* on the very same night.

The two fake news anchors announced real news for the very first time.

The hour-long show was filled with correspondents reporting stories in front of green screens that made it seem like they were at the various campaign headquarters, but mixed in were factual updates on percentages and reports on states that had declared a clear winner. They were supposed to sign off at 11 P.M., because no one thought the election would be confirmed that night, but then one of the producers saw that CNN was going to call the election for Obama.

So they kept the cameras rolling. Rob Kutner, a *Daily Show* writer, set the scene:

"It's a few minutes after 11. The *Colbert* writers have occupied our writers' lounge and are stinking drunk on Crystal Head Vodka," he said. "We stall it just a little longer. The producer signals to Jon and Stephen at the desk, giving them the thumbs up. Then, Jon made the announcement, for the first time ever, delivering a piece of real news."

"I would just like to say, if I may," Stewart said, his voice catching slightly, "that at 11 o'clock at night, Eastern Standard Time, the president of the United States is Barack Obama. We don't normally do this live. We're a fake news show."

Though Colbert whooped it up during the show when a state was announced for McCain and despondently groaned when one went for Obama, when it was all over, he actually felt a bit uncomfortable. "I've never had this feeling before," he said. "Things actually went well on Election Night. I'm a little stunned. I don't know what to do with my happiness. I'm still afraid someone's going to take it away."

As usual, there was no time for retrospection, because in addition to continuing to crank out *The Colbert Report*, Colbert's first holiday special, *A Colbert Christmas: The Greatest Gift of All!*, was about to debut.

The hour-long show was designed as a Colbert-inspired spoof of the variety show Christmas specials from the 1960s, in which a famous celebrity is shown relaxing at home in front of the Christmas tree, and all of his friends just happen to drop by. In Colbert's case, his "friends" just happened to include John Legend, Willie Nelson, and Elvis Costello, among others. Also, the special marked a first, when all three of Stephen's children—Madeleine, Peter, and John—appeared briefly on the show. As Colbert has done with all of his other activities outside *The Colbert Report*, he designated that all profits from the sale of the DVD and the iTunes album that later came out would go to Feeding America, a nonprofit network that serves as an organization of several hundred food banks all over the country. He also auctioned off the sweater he wore in the special, the "Stephen" and "Colbert" Christmas stockings, and his boots, all to raise money for the charity.

Ironically, *A Colbert Christmas* was originally supposed to be released during the 2007 holiday season, but both Colbert and the *Daily Show* executive producer, David Javerbaum, postponed the project a year because of their heavy schedules, which of course only got more hectic.

The show was a bit of a twist on the old-fashioned holiday shows. "A lot of the scenes in the show followed the music rather than vice versa," Javerbaum explained. "In most cases, the subject of each song was dictated by the access we had to the artists. For example, we needed a song that was going to fit Toby Keith, since the point was to make Toby Keith and everyone else look good."

Oddly enough, politics were totally missing from the show. Colbert and guests focused on celebrating the holiday with cheesy, forced songs that still convey the insincerity that Colbert oozes on *The Colbert Report*, only without the politics, though he does toss a few well-hated books on the roaring Yule log fire. The Colbertesque reason for holing up in the cabin: a much-feared bear is on the prowl right outside, which forces his friends to come to him.

The reviews were mixed. "Mr. Colbert is delightful, a few of the song parodies are clever, but over all, the show is too long and more than a little strained, much like the holiday specials it mocks," said one reviewer. "If you're looking for something slick, look elsewhere," said another. "*A Colbert Christmas* looks as if it was put together in about an hour for just under a hundred dollars, but that's part of the reason it's so funny."

There may actually be a *Colbert Christmas* redux in the future, since Colbert and Javerbaum wrote more songs than they ended up using in the show. "There were a lot of songs that either we didn't finish, or they just didn't fit," said Javerbaum. One song that they really wanted to do was a Metallica spoof called "Enter, Santa," patterned after Metallica's hit "Enter, Sandman." The song would be delivered in Metallica's typical headbanging tradition, but the lyrics would fall more along the lines of "Rudolph the Red-Nosed Reindeer." But Metallica wouldn't commit to doing the show.

. . .

The Colbert naming frenzy continued. However, for the first honoree in 2009, Colbert didn't have to rally his nation. A peregrine falcon in San Jose, California, was named after him; residents of the city settled on the name in an online vote, christening the new male falcon "Esteban Colbert." A "falcon cam" had been set up in 2006 when baby falcons were first spotted on the roof of city hall.

San Jose's mayor, Chuck Reed, a regular viewer of *The Colbert Report*, quipped, "Like the City Hall falcons, the original Colbert has proven that with primitive instincts and sharp talons, anyone can survive in modern society."

Next up was NASA, and this time the naming had Colbert's fingerprints all over it. NASA was conducting an online contest to vote and choose from names for a new module on the International Space Station: Earthrise, Legacy, and Serenity were among them. On March 3, Colbert implored his nation to write in his name on the Web site.

Of course Colbert won—with just over 230,000 votes; the second-closest name was Serenity, with 130,000 votes—but NASA reserved the right to choose the final winner. Sunita Williams, an astronaut, appeared on *The Colbert Report* to announce the results of the contest, which she then announced was Tranquility, named after the Sea of Tranquility, where *Apollo 11* landed on the moon in 1969. In any case, Williams cited a rule similar to the Hungarian government when it refused to name a bridge after Colbert because he wasn't deceased.

Colbert was visibly disappointed, but Williams told him they had reached a compromise, deciding to name a $5 million treadmill after him with the following acronym: Combined Operational Load-Bearing External Resistance Treadmill. "Those will be the words that will be passed down on space-to-ground [communications]: 'It's time for me to jump on COLBERT,'" Williams told him.

Colbert was vindicated, and NASA was thrilled at the Colbert Bump it received. "We received more than a million entries, in large part because social media Web sites and television programs, such as *The Colbert Report*, took an interest," said Bill Gerstenmaier, an associate administrator at NASA.

The naming obsession then took a bizarre twist when a woman with a Pomeranian-Chihuahua puppy named Colbert el Dos entered the dog in an online cutest-dog competition sponsored by All American Pet Brands, with a grand prize of one million dollars. Another competitor cried foul, claiming that any dog with the name of Colbert had an undeserved leg up. Cara McCool announced that if her Cavalier King Charles spaniel named Mozart—aka MoMo—won the contest, she'd donate the money to New Orleans relief organizations. Colbert el Dos had not been invited onto *The Colbert Report*, but the dog's owners posted an announcement about the contest on an online Colbert forum, which bumped up the votes.

In the end, while more than sixty thousand people entered the contest, neither MoMo nor Colbert el Dos won. Instead, a Chihuahua from Denver named Dr. Papidies took the prize; her owner announced that she would set up a trust and donate the entire sum to humane organizations.

Charleston called Colbert back twice that spring. First, the board of trustees at MUSC had voted to name its education center and library in memory of Dr. James W. Colbert, Jr., and Stephen and his family attended the dedication of the building on April 10. "In many ways, Dr. Colbert helped the Medical University become the diverse, first-rate academic medical center it is now," the MUSC president, Ray Greenberg, said at the ceremony. "He took what was a little understood concept on our campus at the time—interdisciplinary health care—and turned it into a model that thoroughly permeates our culture today. I can't think of a more fitting tribute than to have his name on our education center and library."

Despite his success, the fact was that his father was still gone. His brother Ed perhaps put it best: "The only thing I'd say at the end is here we are, it's been thirty-five years since he died, and I still think of him all the time," he said. "It still hurts."

In the spring of 2009, *The Colbert Report* was flying high. Ratings were up, with each show averaging a million and a half viewers, an increase of 10 percent over the previous year, and in terms of demographics, more men between the ages of eighteen and thirty-four watched *The Colbert Report* than Letterman, Leno, and the rest of the late-night shows.

Colbert could be fully excused for resting on his laurels, for coasting, for continuing to take the same path, and his loyal fans would still show up in droves each night. After all, between the public appearances, the grueling schedule, and trying to have a family life, he more than deserved it.

But then he decided to up the ante and go ahead with his plan to shoot a full week of shows from Iraq. The week was dubbed "Operation Iraqi Stephen: Going Commando," and he and his staff had been planning the project since Bing West gave him that photo of the marines less than a year earlier.

"There's a thesis statement there, which is something for my character to hang on to," said Colbert. "My character thinks the war is over because he doesn't hear about it anymore. He's like a child. A ball rolls behind the couch and he thinks it's gone forever."

"My character thinks the war is over because he doesn't hear about it anymore. He's like a child. A ball rolls behind the couch and he thinks it's gone forever."

"Operation Iraqi Stephen" was scheduled to air the week of June 8. The crew taped and edited a few segments stateside that were scheduled to run between the segments that were shot in Iraq.

"Each of the shows had a weighty chunk that was pre-recorded because we couldn't bring many people over to Iraq," Allison Silverman explained. "We could only bring about a third of our staff over, and there was just no way to produce a lot of material there, and we have a tough enough time getting the show up at a reasonable hour every day with a full staff."

So they had to work in tandem with the staff back in New York; to account for the time difference, the writers in New York had to work the night shift, coming into the office at three in the morning before leaving around noon.

First, Colbert attended basic training at Fort Jackson, South Carolina. Then he flew with the Thunderbirds, an elite air force acrobatic-demonstration team, which made a lasting impression on him.

"After that, I'll never be afraid to fly again," he said. "Nothing will ever be as terrifying as that. We flew for about forty-five minutes, and when I got off the plane I had to speak to about two hundred people. They gave me a plaque, but I was so out of it, I had to lie on the ground for a while. I went into the men's room to splash water on my face and just collapsed. The airmen were worried. Instead of saying, 'Hey, thanks for coming!' when I left, they said, 'Hey, take care.' "

"After that, I'll never be afraid to fly again. Nothing will ever be as terrifying as that."

Once they got to Iraq, they set up shop at Camp Victory. The first thing he had to adjust to was having a security detail attend to him 24-7. A female army sergeant by the name of Mouse made sure of that.

"She was small, freckly, Irish-looking, maybe five foot one, but really tough," he recalled. "When she walked in, people got to their feet. She assigned me my personal security so there was another sergeant with me at all times. But I was so busy running all over the place that I shook my guard twice. He'd sit there with a newspaper, but suddenly look up and couldn't find me.

"Finally, Mouse came up to me and said, 'Mr. Colbert, this is Ritzy. He's your *guard*. You are not to go anywhere without him, sir.' "

"Am I in trouble?" Colbert asked.

"Yes, sir, you kinda are," Mouse replied, and from that point on,

Ritzy—whose real name was Tony and who was from South Carolina—never let Colbert out of his sight.

"I couldn't go anywhere without him from then on, even the bathroom. I'd say, 'Okay, Tony, let's go to the pisser,' and off we'd go."

Though there were a number of different places they could have set up the studio, the technical staff chose the Al-Faw Palace, one of Saddam Hussein's former residences. "We scouted all the possible locations, but the Al-Faw Palace atrium was our first choice," said the coexecutive producer, Meredith Bennett. "It's the most iconic image of the war, and any time there is a big announcement or dignitary in town they hold conferences in the atrium." More important than the sheer opulence of the palace was the fact that the military had already set up a broadcast studio in Al-Faw.

Another thing Colbert and his staff had to adjust to was the fact that the army had to review every script before taping began. Though they didn't need to approve it, they just wanted to see it, and when they saw the script for "Formidable Opponent" the second night—based on the Don't Ask, Don't Tell policy regarding gays in the military—the top brass tried to talk Colbert and the producers out of doing it.

"They said they couldn't guarantee that we wouldn't be shut down," he said. "'The Word' is pretty hard to do on a consistent basis, but so is "Formidable Opponent," and in Iraq I really wanted to do one on Don't Ask Don't Tell. One of the rules I make for myself as well as the writers who work on 'Formidable Opponent' is that you must come up with a reasonable argument on both sides. A reasonable person must be able to say the things that come out of these characters' mouths."

Probably the most memorable part of the entire week was when Stephen got his head shaved, primarily because they wanted to make it look like General Ray Odierno was receiving orders directly from President Obama. This provided another technical challenge, because while Odierno was offering up his spiel, they had to pipe in a live feed from the White House, while also working in time for reaction from the troops.

While wielding an electric razor, Odierno filed the first volley. "Stephen, if you want to do this right, you're going to have to get your hair cut," he said.

"But without my hair, what would I blow dry?" Colbert shot back.

"Frankly, sir, it's going to take more than a four-star general to get me to cut my hair."

After a bit of back and forth, President Obama appeared on the rear projection screen and ordered the general to give Colbert the regulation buzz cut in front of five hundred cheering and stomping soldiers.

The shows from Iraq also featured taped messages from a number of dignitaries, including John McCain, and vice president Joe Biden. Former President George Bush—number 41—even had a cameo as he addressed the troops. "Your achievements in Iraq have earned you a special place in American history," he said. "You are men and women of great courage and endurance, and that's gonna come in handy, because I've sat through Stephen's stuff before."

"You are men and women of great courage and endurance, and that's gonna come in handy, because I've sat through Stephen's stuff before."

At the same time, just as Stephen honored the countless Christmas variety shows that came before him with *A Colbert Christmas*, he also wanted to convey his respects to the entertainers of years past who had traveled overseas to put on shows for the troops. The USO and other organizations had been sending actors, singers, and comedians to entertain soldiers since World War II.

"We decided to do a number of jokes that were a kind of homage to Bob Hope," said Silverman. "They were jokes that were less coming from the view of a right-wing blowhard and more as from a Bob Hope kind of character, almost cowardly." She cited the segments taped at Fort Jackson as falling into that category, where Stephen tried performing—and failed at—tasks that are second nature to the military. They especially wanted to do this since the USO was instrumental in helping *The Colbert Report* coordinate the shoot, just as it had been when Hope entertained the troops overseas during World War II.

The technical challenges continued. Even though a group of technical staff and producers had visited Iraq and the Green Zone in April on a scouting trip to make sure they knew what kind of space they were working with, of course they discovered new problems once they got rolling.

For one, the Al-Faw Palace was a gigantic, cavernous, circular room mostly constructed of marble. Silverman was amazed to find that even the air-conditioner vents were made from marble, and she began to think that the technical staff in charge of handling audio would have a hard time fine-tuning the sound in such a large space primarily filled with hard surfaces.

"The pillars alone were about 150-feet high, the ceiling was plenty tall and all marble," she said. "So we draped various materials everywhere so that the sound would stay in one place and not bounce all over, but it was sometimes difficult."

"One of the biggest challenges we faced was that we were constrained in the amount of equipment we could transport to Baghdad because we were relying on military transport," said the supervising producer, Tanya Bracco. "When we realized how much equipment we would actually need to ship, we had to be extremely resourceful and judicious in deciding just what to bring."

Even with a pared-down list, the amount of stuff they had to bring was substantial: Two military cargo planes—a C130 and a C17—made three trips to transport not only thirteen pallets of equipment (sets, lighting, video editing equipment, office desks and computers) but also thirty helmeted and flak-jacketed crew members. During the week, two hundred troop members worked overtime to build the set, help set up the equipment, and provide general and specialized assistance to the staff, as well as create housing for thirty extra people.

The typical infrastructure of the office environment also presented problems. For instance, the computers that the writers used couldn't be networked, so they had to share information in a somewhat old-fashioned way, by trading scripts and ideas back and forth on USB memory sticks. Plus, there was only one printer.

Despite the difficulties, there was never any question that they'd proceed as planned. "We thought it would be patronizing not to do everything we normally do content-wise," said Colbert. Though he did tell his staff to let him know when they couldn't solve a particular problem, they always told him they'd come up with a way to handle it. And they did.

"After all, there really is only one way to write the show, and that is to write the show," he said. "Whether it was 'Formidable Opponent' or 'Better Know a District'—or, in this case, it turned out to be 'Better Know a Coalition Partner,' or 'Better Know a Cradle of Civilization'—every night we wanted to do something that was signature to the show, so it felt like we were really doing our home show over there."

The only segment that created a real problem was "Formidable Opponent," which back in the New York studio already had the reputation of being one of the most technically challenging pieces on the show, but they did it without a hitch. "Technical director Jon Pretnar, who has a big mustache, was operating the board, and my joke is that he used both hands and his mustache to push the buttons," said Colbert.

The Sunday after he returned from Baghdad, Colbert first caught up on his sleep—he rarely got a chance to close his eyes during the week he spent in Iraq—and then he and Evie sat down at their Montclair home and watched the shows one right after the other. "I wish we had more time, because there were parts of interviews we had to cut, but I was perfectly happy," he said.

For Colbert, the most poignant part of the week was after the last show had ended and he asked his staff to stand with him onstage. "I thanked the audience and tried to explain what my staff had done, and that no one would know how difficult it had been because they pulled it off flawlessly," he said. The troops then applauded for the staff while they, in turn, with Colbert, clapped for the audience. "That was the sweetest moment of the trip, to see how genuine their gratitude was for how hard my staff worked, and how grateful I was to the soldiers for having invited us and for what they were doing for our country," he continued.

To coincide with the week in Iraq, Colbert had another trick up his sleeve in order to get the word out. He signed on as the very first guest editor of *Newsweek* magazine, for the June 15 issue.

When the editor, Jon Meacham, first floated the idea by Colbert in the spring, he didn't necessarily intend to tie it in with the Iraq shows. "When Colbert and I first spoke about his guest-editing, he initially doubted he would have the time to do it," said Meacham. "As he thought about it, however, he found the idea intriguing because of the trip to Iraq he was planning, and he agreed to do it."

As part of his responsibilities, Colbert had input into the cover design and also suggested departments and sections in the magazine that he wanted to write. He wrote the letter from the editor as well as the letters *to* the editor, which consisted of all of the letters he'd supposedly written to the magazine over the years that they never ran, as well as several other sections.

He handled the assignment in his typical style. In his editorial, he wrote, "There are still 135,000 troops in Iraq, which I don't understand because we've already won the war," he quipped. "And we've won it so many times. We should win something for the number of times we've won it. We eliminated the weapons of mass destruction by having them not exist. We took out Saddam Hussein, or a really convincing and committed Saddam Hussein double. And by August of next year we'll withdraw every single one of our troops, leaving behind only memories and 50,000 troops."

Unfortunately, despite Colbert's dual efforts, between the week of shows in Iraq and the *Newsweek* issue, interest in the war had actually declined. Each show from Iraq was viewed by an average of 1.4 million people, which was a decrease from his previous week's shows. However, the median age of viewers actually rose during the Iraq week, up to forty years old; a year earlier, the median age was just under thirty-four years of age.

A couple of months later, Colbert suffered another blow when his long-time executive producer, Allison Silverman, decided to leave the show after four years. She made the announcement during the summer hiatus, citing not only the need to move on but also the desire not to spend every waking moment working, since she had recently married.

Colbert was understandably upset—Silverman had been with him since the show launched four years earlier. "It has been a great joy to work with Allison and watch her grow from a devastatingly funny writer to a devastatingly funny leader," he said. "I am happy for my dear friend, but I will miss her. And this statement would be much funnier if she would just stay and help me write it."

"Not many people get to work on a kind-hearted show with a brilliant staff and a host who thinks *Watership Down* is nonfiction."

Silverman continued the mutual love fest: "I will always treasure my time at *The Colbert Report*," she said. "Not many people get to work on a kind-hearted show with a brilliant staff and a host who thinks *Watership Down* is nonfiction. For me, the only thing that could top working with Stephen Colbert would be having Stephen Colbert as a lifelong friend, and I am very excited to start that project."

CHAPTER 14

In January 2010, Colbert won his first Grammy for Best Comedy Album for the soundtrack to *A Colbert Christmas: The Greatest Gift of All!* He was nominated for a Grammy once before, for Best Spoken Word Album back in 2008.

This time, however, he hosted the show as well and involved his daughter, Madeleine, in his opening speech by asking if she thought he was finally cool. When the camera showed her shaking her head, he said, "Stay away from Katy Perry."

Later on, when he walked onstage to accept his award, he quipped, "It is a Christmas album, so obviously I should thank Jesus Christ for having such a great birthday."

This time, when he asked Madeleine, "Am I cool now?" she nodded her head.

When the Winter Olympics began in 2010, Colbert jumped in pretty much in the same way he did when he brought his show to Iraq: with both feet.

"My character is a patriot, and he believes that the Olympics are war. . . . It's a way to prove who's got the best country, only nobody gets hurt." he said. "We wanted to get everyone focused on the Games. And saber rattle—in the nicest possible way, of course."

The worldwide financial crisis that had hit in the fall of 2008 was having

"My character is a patriot, and he believes that the Olympics are war. It's a way to prove who's got the best country, only nobody gets hurt."

repercussions on the corporate sponsorship of some Olympic sports teams. Most notably, the U.S. speed-skating team lost its primary sponsor when the Dutch bank DSB went bankrupt in October 2009 after depositors made a run on the bank. The team had to scramble to fill a budget gap of more than $300,000, and athletes and coaches were frantically pondering how to deal with the shortfall when Colbert got wind of it.

It was Colbert who actually came up with the idea of having the Colbert Nation sponsor the team, and he called Bob Crowley, the executive director of United States Speedskating, on October 29 to make him a deal: Colbert would talk about speed skating on the show on a regular basis leading up to the games and ask viewers to donate money to go toward the shortfall, and in exchange members of the team would wear uniforms emblazoned with the Colbert Nation logo. "I don't know if he blinked," Colbert later said. "It was long distance."

"We were stunned," said Crowley. "We were looking for a knight in shining armor."

Though Colbert's philanthropic streak was definitely aroused by the idea of sponsoring the team, he also knew that the concept would provide him with hours of material for *The Colbert Report*. "They look like members of Blue Man Group," he said. "But there's nothing comedic about speed skating; they're incredible athletes."

Colbert mentioned the speed skaters' plight on his show on November 2—joking that DSB stood for "Deposit Savings in Bong"—and hosted both Crowley and the gold-medalist speed skater Dan Jansen on the show. He pitched his nation the same way he pitched Crowley, and donations started to pour in. In just over the first week, $200,000 rolled in, with the rest raised in the next few weeks. By the time it was over, almost ten thousand members of the Colbert Nation had donated an average of $30 each.

"I'm so surprised that so many people have offered to help out," said the three-time Olympic speed skater Apolo Anton Ohno. "I think it's great exposure for the sport." To sweeten the pot, Colbert was the cover boy on the December 21 issue of *Sports Illustrated* magazine, clad in spandex—the official U.S. speed-skating uniform emblazoned with the Colbert Nation logo—and skates.

Other teams and sponsorship consultants definitely noticed. "When Colbert did this, all of us in the business went, 'Why didn't we think of that?'" said Rob Prazmark, an Olympic marketing consultant.

There was only one detractor on the team: the 2006 U.S. gold medalist Shani Davis didn't care for Colbert the character's tendency to make fun of Canadians. "He's a jerk," he said.

True, Colbert has often referred to Canadians in less than complimentary terms on his show: "syrup-suckers" and "iceholes," for example. But he made amends once the Olympics got underway. "I've forgiven Canada," he said. "I'm there to celebrate Canada at this point."

Then, to make up with Davis, he scheduled a speed-skating race against him for the last spot on the team that turned into a skit on *The Colbert Report*; Stephen took almost fourteen minutes to make two laps, while Davis did it in thirty-five seconds. When it was announced that Davis would take the slot, the coaches quickly appeased Colbert by making him official assistant sports psychologist of the team, and he went to Vancouver after all.

As if there was ever any doubt that Comedy Central wouldn't extend Colbert's contract to continue doing *The Colbert Report* for the foreseeable future, in May the cable channel made it official and committed to continue airing the show through the end of 2012.

"I'm tired all the time," he admitted. Indeed, there were many pivotal events in the last two years.

Election night 2008. *A Colbert Christmas*. Doing a week's worth of

Colbert appeared with Jon Stewart on the National Mall in Washington at the Rally to Restore Sanity and/or Fear on October 30, 2010. *(Courtesy Reuters/Corbis)*

shows from Iraq. The writers strike. The week of shows from Philadelphia during the presidential primary. Running for president. Publishing a number-one bestseller.

And then doing all this in addition to putting out 162 shows a year, with the help of a staff of close to one hundred. How does he do it all and still manage to maintain the normal family life that he says is so important to him? And how long can he feasibly continue at this breakneck pace?

"The short answer is, I don't know," he said. "Maybe the true answer is, as long as it's fun. And as long as I can keep up the energy to do it. I can't imagine not wanting to do this, and yet, it's a very difficult and complicated thing that we do, keeping it fresh. When we were first planning *The Colbert Report*, Jon asked me, 'What interests you? Make it about what interests you, and you won't get tired of it.' So I'll do the show until I don't enjoy it anymore," he said.

"I always got the sense from the way he was off-camera that show business is not the end-all and be-all for him," said John Obrien, who interned on *The Daily Show* in 2002. "One day we might see him in a more serious role. I could see him leaving the spotlight and writing a TV series and enjoying being behind the scenes. On *The Daily Show*, he considered himself to be more of a writer than a correspondent/performer. He was proud of the fact that he was lead writer, and he treated all the writers equally."

"I would have to say that I'm still unambitious, simply because I get to do anything I want on *The Report.*"

Despite his prodigious output, some have actually accused him of being unmotivated because he hasn't yet made a movie based on his character. Surprisingly, he admits it. "I would have to say that I'm still unambitious, simply because I get to do anything I want on *The Report*," he said. "It takes everything I've got to do it, so I don't have the luxury of thinking about the next thing, nor do I have any desire, because I like it so much. When I sit down in that chair and my stage manager shakes my hand and asks, 'Are you ready to do this?' I say, 'Yeah!' "

And he still loves loves loves Charleston, as does the rest of his family. His brother Ed referred to the city as "a big hot cluster of Colberts."

"They call it a hot zone," Stephen added. "It should be isolated, really. Once I cross the Ben Sawyer Bridge [into Sullivan's Island, where Colbert has a house], I try not to cross back over. I try not to drive. I try not to wear long pants. I try to go swimming, no matter what time of year it is. We spend as much time in Charleston as we can, so our children will know how to crab, how to open an oyster, and what low tide smells like."

He said that this visceral appreciation of everything Charleston was one thing that had attracted him to Evie, and vice versa. "Those were the things that were inexplicable to the people my wife and I dated before we met each other," he said. "They were poetic expressions we could give, merely by appreciating each other's love of the Lowcountry.

"When I was a kid, there was a Japanese monster TV show called Ultraman," he continued. "Ultraman could do anything, fighting monsters in his big silvery suit, but he could only fight so long before he had to return to his solar system to be recharged by the light of his home sun. That's what Charleston is like for me—I've got to go home every so often to be recharged by my home sun."

He also considers himself to be unusual among his peers in the entertainment world, and not just because he goes to Mass every week, teaches Sunday school, and is happily married.

"I desire to have what I would consider a normal life, to have a wife and kids, and live in a suburban house, and wear khaki pants, and pick them up from the dry cleaner," he said. "I don't see anything wrong with that. I think a lot of people who perform have a fear of being ordinary. But they confuse ordinary with common."

And for someone in the public eye with so many demands on his time that he already has trouble fulfilling, he says that his family is very understanding.

When he was working on *I Am America (And So Can You!)*, he hadn't taken a vacation with his family for over six months. He told Evie and the kids that it was only temporary, and when he handed in the book things would return to normal. "My wife has been very patient, and so have the kids, and I think they're proud of the success of the show, but that only lasts so long because I miss them terribly," he said. "Just spending two [vacation] weeks with them was incredibly medicinal, incredibly important. And since we've come back, I've come home for dinner and put them to bed, and that's the way I want it to be."

To help keep things in perspective, Colbert often calls upon the lesson of the Sermon on the Mount: "Being fearless," he said. "Not living in fear is a great gift, because certainly these days we do it so much. And do you know what I like about comedy? You can't laugh and be afraid at the same time—of anything. If you're laughing, I defy you to be afraid. That's not a philosophical statement, it's a physiological statement because when you laugh, you're not afraid. Sometimes you laugh *because* you're afraid, but when you laugh the fear goes away. That's why I don't think I could ever stop what I'm doing, because I laugh all day long. If I stopped, I'd just cry all day long.

"It's a great life. I couldn't ask for more. I'm so very lucky."

ACKNOWLEDGMENTS

Is there anyone but Superagent, aka Scott Mendel, who should go first? Of course not.

Next up are Peter Joseph at St. Martin's, as well as Katy Hershberger, Loren Jaggers, Tom Dunne, Sally Richardson, and Matthew Shear.

Thanks to Charles Best, Lewis Black, Sue Chanson, Mandy Ganis, Charna Halpern, Ben Hutto, Angela Katsos Kiehling, Amos Lee, Joe Legaz, Dr. Maxwell Mowry, Jon Obrien, Marj Wentworth, Bob Wiltfong, and Seth Zimmerman.

And for valued assistance in research matters, thanks be to Mike Tuttle, Brink Norton at Porter-Gaud, the archivist Brooke Fox at MUSC, and Libby Wallace Wilder at the *Post & Courier.*

Finally, for coming up with the first stellar title, thanks to my son, Brendan Rogak.

NOTES

Introduction

"My name is . . . let you figure it out": Knox College commencement address, June 3, 2006

"I can never . . . what he is": South Carolina ETV, May 2008

"His humor . . . Trickled Down": *Rolling Stone*, November 16, 2006

"What did . . . what happens": MUSC interview with Colbert family, July 3, 2009

"She's bright . . . *so* Irish": *Faces of America*, p. 194

"I'm not entirely . . . I believe": *Newsweek*, February 13, 2006

"I don't have to pretend . . . on camera": *New York Times*, August 27, 2004

"I'm not someone . . . I love hypocrisy": *Washington Post*, October 10, 2005

"Generally speaking . . . I'm a liberal": *Satiristas*, p. 30

"I like talking . . . have no rights": *New York Times*, September 24, 2010

"Stephen is . . . brilliant": *And Here's the Kicker*, p. 238

"Isn't that . . . Bayreuth?": MUSC interview with Colbert family, July 3, 2009

"His basic decency can't be hidden": *Rolling Stone*, November 16, 2006

"I have a boring . . . decision": *60 Minutes*, April 30, 2006

"I have a wife . . . oddly normative": *New York Times*, September 25, 2005

"I live . . . groups that often": *NPR Talk of the Nation*, March 1, 2004

"I love . . . of this earth": *Time Out New York*, June 9–15, 2005

"'They immediately ask . . . came before God?'": *New Yorker* festival, October 5, 2008

"Stephen . . . around the kitchen": *Rolling Stone*, November 16, 2006

"His own family . . . grounded": *Vanity Fair*, October 2007

"Colbert is more than . . . the story": *Gold Coast Bulletin*, January 2, 2008

"I like preserving . . . any good": *Vanity Fair*, October 2007

"There couldn't be . . . working for him": *Newsweek*, February 13, 2006

"He always . . . cult": *Charleston Magazine*, May 2006

"I drive myself . . . normal again": *Vanity Fair*, October 2007

One

"My three sisters . . . me": *San Francisco Chronicle* podcast, January 16, 2006

"He had lots . . . tricks with him": South Carolina ETV, May 4, 2008

"I was very loved . . . so much": *New York Times*, September 25, 2005

"That way . . . seconds first": South Carolina ETV, May 7, 2008

"Being the youngest . . . I need attention": *Post & Courier*, March 12, 1996

"I grew up . . . king": *New York Times*, August 27, 2004

"And to this day . . . *listen* to him": *Newsweek*, February 13, 2006

"I'm definitely . . . my family": *Washington Post*, October 10, 2005

"I think my brothers . . . over the years": *Post & Courier*, May 15, 2005

"He used to do . . . comes to humor": *San Francisco Chronicle* podcast, January 16, 2006

"The Ladies of Love to . . . educated by them": *Faces of America*, p. 209

"He evidently . . . dicey characters": *Faces of America*, p. 195

"A lease . . . business success": *WPA Guide to New York City*, 1939

"When . . . Jewish": MUSC interview with Colbert family, July 3, 2009

"I brought . . . stuck with me": Ibid.

"I'd ask . . . look at me?": Ibid.

"He was always . . . so bookish": Ibid.

"There wasn't . . . type of people": Ibid.

"He really didn't . . . at the time": Ibid.

"I wish . . . pickled at the reception": Letter of August 6, 1944, Screamingeagles.com

"It was just a terrible . . . blocked the view": MUSC interview with Colbert family, July 3, 2009
"I'm just . . . disease": Ibid.
"He said . . . joined the army": Ibid.
"There's no point . . . tell him": Ibid.
"They made me . . . what to do?": Ibid.
"There was . . . because of the war": Ibid.
"We had to go . . . that's Paul!": Ibid
"one, two, three": Ibid.
"After that . . . by name": Ibid.
"It was just like . . . roll call": Ibid.
"In our house . . . icon": *Rolling Stone*, November 16, 2006
"My freshman year . . . sort of thing": MUSC interview with Colbert family, July 3, 2009
"The thing that I loved . . . school thing": Ibid.
"I'm just . . . dignity at all times": Ibid.
"As a young girl . . . educated woman.'" *Post & Courier*, February 6, 2010
"It is the exact opposite . . . Americans": MUSC interview with Colbert family, July 3, 2009
"He was really . . . money": Ibid.
"They wanted to hire . . . bolster the company": Ibid.
"He came home . . . plastic white balls": Ibid.
"They . . . hire him": Ibid.
"I specifically . . . want to be that": Ibid.
"Oh . . . Old Fashioned": Ibid.
"Mass . . . breathing out": Funeral eulogy, September 16, 1974
"door from the outside": MUSC interview with Colbert family, July 3, 2009

Two

"It's hard . . . with that many kids": South Carolina ETV, May 4, 2008
"I heard . . . my father let it go": *Charleston Magazine*, May 2006
"He adored . . . especially tight": Ibid.

"My father's . . . French Christian philosophy": South Carolina ETV, May 7, 2008

"Singing . . . highly encouraged": *Parade Magazine*, September 23, 2007

"and he'd be just fine": Harvard University Institute of Politics talk, December 1, 2006

"My father's words . . . about bears": *San Francisco Chronicle* podcast, January 16, 2006

"We all wanted . . . adventure": MUSC interview with Colbert family, July 3, 2009

"He told us . . . blow up": Ibid.

"The Medical College . . . suggested to us": Letter from William M. McCord, M.D., July 30, 1968

"They gave . . . turn it down?": MUSC interview with Colbert family, July 3, 2009

"The hospital . . . nuts-and-bolts sense": *The Catalyst*, April 3, 2009

"They sent me . . . so Southern": MUSC interview with Colbert family, July 3, 2009

"My mother said . . . we kept going": *Faces of America*, p. 207

"Welcome to the South": MUSC interview with Colbert family, July 3, 2009

"He believed . . . faculty": MUSC archives

"It was perfectly . . . Yankees got down here": MUSC interview with Colbert family, July 3, 2009

"I remember . . . old buildings": Ibid.

"James Island . . . tomato sheds": *Faces of America*, P. 193

"It was like a time warp": Ibid.

"But they didn't . . . going to Hell.' " MUSC interview with Colbert family, July 3, 2009

"I remember . . . strange people": Ibid.

"And that was filled . . . a lot hotter.' " Ibid.

"Oh . . . this is my boy": Ibid.

"He always tried . . . losing their heads": MUSC archives

"He had this vision . . . persistence": MUSC archives

"Dad . . . going places": MUSC interview with Colbert family, July 3, 2009

"We talked . . . supporting the strikers": *The Colbert Report*, January 22, 2008

"He told me . . . loved it": MUSC interview with Colbert family, July 3, 2009
"By contrast . . . pin drop": Ibid.
"We worked . . . very unusual": *The Colbert Report*, January 22, 2008
"At a very young age . . . seem smart": *60 Minutes*, April 30, 2006
"Do what . . . offend anybody": *Rolling Stone*, November 16, 2006
"He was the first . . . Herman Munster's": *Meet the Press*, October 21, 2007
"Everybody . . . punch line": *Larry King Live*, October 14, 2007
"He was so liberal . . . Nixon!": *New York Magazine*, October 16, 2006
"Dad . . . moved to Charleston": MUSC interview with Colbert family, July 3, 2009
"We'd put the boat . . . never see him again": Ibid.
"Jim and Stephen . . . rough day": Ibid.
"Once . . . shark-infested waters": Ibid.
"He was also . . . waves": Ibid.
"They hoped . . . pay the rent": *IGN.com*, August 11, 2003
"Even though . . . legitimate adventure": *O, The Oprah Magazine*, October 2005

Three

"I heard the jet . . . explosion": *Evening Post*, September 12, 1974
"I thought . . . saw flames": Ibid.
"I saw a tree . . . we hit": *Evening Post*, September 14, 1974
"I felt . . . running through the woods": *Evening Post*, September 12, 1974
"Everything was on fire": *News & Courier*, September 12, 1974
"As I unbuckled . . . get the people out": *Charlotte Observer*, September 12, 1974
"As we were going . . . people that were hurt": *Charlotte Observer*, September 12, 1974
"There were tremendous . . . silenced": Ibid.
"Now . . . find the airport": NTSB aircraft accident report, May 23, 1975
"Rescue . . . equipment arrived": Ibid.
"My first . . . terrible": *Charleston Evening Post*, September 11, 1987
"You need . . . accident": *Post & Courier*, February 6, 2010
"My brother . . . people and food": *Faces of America*, p. 193

"Purchased . . . survivors": *News & Courier*, September 12, 1974
"We hit . . . Come on!" *Post & Courier*, February 6, 2010
"It affected . . . plane": *Post & Courier*, September 11, 2009
"It was really . . . community": *Vanity Fair*, October 2007
"We concentrate . . . had with his family": MUSC interview with Colbert family July 3, 2009
"Unlike . . . positive and creative": eulogy
"They were true . . . arrived": Ibid.
"There is nobility . . . education and growth": Ibid.
"trapped in amber": *Post & Courier*, May 16, 2009
"Experience . . . rare": NTSB aircraft accident report May 23, 1975
"I must have . . . altimeters": *News Courier*, December 6, 1975
"It is noteworthy . . . professional conduct": NTSB aircraft accident report, May 23, 1975
"Probable cause . . . prescribed procedures": Ibid.

Four

"I went . . . book a day": *Charlie Rose*, December 8, 2006
"I don't think . . . ten and eighteen": Ibid.
"I learned . . . nothing seemed threatening to me": Ibid.
"I escaped . . . grief in books": *Post & Courier*, April 29, 2006
"I was detached . . . children around me": *60 Minutes*, April 30, 2006
"This is what . . . else did I know?": *Larry King Live*, October 14, 2007
"The shades . . . very quiet": *Parade Magazine*, September 23, 2007
"Because . . . impression on me": *Faces of America*, p. 194
"It was a constant . . . home with her": *Parade Magazine*, September 23, 2007
"I don't see . . . faith": *Charleston Evening Post*, September 11, 1987
"I felt . . . finish raising": MUSC interview with Colbert family, July 3, 2009
"As you can imagine . . . comfort": Letter to Dr. William H. Patterson, November 7, 1974
"MUSC survived": MUSC archives
"I wasn't from downtown . . . kids": *Post & Courier*, April 29, 2006
"I was beaten . . . regular basis": *Parade Magazine*, September 23, 2007

"When I was . . . wall": Gates Foundation interview, April 21, 2009
"One day . . . talking about": *GameSpy.com*, August 17, 2004
"It was . . . books I was reading": Ibid.
"I put . . . my schoolwork": *University Wire*, March 6, 2008
"It's an opportunity . . . teenagers?": *GameSpy.com*, August 17, 2004
"We were all . . . outcast we were": Ibid.
"We'd do huge . . . mother and father": Ibid.
"She was . . . sex your character was": Ibid.
"Who'd . . . real at times": Ibid.
"We started . . . felt about each other": Ibid.
"Aragorn . . . peacemaker": *Parade Magazine*, September 23, 2007
"I used . . . all over again": Ibid.
"His *Dungeons & Dragons* cult": *Vanity Fair*, October 2007
"The thing . . . room": Ibid.
"I was . . . comedy album": *Satiristas*, p. 28
"I read . . . *Lazlo Letters*": Ibid.
"I loved . . . emotional ignorance": Ibid.
"Most of it . . . humor at the time": *Onion AV Club*, January 25, 2006
"The beginning . . . parties": *Parade Magazine*, September 23, 2007
"Almost . . . car kind of way": *IGN.com*, August 11, 2003
"I thought I'd like . . . appealing": *Vanity Fair*, October 2007
"He checked . . . aspirin": *Post & Courier*, November 8, 1998
"There was no . . . pedophile": Ibid.
"I'd put . . . more than once": MUSC interview with Colbert family, July 3, 2009
"I barely . . . homework": *San Francisco Chronicle* podcast, January 16, 2006
"It was . . . tough on her": *Larry King Live*, October 14, 2007
"As Manuel . . . intermission": *Evening Post*, May 25, 1982
"They were very encouraging . . . anything": *Charleston Magazine*, May 2006

Five

"It was . . . rhetoric and grammar": *Onion AV Club*, January 25, 2006
"an inorganic rock of ultraconservatism": *New York Times*, August 27, 2004

"The school . . . love-in": *San Francisco Chronicle* podcast, January 16, 2006
"[The professors] . . . better students": *Onion AV Club*, January 25, 2006
"My dad . . . your answer": *San Francisco Chronicle* podcast, January 16, 2006
"He was very different . . . Hampton-Sydney": *IGN.com*, August 11, 2003
"I thought . . . getting away with it": Ibid.
"I weighed . . . depressed": *San Francisco Chronicle* podcast, January 16, 2006
"The minute . . . believe": *Parade Magazine*, September 23, 2007
"I went out . . . Love, Stephen": Talk for Charleston Stage, December 23, 2007
"When I walked . . . Colbear": *Charlie Rose*, December 8, 2006
"I came . . . remarkable": *Glenview Announcements*, October 13, 2005
"And I was calling . . . couch": *Vanity Fair*, October 2007
"It was like living . . . fit that at all": *IGN.com*, August 11, 2003
"The point . . . went through that": Ibid.
"She insisted . . . fuse back then": *San Francisco Chronicle* podcast, January 16, 2006
"I was constantly . . . insufferable": *Vanity Fair*, October 2007
"I was a real . . . grief with you": *Chicago Sun-Times*, October 18, 2006
"He was masculine . . . onstage": Ibid.
"It's like . . . hummus": Ibid.
"I can't imagine . . . fraternity boy": Ibid.
"I like . . . betrays him": *IGN.com*, August 11, 2003.
"I had no . . . bed at night how much I wanted to do it": *Chicago Sun-Times*, October 18, 2006
"I went . . .": *Onion AV Club*, January 25, 2006
"What Stephen . . . extreme situations": *Chicago Sun-Times*, October 18, 2006
"Del . . . new-moon celebrations": *New Yorker*, July 25, 2005
"Instead . . . scrawled on it": Knox College commencement address, June 3, 2006
"Let me . . . humbling experience": Ibid.
"To this day . . . college": Ibid.
"It's food": *Charleston Magazine*, May 2006
"horrible . . . mattresses": *Chicago Sun-Times*, October 18, 2006
"I wanted . . . make a living at": *Parade Magazine*, September 23, 2007
"Improve Olympic . . . proud of ourselves": *Onion AV Club*, January 25, 2006
"A typical . . . young people": *NPR All Things Considered*, June 3, 2008

"The notion . . . actor by Paul": Ibid.
"a group of performers . . . punch lines": *And Here's the Kicker*, p. 234
"In my mind . . . pretentious person": *Chicago Sun-Times*, October 18, 2006
"He showed up . . . attitude": *Vanity Fair*, October 2007
"I thought . . . cold": *Chicago Sun-Times*, April 27, 2003
"I thought . . . dolt": Ibid.
"I was very actorly . . . stupider behavior": *Second City Unscripted*, p. 200
"Stephen approaches . . . jump in": Ibid.
"In the improv . . . watching you die": *Elle*, March 20, 2009
"All of a sudden . . . about it": *Second City Unscripted*, p. 200–01
"He got . . . broke onstage": *Chicago Sun-Times*, April 27, 2003
"I was so mad . . . rage": *Second City Unscripted*, p. 201
"But something . . . high horse": *Parade Magazine*, September 23, 2007
"As soon . . . sillier": *Vanity Fair*, October 2007
"And then . . . each other": *Chicago Sun-Times*, April 27, 2003
"God . . . inseparable": Ibid.
"They . . . trio": Ibid.
"Colbert . . . the rest": *Second City Unscripted*, p. 201
"There were . . . all over again": Ibid.
"You know . . . audience": *Post & Courier*, April 29, 2006
"Imagine . . . beer was free": *Chicago Tribune*, April 27, 2003
"I wasn't . . . need for importance": *Charlie Rose*, December 8, 2006
"People . . . gave in to it": *Chicago Sun-Times*, October 18, 2006
"It was so cold . . . spoke to me": *Parade Magazine*, September 23, 2007
"It gave me . . . world": *The Second City Unscripted*, p. 198
"Second City . . . audience blows": *Second City Unscripted*, p. 199
"Learn . . . *love* it" " Ibid.
"Colbert . . . money": Ibid.
"That's when . . . wanted to do": *Parade Magazine*, September 23, 2007
"it was a hit [with audiences]": *Second City Unscripted*, p. 202
"Stephen . . . straight face": Ibid.
"I tended . . . lawyer": *Onion AV Club*, January 25, 2006
"I wish . . . person?": *Second City Unscripted*, p. 208
"The basic tenet . . . don't block": *Second City Unscripted*, p. 203
"Hi . . . sweatpants": Ibid.

"The *yes-and* . . . audience": Knox College commencement address, June 3, 2006
"I'm proud . . . your work": *Onion AV Club*, January 25, 2006
"People . . . improvise high": *Larry King Show*, October 14, 2007
"I just got . . . wonderful": Ibid.
"In the touring . . . a first": *Austin Chronicle*, July 21, 2006
"It's not easy . . . hungry": *Second City Unscripted*, p. 200
"If . . . we play": *Charleston Magazine*, February/March 1992
"We were all . . . I made it": *Second City Unscripted*, p. 200
"A lot . . . more physical": Ibid.
"huge . . . doomed squirrel": *Chicago Sun-Times*, April 23, 2003
"Second City . . . misfits even there": *PaulDinello.net*
"Between . . . wonderful team": *Chicago Sun-Times*, January 24, 1992
"The best wackos this side of *Twin Peaks*," *Chicago Sun-Times*, June 30, 1992
"These folks . . . groin pulls": *Chicago Sun-Times*, June 30, 1992
"He's an incredible . . . try anything": *Second City Unscripted*, p. 207
"It was absolutely . . . grapes?": Ibid.
"I was . . . light of day": Ibid.
"By the time . . . rules away": *Second City Unscripted*, p. 201
"They completely . . . broke me": Ibid.
"The rats . . . somewhere": *Second City Unscripted*, p. 203
"thirty . . . backstage": Ibid.
"I'd dig . . . put it on": Ibid.
"Once . . . skirt": Ibid.
"I told him . . . not right": *Post & Courier*, April 29, 2006
"I'll never forget . . . right": Ibid.
"He spent . . . again": Ibid.
"I was there . . . stupid seriously": *Second City Unscripted*, p. xi

Six

"We try to amuse ourselves . . .": *IGN.com*, August 11, 2003
"They left . . . freedom": Comedy Central online chat, June 12, 2000

"We had no budget . . . jackhammer.' " Ibid.

"You shoot . . . guessing": Ibid.

"never beat . . . good taste": *Chicago Sun-Times*, April 19, 1995

"*Exit 57* . . . choose to ignore": *Chicago Sun-Times*, September 21, 1995

"I actually held . . . completely desperate": *New York Times*, May 10, 2009

"I was parodying . . . 'flesh.' ": *Chicago Sun-Times*, April 28, 2006

"I think . . . network show?": *Post & Courier*, March 12, 1996

"One of the nicest . . . business": *New York Times*, May 10, 2009

"If you . . . camera": Ibid.

"The show . . . prime time": *Chicago Sun-Times*, March 26, 1996

"The first sketch . . . old": *New York Times*, March 14, 1996

"It was probably . . . bizarre": *New York Times*, May 10, 2009

"It's definitely . . . this particular one": Ibid.

"de-potted plants the whole time": *New Yorker* festival, October 5, 2008

"I was desperate . . . chimp": *Washington Post*, October 10, 2005

"I thought . . . living": *IGN.com*, August 11, 2003

"It was too late . . . die was cast": Ibid.

"my crisis of confidence": *Parade Magazine*, September 23, 2007

"I thought . . . terrible idea": *Charleston Magazine*, May 2006

"I really . . . type of show": *Post and Courier*, April 29, 2006

"I get . . . cracked me up": *Paley Center Daily Show* chat, April 19, 2001

"I pitched . . . hire me": *Larry King Show*, October 14, 2007

"To me . . . paycheck to show up": *Mediabistro*, May 6, 2003

"They were all . . . elevated it": Ibid.

"If they asked what kind . . . leave": Harvard University Institute of Politics talk, December 1, 2006

"And then I found . . . morning": *Mediabistro*, May 6, 2003

"Once . . . working with": *Charleston Magazine*, May 2006

"It helps . . . asshole personas": *Onion AV Club*, January 22, 2003

"I spent . . . host-driven": *Minneapolis Star Tribune*, February 8, 1998

"The take-no-prisoners . . . nonsense": *New York Daily News*, October 7, 1996

"In the world . . . edited": *New York Times*, August 23, 1998

"You wanted . . . something funny": *Onion AV Club*, January 22, 2003

"He was . . . TelePrompTer": Benefit for Charleston Stage, December 23, 2007
"We can say . . . honest": *Chicago Sun-Times*, April 27, 2003
"I don't know . . . something, right?": Ibid.
"This is the character you should do": Comedy Central online chat, June 12, 2000
"Sitting around . . . tape and string": *Virginian-Pilot*, January 11, 1999
"Whenever . . . time to evolve": *Chicago Sun-Times*, January 4, 1999
"You go down . . . get back in it": *Bergen Record*, January 11, 1999.
"He once seemed destined for more": *Chicago Sun-Times*, January 4, 1999
"There are no mirrors . . . until I get there": *Bergen Record*, January 11, 1999
"I'm doing everything . . . tailoring it to that": *Chicago Sun-Times*, January 4, 1999
"Hopefully . . . shower afterward": Ibid.
"When I started . . . national significance": *Daily Variety*, April 25, 2006
"[My character] . . . what's true": Ibid.

Seven

"Happily . . . return": *Seattle Post-Intelligencer*, January 14, 1999
"[The show] . . . before *The Daily Show*": *Campus Progress*, October 2005
"I didn't enjoy . . . imagined": *IGN.com*, August 11, 2003
"He'd do . . . opposition to them": Ibid.
"There's nothing he can't make funny": Ibid.
"It's *My So-Called Life* on acid": *Chicago Sun-Times*, December 17, 1998
"Then Stephen . . . supposed to write": *Onion AV Club*, January 21, 2004
"We all have . . . script form": Ibid.
"Stephen remembers . . . story arc": *Dallas Morning News*, July 20, 2006
"If we don't . . . what lines happen": *NPR Weekend Edition*, June 25, 2006
"I'm an idea person . . . group": *Oakland Tribune*, July 25, 2003
"Who's gonna watch this?" *Uproar*, December 2003
"He's just . . . other than teach": Comedy Central online chat, June 12, 2000
"He used . . . one of them": Ibid.

"They'd been . . . Noblet": *Uproar*, December 2003
"In the after-school . . . extreme": *Dallas Morning News*, July 20, 2006
"Whereas . . . twisted": *Washington Post*, April 7, 1999
"We get . . . damaged people": *Los Angeles Daily News*, July 28, 2003
"Damaged people . . . very entertaining": *IGN.com*, August 11, 2003
"It started as a happy accident": Comedy Central online chat, June 12, 2000
"One thing . . . dance party": Ibid.
"I like . . . about them": Ibid.
"We get . . . whatever we want": *Charleston Daily Mail*, April 26, 1999
"We are stunned . . . no one ever does": Comedy Central online chat, June 12, 2000
"We could say . . . other one": *Uproar*, December 2003
"But there . . . never consistent": *Underground*, May 2003
"We had a total . . . take some notes": *Modest Proposal*, Fall 2003
"We were always behind . . . that's it": Ibid.
"I don't know . . . fun again": *Uproar*, December 2003
"Boy . . . like the show, too": *Dallas Observer*, November 20, 2003
"She brought . . . network": Ibid.
"Since . . . decision has been made": Ibid.
"I think we could . . . figure it out": *Underground*, 2003
"There was no better . . . all felt that way": *San Francisco Chronicle* podcast, January 16, 2006
"Infected me . . . perfect job for me": *Parade Magazine*, September 23, 2007
"Stone Phillips . . . There were none": *Campus Progress*, October 2005
"Stone . . . Gypsum": *60 Minutes*, April 30, 2006
"If . . . porn star name": *Campus Progress*, October 2005
"He always looks . . . going on": Ibid.
"I read . . . on patrol": *Charlie Rose*, December 8, 2006
"I'm not entirely . . . adorable": *Parade Magazine*, September 23, 2007
"Anderson . . . attractive that is": Ibid.
"a Bill O'Reilly . . . idiot": *Chicago Sun-Times*, May 4, 2005
"O'Reilly's . . . great about yourself?": *Onion AV Club*, January 25, 2006
"Like everyone . . . victimhood": *New Yorker* festival, October 5, 2008
"On *The Daily Show* . . . is that I'm stupid": *IGN.com*, August 11, 2003

"I am a button-down . . . quality": Ibid.

"Stephen . . . threatening": *Chicago Magazine*, April 2006

"I did not intend . . . snuck up on me": *New Yorker* festival, October 5, 2008

"The last thing . . . improv scene": *Rolling Stone*, November 16, 2006

"Essentially . . . later and cry": *Paley Center Daily Show* chat, April 19, 2001

"I don't care . . . feelings": *New Yorker* festival, October 5, 2008

"They sometimes . . . editing": *Campus Progress*, October 2005

"I kept . . . bio-ethicist": *IGN.com*, August 11, 2003

"I was thinking . . . Joan Lunden": *Washington Post*, February 7, 2002

"We'll use it anyway": Ibid.

"The whole time . . . but I promised": *Time Out New York*, June 9–15, 2005

"We've always wanted . . . come and talk": *University Wire*, April 4, 2002

"How could I . . . most important show ever": *Newsweek*, July 31, 2000

"We rarely . . . reality": *Rolling Stone*, November 16, 2006

"We claim . . . defend anything": Ibid.

"The show . . . who we are": *Paley Center Daily Show* chat, April 19, 2001

"I think what we do . . . real journalism": *Rocky Mountain News*, July 21, 1999

"I'm a comedian . . . know about the news": Harvard University Institute of Politics talk, December 1, 2006

"It sounds . . . half of our joke": *Mediabistro*, May 6, 2003

"The most common . . . or hypocrisies that politicians have?": *Washington Post*, October 10, 2005

"Because . . . fake": *Washington Post*, July 27, 2004

"We try . . . this time": *University Wire*, April 4, 2002

"Obviously . . . everything stupider": *Campus Progress*, October 2005

"So we went . . . idiocy. *Mediabistro*, May 6, 2003

"I liked . . . tragedy news": Ibid.

"As soon . . . begin to change": Ibid.

"I put . . . happening at the desk": Ibid.

"Some of the correspondents . . . his own stuff": *University Wire*, April 4, 2002

"Writing . . . material that way": *Mediabistro*, May 6, 2003

"You can't feel . . . immediately enjoyable": Ibid.

"I'm more involved . . . rest of the day": *IGN.com*, August 11, 2003

"It's like . . . shtick": *New York Times*, November 22, 2000

"Make sure . . . He'll see me": White House press conference, January 19, 2001

"While we were there . . . places that [we're not]": *NPR Morning Edition*, November 1, 2002
"I remember . . . out of office?": Ibid.

Eight

"Jon deconstructs . . . Colbert guy": *Charlie Rose*, December 8, 2006
"Jon is . . . mock": Ibid.
"a narrow . . . dorm": *Boston Globe*, May 1, 2005
"We have dogs . . . Headquarters": *No Fact Zone*, October 28, 2009
"It's about people . . . come from": *Post & Courier*, December 28, 2002
"I'm very happy . . . too excited": Ibid.
"This is a coup . . . finished product": Associated Press, December 9, 2002
"In theory . . . back it up": *Rolling Stone*, November 16, 2006
"The biggest mistake . . . get a laugh": Ibid.
"Colbert would be . . . Internet": *Newsweek*, February 13, 2006
"Jon's very generous . . . every day": *Charlie Rose*, December 8, 2006
"We had him . . . so did Hack": Paley Center *Daily Show* chat, April 19, 2001
"He said we claimed . . . And he did": Ibid.
"If they ask . . . *Grandfatherland* again": Ibid.
"We all know . . . body in his trunk": *Salon*, April 4, 2001
"We named him . . . adventures": *Onion AV Club*, January 21, 2004
"Somehow the worm . . . lowest star": Ibid.
"He wasn't particularly . . . goes through life": *Believer*, March 2004
"gape-mouthed stares": *Oakland Tribune*, July 25, 2003
"When I was growing up . . . Wigfield": *Travel & Leisure*, April 2003
"I had been making . . . wacky captions": *Oakland Tribune*, July 25, 2003
"I work . . . anything funny": *New York Times*, August 27, 2004
"It was one . . . three and a half": *Chicago Tribune*, April 27, 2003
"The town council . . . chief of police": *Boston Herald*, June 12, 2003
"Plus . . . horrible place": *Bay Windows*, June 12, 2003
"Since none . . . rules of grammar": *Los Angeles Daily News*, July 28, 2003
"We thought . . . joking": *NPR Weekend Edition*, May 31, 2003
"We needed . . . panicked": *Oakland Tribune*, July 25, 2003

"thanks . . . thrusting there": *Chicago Sun-Times*, April 27, 2003

"Being in costume . . . word count": *Oakland Tribune*, July 25, 2003

"Russell . . . page that way": *NPR Weekend Edition*, May 31, 2003

"The show . . . on the road": *Bay Windows*, June 12, 2003

"They're very nice . . . *Strangers With Candy*": *Dallas Observer*, November 20, 2003

"This will be . . . left out": *Zap2it.com*, June 6, 2003

"It's going . . . action verbs": *Oakland Tribune*, July 25, 2003

"The intention . . . never changed": *Dallas Observer*, November 20, 2003

"We have this little saying . . . words?": *Boston Herald*, June 12, 2003

"The thing about . . . Mr. Goodwrench": *USA Today*, December 6, 2004

"I don't think . . . apogee of pimping": *Washington Post*, October 10, 2005

"My kids . . . inanimate objects": *Parents*, March 2004

"For a solid year . . . mouth": Ibid.

"It's hard . . . ear very badly": Ibid.

"Kids . . . mean to them": Ibid.

"During the week . . . History Channel": Ibid.

"I want them . . . very dry": *Meet the Press Take Two*, msnbc.com, October 21, 2007

"Comedy often relies . . . had to laugh": *Parents*, March 2004

"Never underestimate . . . waffles are vegetables": Ibid.

"The way . . . what could I do?": *Larry King Live*, October 14, 2007

"We heard . . . shook": *Post & Courier*, February 6, 2010

"It was one . . . your mind": Ibid.

"I tried . . . cable news": *Charlie Rose*, December 8, 2006

Nine

"We shoot . . . people all the time": *NPR Talk of the Nation*, March 1, 2004

"We'll do it . . . farmers": Ibid.

"The Dean . . . talk to anybody": Ibid.

"We reminded . . . never forget that we're not": Ibid.

"Republicans . . . very interesting": Ibid.

"They're sales . . . easy pickings": *New York Times*, August 27, 2004
"I couldn't get . . . brick wall": *Campus Progress*, October 2005
"Republicans . . . friend of mine": Ibid.
"At first . . . to that point": Ibid.
"I knew . . . desk together": *Daily Variety*, January 21, 2009
"Jon . . . entire thing": *Daily Variety*, January 21, 2009
"I don't think . . . gonna laugh": *Entertainment Weekly*, August 13, 2004
"*The Daily Show* . . . revenue": *Advertising Age*, September 27, 2004
"It's in advertisers' niche": Ibid.
"No predictions . . . milestones": *Seven Days*, November 10, 2004
"After this . . . what I'm saying": *Washington Post*, November 4, 2004
"I couldn't imagine . . . *not* like it": *New York Magazine*, October 16, 2006
"He'd been there . . . Stephen could do": *Vanity Fair*, October 2007
"Bill O'Reilly's . . . never got to see": *NPR All Things Considered*, May 4, 2005
"Besides . . . rip us off": *Washington Times*, May 13, 2005
"But I can't be an asshole": *New York Magazine*, October 16, 2006
"You're not . . . difference": Ibid.
"The audience . . . this character": Ibid.
"The challenge . . . keys": *Washington Post*, October 10, 2005
"It's as if . . . this character": Associated Press, May 3, 2005
"At the same time . . . host's chair": *New York Times*, September 25, 2005
"Stephen . . . so perfectly": Associated Press, June 9, 2008
"Colbert . . . money": *Daily Variety*, May 17, 2005
"It doesn't break . . . business": Associated Press, May 12, 2005
"Nora Ephron's . . . broomstick": *Variety*, June 16, 2005
"Oh . . . wastes his time": *New York Magazine*, June 26, 2005
"It'll be like . . . pacing": *New Yorker*, July 25, 2005
"I loved . . . crisp": *Newsweek*, February 13, 2006
"Plus . . . person himself": *Post & Courier*, May 15, 2005
"Seat belts . . . upper torso?": *Los Angeles Times*, September 8, 2005
"Now analysis . . . factory": *Arlington Heights Post*, October 20, 2005
"With the 24-hour news . . . clearer": *NPR Talk of the Nation*, March 1, 2004
"I could just take . . . written it for me": *Post & Courier*, May 15, 2005
"We wanted . . . redundant?": *Daily Variety*, June 14, 2006

"I see . . . half-hour": *Post & Courier*, May 15, 2005

"My friends . . . life-threatening": *Late Show with David Letterman*, September 2, 2005

"We found . . . exception": *Late Show with David Letterman*, September 2, 2005

"We lost . . . experience": Ibid.

"I think we reached . . . cannibal": Ibid.

"I remember . . . Jew": *And Here's the Kicker*, p. 232

"I very much . . . failure": *And Here's the Kicker*, p. 240

"I left . . . something good": *Television Week*, June 16, 2008

"I was hesitant . . . terrified": *San Francisco Chronicle*, January 16, 2006

"[We viewed] . . . farcical": *New York Magazine*, October 16, 2006

"["The Word"] . . . exist": Ibid.

"They don't need . . . mouth like that": *Glenview Announcements*, October 13, 2005

"All the architecture . . . set around me": *Onion AV Club*, January 21, 2004

"There are no . . . source": Ibid.

"For me . . . attention to himself": *And Here's the Kicker*, p. 232

"*The Colbert Report* . . . four nights a week": *Daily Variety*, October 20, 2005

"It became . . . virtuoso performance": *Vanity Fair*, October 2007

"The Colbert Report . . . second language": Ibid.

"Maintaining . . . bring that across": General Motors press release, October 24, 2005

"Letterman . . . happened": Associated Press, November 6, 2005

Ten

"People . . . error at a time": *Newsweek*, February 13, 2006

"Besides . . . Hannity does": *Onion AV Club*, January 25, 2006

"I feel . . . research for his writers": *Newsweek*, February 5, 2005

"People I can see under . . . wearing": *Philadelphia Inquirer*, April 13, 2008

"I think it . . . likable way": *Daily Variety*, June 14, 2006

"He's able . . . real world": *Vanity Fair*, October 2007

"It does not . . . press agrees": Associated Press, June 9, 2008

"We've got . . . next step": *NPR Fresh Air*, November 19, 2008

"You don't want . . . their show": *Stand Up with Pete Dominick*, August 20, 2009
"It's a sliding . . . down": *Meet the Press Take Two*, msnbc.com October 21, 2007
"I'm a satirist . . . reveal myself": *Vanity Fair*, October 2007
"There's only one . . . not me": *Rolling Stone*, September 17, 2009
"I try . . . *Most* of the time": *Satiristas*, p. 30
"At Second City . . . I do that on the show": *Meet the Press Take Two*, msnbc .com October 21, 2007
"I like jumping . . . confuse the audience": *Satiristas*, p. 30
"Probably . . . the person": *NPR Fresh Air*, November 19, 2008
"There are times . . . my jokes": *Newark Star Ledger*, October 26, 2009
"The media . . . crouton": *Vanity Fair*, October 2007
"I am always . . . sadness in his life": *Ibid.*
"A lot . . . play with Stephen Colbert": *And Here's the Kicker*, p. 239
"They wanted . . . acknowledge it": *Rolling Stone*, September 17, 2009
"What makes . . . pick that up": *Boston Globe*, October 18, 2009
"He's new . . . over it": *Rolling Stone*, November 16, 2006
"The funny thing . . . means it's working": *New York Magazine*, October 16, 2006
"The letters . . . are not great": *Parade Magazine*, September 23, 2007
"People see . . . something like that": Ibid.
"I don't really know . . . they've noticed": *Rolling Stone*, September 17, 2009
"It's not so much . . . fall over": *Baristanet*, February 2, 2006
"I'll be stopped . . . map": *Parade Magazine*, September 23, 2007
"to humanize . . . ignorance": Associated Press, June 9, 2008
"My character calls . . . what to make of the character": Associated Press, February 21, 2010
"Some people . . . comfortable as possible": *Onion AV Club*, January 25, 2006
"I like political . . . junior high school": *Boston Globe*, November 10, 2005
"Barney Frank . . . wrong": Harvard University Institute of Politics talk, December 1, 2006
"I've climbed . . . real threat": *Rocky Mountain News*, November 17, 2005
"Oh . . . foolish": *Long Beach Press-Telegram*, March 6, 2006
"Thank you, Mr. Stewart": Ibid.
"That was the most . . . enjoying himself so much": *Vanity Fair*, October 2007
"I'm just stunned . . . consensual rape": Ibid.

"It was the biggest . . . happen in the interview": *Charlie Rose*, December 8, 2006
"The writers . . . talking about it": *NPR Talk of the Nation*, March 1, 2004
"Sometimes I really want . . . talk": *Charlie Rose*, December 8, 2006
"Boy . . . fire": *Pittsburgh Post-Gazette*, October 14, 2005
"She once said . . . good enough actor": Harvard University Institute of Politics talk, December 1, 2006
"We want people . . . credibility to lose": *Rolling Stone*, November 16, 2006
"One of the things . . . gay baby": *Entertainment Weekly*, July 2, 2007
"Facts . . . section of the country": *Rolling Stone*, November 16, 2006
"Some people . . . everything will be fine": Ibid.
"We wanted . . . validity of that feeling": Ibid.
"my character . . . sell a magazine": *Daily Variety*, June 14, 2006
"Oh, it had to happen sometime": *Rolling Stone*, November 16, 2006
"He said . . . sense of it": Ibid.
"But you saw . . . seriously": Ibid.
"Not everybody . . . as I do": Ibid.
"I thought . . . thrilled": Ibid.
"This book . . . error at a time": *Mediabistro.com*, March 21, 2006
"I'm so excited . . . levitate": *Newsweek*, February 13, 2006
"A group . . . might be a problem": *And Here's the Kicker*, p. 242
"The only time . . . blow it": *NPR Wait Wait . . . Don't Tell Me*, October 20, 2007
"Whether or not . . . rehearsing the jokes": *Stand Up with Pete Dominick*, March 13, 2008
"We actually . . . get to do this": *Rolling Stone*, November 16, 2006
"It's hard . . . upsetting anyone": *Charlie Rose*, December 8, 2006
"The speech . . . inspiring": *And Here's the Kicker*, p. 242
"I believe . . . magical!": White House Correspondents' Dinner speech, April 29, 2006
"So the White House . . . Hindenburg!": Ibid.
"Jesse Jackson . . . what a glacier is": Ibid.
"I stand by . . . photo-ops in the world": Ibid.
"Well done": *Charlie Rose*, December 8, 2006
"Then he gave . . . spine": *Larry King Show*, October 14, 2007
"I saw . . . looking away": *Charlie Rose*, December 8, 2006

"Colbert crossed . . . been there before": *U.S. News & World Report*, May 1, 2006

"We were surprised . . . moment in time": *And Here's the Kicker*, p. 242

"And as excited . . . courtesy not to try to find out": White House Correspondents' Dinner speech, April 29, 2006

"Comedy Central's . . . Dinner": *Washington Post*, May 2, 2006

"bombed badly": *NY Daily News*, May 1, 2006

"Do I like . . . right back": *New Yorker* festival, October 5, 2008

"And I did . . . Dr. Colbert": *Wired*, August 2006

"I think this year . . . but thank you": *Boston Globe*, August 28, 2006

"He's so busy . . . sleep deprived": *Baristanet*, February 2, 2006

"Nothing says '08": *Albany Times Union*, October 10, 2006

"I can't tell Jon . . . Barack": *Rolling Stone*, November 16, 2006

"When we were working . . . write a movie": *Philadelphia Weekly*, July 5, 2006

"We like playing . . . really it": *Dallas Morning News*, July 20, 2006

"I guess . . . hold a film": *San Francisco Chronicle* podcast, January 16, 2006

"So we . . . released it": *San Francisco Chronicle* podcast, January 16, 2006

"*Strangers* . . . one last time": *Toledo Blade*, July 21, 2006

"The only character . . . sleep through the movie": *NY Newsday*, June 28, 2006

" 'Truthiness' is a playful way for us to think about a very important issue": Associated Press, December 9, 2006

Eleven

"I read . . . six hours later": *Meet the Press Take Two*, msnbc.com October 21, 2007

"It can get . . . something important": *Television Week*, June 16, 2008

"Then the writers . . . another idea' ": Ibid.

"You may throw . . . ten years": *Elle*, March 20, 2009

"We're constantly . . . all the time?": *Satiristas*, p. 27

"The clock . . . real or not": Harvard University Institute of Politics talk, December 1, 2006

"Ernie Kovacs . . . trying to meet them": *NPR Fresh Air*, November 19, 2008

"It's a little bit . . . slow process": *NPR Fresh Air*, December 7, 2005

"Generally . . . feel great": *Satiristas*, p. 27

"It can become . . . overwhelming": *And Here's the Kicker*, p. 239

"Sometimes . . . Stephen Colbert character": *Elle*, March 20, 2009

"Both Stephen . . . pull it off": *And Here's the Kicker*, p. 238

"Comedy writers . . . own writing": *IGN.com*, August 11, 2003

"It'll always . . . difficulty of it": *NPR Fresh Air*, June 22, 2009

"Both writers . . . sound like his character": *And Here's the Kicker*, p. 241

"Sometimes the news . . . in the case of health care": *Stand Up with Pete Dominick*, August 20, 2009

"The game . . . food to go around": *New York Magazine*, October 16, 2006

"It's the Jewish . . . salads": Ibid.

"Every . . . horny": Ibid.

"He looks . . . comedic idea": *Orlando Sentinel*, October 13, 2005

"We actually talk . . . frequently.": *NPR Talk of the Nation*, March 1, 2004

"I don't actually . . . releases the gas": *Larry King Show*, October 14, 2007

"We decided . . . wants to be liked": *Entertainment Weekly*, March 5, 2007

"He's amazingly . . . juice before he goes on": *Chicago Sun-Times*, July 27, 2008

"I think the staff . . . host is a prick": *Stand Up with Pete Dominick*, August 20, 2009

"If you look . . . reels": *Westword*, April 23, 2008

"It's a lot of work . . . perform more": *NPR Fresh Air*, December 7, 2005

"Like every performer . . . law school": *Post & Courier*, December 28, 2002

"Now we just . . . time for anything else": *Charlie Rose*, December 8, 2006

"The hardest thing . . . eat you up": *New Yorker* festival, October 5, 2008

"The show is a daily . . . desire to do anything else": *Daily Variety*, April 25, 2006

"But I could . . . come back tired": *New York Times*, March 7, 2009

Twelve

"I look forward . . . same way about Mr. O'Reilly": Associated Press, January 9, 2007

"I have a genuine . . . do his show": *Rolling Stone*, November 16, 2006

"I'm really looking . . . career to me": Associated Press, January 9, 2007

"I want you . . . vertigo,": *O'Reilly Factor*, January 18, 2007

"I spoke . . . right?": Ibid.

"In South Carolina . . . tell you that much": Ibid.

"It is? . . . money?": Ibid.

"Well . . . big difference": Ibid.

"So . . . Col-bear?": Ibid.

"Bill . . . mat here": Ibid.

"This was a huge mistake . . . show": *The Colbert Report*, January 18, 2007

"This would play . . . San Francisco like that": Ibid.

"I'm effete . . . act": *The Colbert Report*, Ibid.

"If you're . . . what am I?" Ibid.

"I thought . . . going at each other": *Entertainment Weekly*, March 5, 2007

"After his visit . . . record straight": *O'Reilly Factor*, February 1, 2007

"Such a proud . . . Jon laugh": *Entertainment Weekly*, August 13, 2004

"There's a little Barbarella left": *New Yorker* festival, October 5, 2008

"She brought . . . off my game": Ibid.

"Well . . . I don't want them!" Ibid.

"Don't ever let . . . show again!" Ibid.

"But honey . . . table!" Ibid.

"It doesn't matter . . . higher status": Ibid.

"Jane Fonda was my squirrel monkey": Ibid.

"That was the most . . . tongue in my ear": *Star Ledger*, October 26, 2009

"They sent me . . . thumbs up": *USA Today*, March 7, 2007

"It actually tastes . . . Very sweet": *New York Magazine*, March 6, 2007

"Stephen Colbert the character . . . internally at the same time": *USA Today*, March 7, 2007

"You trashed . . . *The Kite Runner*": *Albany Times Union*, June 4, 2007

"I was a little mad . . . women's book clubs": Ibid.

"We wrote it . . . girlfriend after girlfriend": *Entertainment Weekly*, July 2, 2007

"There was quite . . . close attention": Ibid.

"It's a fictional character . . . fun": Ibid.

"They particularly . . . not an ant": *Nofactzone.net*, April 5, 2007

"I try to draw . . . arrogance across in every frame": Ibid.

"He had a very clear . . . straight as he does on the show": Ibid.

"This is a gods end . . . golden ticket": *Parade Magazine*, September 23, 2007

"If I had known . . . triquetrum a long time ago!": *Washington Post*, August 22, 2007

"Not until the war is over": Associated Press, June 12, 2008

"It's just like . . . don't even think them": *Entertainment Weekly*, March 5, 2007

"There are sections . . . feeling's sake": *NPR All Things Considered*, October 9, 2007

"Colbert's opus . . . forced": *Entertainment Weekly*, October 12, 2007

"*I Am America* . . . page": *New York Times*, October 8, 2007

"One of the things . . . grateful to have it": *Parade Magazine*, September 23, 2007

"That way, I can lose twice": *Beaufort Gazette*, October 17, 2007

"I'm running . . . Dixville Notch": *Meet the Press*, October 21, 2007

"Anybody can run . . . filing": *Beaufort Gazette*, October 17, 2007

"If Stephen . . . his right": Ibid.

"I'm shocked . . . overqualified for the job": *The State*, October 17, 2007

"We are happy . . . *(And So Can You!)*": Ibid.

"I don't want . . . so can you": *Meet the Press*, October 21, 2007

"The Governor . . . tit for tat": *Larry King Live*, October 14, 2007

"This is a serious . . . look where it got us": *The Times UK*, October 27, 2007

"They're more numerous . . . unparalleled": Campaign speech, October 9, 2007

"Over my dead body will Colbert's name be on the ballot": CNN, October 31, 2007

"He's just trying . . . candidates on the ballot": *The State*, October 17, 2007

"Would be better off . . . girlfriend": *The Times UK*, October 27, 2007

"They tell you . . . not you, Stephen Colbert": *New Yorker* festival, October 5, 2008

"the only hope . . . crap": *60 Minutes*, April 30, 2006

"I came close . . . is this real?": *Stand Up with Pete Dominick*, March 13, 2008

"You touched . . . got on you": *Entertainment Weekly*, September 30, 2008

"They were lying . . . lied to *a lot*": Ibid.

"I couldn't have the Presidential election *not* be about me": *New Yorker* festival, October 5, 2008

"I get asked dollars": *Stand Up with Pete Dominick*, August 20, 2009

"We'll be affected . . . four nights a week": *Multichannel News*, October 29, 2007

"Our position . . . material on the show": Ibid.

"In receiving . . . Al Gore": *Gold Coast Bulletin*, January 2, 2008

Thirteen

"The first thing . . . yoga pants": *Stand Up with Pete Dominick*, March 13, 2008

"I love being onstage . . . improvising": *Vanity Fair*, October 2007

"When I don't . . . connect to the audience": *Parade Magazine*, September 23, 2007

"An ultimatum . . . What's your answer?'" Associated Press, December 25, 2007

"We would like . . . nuanced as ambivalence": Associated Press, December 21, 2007

"Doing the show . . . hardest thing I've ever done": *Stand Up with Pete Dominick*, March 13, 2008

"You watch . . . go far": MUSC interview with Colbert family, July 3, 2009

"Do you remember my father?" Ibid.

"Very . . . well": Ibid.

"I wanted him . . . happy to": Ibid.

"The Democrats . . . being made fun of by Stephen Colbert": *NPR Day to Day*, April 11, 2008

"We didn't know . . . in case it didn't happen": *NPR Fresh Air*, November 19, 2008

"The whole night . . . everybody on it": Ibid.

"I love . . . trouble": Ibid.

"I proudly accept . . . Sherman": *Entertainment Close-up*, April 9, 2008

"I think . . . involving his audience": *Daily Variety*, June 11, 2008

"I talk about the war . . . if I didn't do it": *Stand Up with Pete Dominick*, August 20, 2009

"We became . . . watching at home?": *NPR Fresh Air*, June 22, 2009

"What resources . . . even possible?" *Post Magazine*, September 1, 2009

"When we told them . . . impossible to do": *Stand Up with Pete Dominick*, August 20, 2009

"You can . . . This is possible." *Rolling Stone*, September 17, 2009

"Everyone likes . . . cover one thing": *Entertainment Weekly*, September 30, 2008

"Guys . . . endorsed him": *NPR Fresh Air*, June 22, 2009

"I know this is shocking . . . winning this thing": *The Colbert Report*, October 29, 2008

"It's a few minutes . . . piece of real news": *Nofact Zone*, December 2, 2008

"I would just like . . . fake news show": Ibid.

"I've never had . . . take it away": Associated Press, November 5, 2008

"A lot of the scenes . . . everyone else look good": Ibid.

"Mr. Colbert . . . specials it mocks": *New York Times*, November 20, 2008

"If you're looking . . . reason it's so funny": *San Francisco Chronicle*, November 21, 2008

"There were . . . didn't fit": *Nofactzone.net*, December 1, 2008

"Like the City Hall falcons . . . modern society": *SanJoseCa.gov*, February 24, 2009

"Those will be . . . jump on COLBERT": *The Colbert Report*, April 14, 2009

"We received . . . took an interest": *Townsville Bulletin*, April 14, 2009

"In many ways . . . education center and library": *The Catalyst*, April 3, 2009

"The only thing . . . still hurts": MUSC interview with Colbert family, July 3, 2009

"There's a thesis . . . gone forever": *New York Times*, June 8, 2009

"Each of the shows . . . full staff": *NPR Fresh Air*, June 22, 2009

"After that . . . take care": *Stand Up with Pete Dominick*, August 20, 2009

"She was small . . . couldn't find me": Ibid.

"Finally, Mouse . . . sir": Ibid.

"Am I in trouble?" Ibid.

"Yes, sir, you kinda are": Ibid.

"I couldn't . . . off we'd go": Ibid.

"We scouted . . . conferences in the atrium": *TV Technology*, August 12, 2009

"They said . . . characters' mouths": Ibid.

"Stephen . . . hair cut": *The Colbert Report*, June 8, 2009

"Your achievements . . . stuff before": Associated Press, June 12, 2009

"We decided . . . almost cowardly": *NPR Fresh Air*, June 22, 2009

"The Pillars . . . sometimes difficult": Ibid.

"One of the biggest . . . what to bring": *TV Technology*, August 12, 2009

"We thought . . . content-wise": *Post Magazine*, September 1, 2009

"After all . . . home show over there": Ibid.

"Technical director . . . push the buttons": Ibid.

"I wish . . . perfectly happy": Ibid.

"I thanked . . . for our country": Ibid.

"When Colbert . . . agreed to do it": *Newsweek*, June 15, 2009

"There are still . . . 50,000 troops": *Newsweek*, June 15, 2009

"It has been a great joy . . . help me write it": *PRNewswire*, August 24, 2009

"I will always treasure . . . start that project": Ibid.

Fourteen

"Stay away from Katy Perry": Associated Press, January 31, 2010

"It is a Christmas . . . great birthday": Ibid.

"Am I cool now?": *Seattle Post-Intelligencer*, February 1, 2010

"My character . . . nobody gets hurt": *Sports Illustrated*, December 21, 2009

"We wanted to get . . . possible way, of course": *Crain's New York Business*, January 25, 2010

"I don't know . . . long distance": *Sports Illustrated*, December 21, 2009

"We were stunned . . . shining armor": Ibid.

"They look . . . incredible athletes": Ibid.

"Deposit Savings in Bong": *The Colbert Report*, November 2, 2009

"I'm so surprised . . . exposure for the sport": Ibid.

"When Colbert . . . think of that?" Ibid.

"He's a jerk": Associated Press, December 4, 2009

"I've forgiven . . . Canada at this point": *Charleston Gazette*, February 11, 2010

"I'm tired all the time": *IGN.com*, August 11, 2003

"The short answer . . . fun": *Parade Magazine*, September 23, 2007

"And as long . . . fresh": *Charlie Rose*, December 8, 2006

"When we were first . . . enjoy it anymore": *Stand Up with Pete Dominick*, March 13, 2008

"I would have to say . . . Yeah!": *Rolling Stone*, September 17, 2009

"a big hot cluster of Colberts": MUSC interview with Colbert family, July 3, 2009

"They call it . . . isolated, really": Ibid.

"Once I cross . . . low tide smells like": *Charleston Magazine*, May 2006

"Those were the things . . . Lowcountry": Ibid.

"I desire . . . ordinary with common": *Parade Magazine*, September 23, 2007

"My wife . . . I want it to be": Ibid.

"Being fearless . . . be afraid": Ibid.

"That's not a philosophical . . . all day long": *Meet the Press Take Two*, msnbc .com, October 21, 2007

"It's a great life . . . lucky": *IGN.com*, August 11, 2003

RESOURCES

Books

And Here's the Kicker: Conversations with 21 Top Humor Writers on Their Craft. By Mike Sacks. Cincinnati: Writers Digest Books, 2009.

Satiristas: Comedians, Contrarians, Raconteurs & Vulgarians. By Paul Provenza and Dan Dion. New York: HarperCollins, 2010.

The Second City Unscripted. By Mike Thomas. New York: Villard Books, 2009.

Stephen Colbert's Tek Jansen. By John Layman and Tom Peyer. Portland, Oregon: Oni Press, 2009.

INDEX